Reflections *on* Afro-American Music

The Kent State University Press

Copyright © 1973 by Dominique-René de Lerma
All rights reserved.
Library of Congress Card Catalog Number 72-619703
ISBN: 0-87338-135-1.
Manufactured in the United States of America
First Printing

Contents

Offered in tribute to those individuals and foundations whose consistent support and interest was essential to the Black Music Center during the two years of my directorship:

Thomas J. Ahrens

C. Howard Allen, Jr.

Thomas Jefferson Anderson, Jr.

Walter F. Anderson

David Baker

William B. Christ

Charles Ellison

Jeremiah Gutman

Madeleine Gutman

Natalie Hinderas

The Irwin-Sweeney-Miller Foundation

Herbert McArthur

Don Malin

The E. B. Marks Music Corporation

Undine Moore

The National Endowment for the Arts

The National Endowment for the Humanities

Paul Rohmann

John A. Taylor

Sharon B. Thompson

Jo Zuppan

1. Preface:
The Black Music Center and Its Projects

It was about 8:30 on the morning of April 5, 1968, that I received a telephone call from our dean, Wilfred C. Bain of the Indiana University School of Music. The president of the university had announced a memorial service to be held on campus at noon to commemorate the death of Rev. Martin Luther King, Jr., and Dean Bain had offered the resident Berkshire String Quartet to provide music for the ceremonies. As music librarian, I was charged with the provision of an "elegiac" work for string quartet, written by a Black composer, which the ensemble could rehearse and perform within three hours.

I paused for a moment and the dean sensed my quandary. Who were the Black composers? Long alert to the essence of Black culture, he had continued the evolution of the jazz program at North Texas State University while he served as dean (it was already developing in 1938 and became a curricular activity under Dean Walter H. Hodgson in 1947, when Dean Bain moved to Indiana). It was Dean Bain who hired Richard Johnson in 1949—Indiana University's first Black professor, and it was he who immediately mentioned the names of several Black composers for my catalog check: Edmund Dédé, Clarence Cameron White, William Grant Still, Ulysses Kay, Harry Burleigh, Howard Swanson, and others. Even though some of these names were known to me, and even though I thought of a few others within the next hour, I had no concept of what the music of these figures was like (excepting a few works of Still, Kay, and Swanson). I promised him I would do my best and ran off to the card catalog of the nation's fifth largest music library to see what was the state of our holdings in this area.

The concept of "integration" which existed up to Dr. King's death in many communities centered around the willingness to ignore color and, with it, culture; it was fashionable to regard all men as brothers and as equals. Such a noble philosophy carried with it the "liberal" implication that Anglo-American society could accept those of other heritages as long as the behavior would be White. This is why Black composers were generally identified as Black only by photograph, reputation, or citation in some of the basic research which had been conducted by such scholars as John Duncan, W. C. Handy, James Trotter, or Maude Cuney Hare. Despite the Moorish blood in my purple veins, despite the pride I had in my own cultural background, despite my residence for a decade virtually next door to a Sanctified church and the extraordinary fragrance of Saturday night's barbeque in my neighbor's yard, despite my own experiences in public school with racism, despite my close association with numerous Afro-American musicians, I had a long way to go before I could understand how my own education had directed my every thought to the exclusive support of European "masterworks."

There were some exceptions in my education, however. Just now it seems that the strongest of these came from the late Paul Nettl, who had been chairman of my graduate committee during my doctoral musicology days at Indiana University. Dr. Nettl was a Czech Jew who escaped from the Nazis at the last moment. Possibly that experience played a major role in his own development, but he told his students he did not teach "micrology," that he was interested in music as an end in itself but also in the extent to which it related to society. His lectures and tests always guided us gently to think of music in these terms, but I am only now beginning to understand the extent to which his teaching opened philosophical doors that might have remained shut had I not had the experience of his guidance. And those doors lead out of the ivory tower, to the people. This is the path his own son has taken, Bruno Nettl, one of the most distinguished ethnomusicologists of our time.

I had not assimilated all of this when, in 1968, I began my search for a string quartet. It came as a shock to my acquisitional self-righteousness, however, when I discovered how very few works by Black composers we had in our library. There was not one composition which would have been suitable. Only then did it dawn on us that, in David Baker, we had a Black composer on our own faculty. How could we have overlooked Dave? Simply because society had encouraged us not to notice the color of one's skin, plus the fact that one not often expects to find a solution so close at hand.

The university auditorium was filled at noon. Probably every Black student and professor on the campus attended the service, and White representation was not minimal. It was a decade of murders. The assassination of John Kennedy was still fresh in our minds. We did not anticipate the events of Jackson State, nor of Kent State. Dr. King had begun to make popular many of the ideas of W. E. B. DuBois, particularly as they applied to the Vietnamese war. He had led us gently to a moral consciousness which truly subversive elements had hidden and euphemized. He had survived attacks from his own people and from White bigoted nationalists, but he became only more devoted to humanity and more resolved to implement his dream. The power of his eloquent lyricism had just ended, hours before, and he became the patron saint of garbage collectors. From the trash cans to the halls of one of the nation's most distinguished universities is a long distance, but this is the fault of the academic institutions. The gap was partially bridged that day, and Blacks and Whites shared a profound grief, but only the Blacks really know why the caged bird sings.

A series of brief talks by the most articulate Black students and faculty of the campus summarized and extended Dr. King's ideas, and one speaker militantly laid out plans for the future. The quartet played David Baker's *Pastorale,* but already in Dave's mind were plans for that evening's initial work of what became a masterwork: *Black America.* I felt the time had come for me to restructure the hostilities of my own minority memberships in a creative manner, to leave the ivory halls if necessary. I did not fully understand just then that my part could be played, using my professional skills, if I accepted the implicit challenges coming from Dr. King, Dean Bain, Dave Baker, Paul Nettl, T. J. Anderson, and the prejudices of former classmates.

It took a few weeks to assimilate enough ideas to plan any potentially viable channel, but I knew I needed guidance and more specific ideas than I could generate on my own. I asked Dean Bain if he would consider the establishment of a Black Music Committee, just to see if we could get something together. He responded immediately by appointing me chairman, to work with Austin B. Caswell and Dave Baker, with administrative advice from Associate Dean William B. Christ, and asked us to report those ideas which might be considered for action by Indiana University.

Fresh from the reference problem of April 5, I suggested we conduct some research to find out exactly who the Black composers were and what they had done. But for jazz names, the initial list was terribly small, and we knew we had to dedicate a lot of time to to the search. Dean Christ, with assistance from IU's grants specialist of the time, Martha Mosier Reynolds, suggested we approach the National Endowment for the Humanities to see if funds could be secured to supplement whatever the campus might provide. Our proposal was accepted. By this time we knew it would be best for us were we to host a seminar which would attract specialists from across the country to give us additional ideas and guidance. That seminar, offered in 1969, was the basis for our first publication, *Black Music in Our Culture,* which was issued by the Kent State University Press in 1970.

The research on the identification of Black composers was conducted from many secondary sources, under the guidance of my secretary Sharon B. Thompson. The primary research, consisting of interviews, was the weekend and holiday activity of Dr. Caswell and, especially, of Dave Baker. When the funding period ended in 1969, we had made enough headway to coast until additional research could be initiated with the establishment of the Black Music Center. By that time, the routines and formats had been established, with the worksheets for bibliographic registration representing the culmination of experiments in format which had been employed in two non-Black composer bibliographies of mine.[1]

The idea of the Black Music Center forced itself on my mind before our 1969 seminar, when I became sensitive to the unexpected intensity of need for information on the subject and the crucial necessity of having established a central location for the registration of such data. A preliminary letter of inquiry was sent to the National Endowment for the Humanities to see if they would be interested in the concept. Their answer arrived during the 1969 sessions, and I met with a large number of the Black registrants in my home that evening to secure their reaction. The major sentiment was that such a project, with substantial potentials, should have the assurance of responsible Black involvement from the start. On this basis was established an *ad hoc* Black committee made up of those at our conference, a group of off-campus advisors who would support locally generated ideas of merit and who would not hesitate to be critical of any misdirected ones.

Only a few weeks after our 1970 seminar, we received notice from the National Endowment that the Black Music Center would be established on September first. I had already cut short a research trip in Europe by six weeks in order to work on the proposal budget; I had no qualms about giving up my scheduled August vacation so that all could be set for the Center's first day in September.

The basic activity of the Center is to serve all communities as a clearing house, depository, and research-reference site for the documentation of Black music history. Our concern is not just with the composers and concert artists, not just with jazz or twentieth-century

---

[1] *Charles Edward Ives, 1874–1954; A Bibliography of His Music* (Kent: Kent State University Press, 1970) and *Igor Fedorovitch Stravinsky, 1882–1971; A Practical Guide to Publications of His Music* (Kent: Kent State University Press, forthcoming).

music, and not just with Afro-Americana; the latitude is open for work to be done with all cultural expressions of all countries and continents, from any historical period.

We are engaged in the collection of materials related to any manifestation of these cultures: books, scores, recordings, journal articles, manuscripts, sketches, letters, photographs, and other items of documentary value. Pending substantial supplementary funding for the acquisition of all bibliographical materials registered in our research, this collection consists primarily of more current publications, often secured as gifts or review copies.

In order to develop a collection strong enough to satisfy the needs of all interested persons, be they graduate college professors or elementary school children, the extent of literature on the subject must be known. This has been the prime activity of the Center and will continue to be so until its two major bibliographies are published. The first of these, *Black Music; A Preliminary Register of the Composers and Their Works* (hereafter cited as *Register*), will put the actual music in primary position and will be followed by an equally exhaustive international bibliography of literature on the music, *The Legacy of Black Music.* A selective stop-gap solution for the latter title will be offered as the second edition of *The Black-American Musical Heritage,* projected for commercial publication in 1973.

Until these initial projects are completed, the Center is pleased to provide limited reference service by mail to individuals and societies, to performers and publishers, to teachers and students. The Center can thus advance the cause of performance and research, and assist in the development of new curricula and innovative approaches to music education. The reference service is, however, of necessity limited to those areas that will not inhibit the satisfaction of the top-priority documentation and research projects, which promise far better and more satisfactory public service when completed.

For reference service of particular detail, patrons are invited to consult the Center's collection in person between 8:00 A.M. and 5:00 P.M. almost every weekday of the year. Published materials are housed in the School of Music Library, which is open eighty-eight hours weekly when school is in session, and forty hours per week at other times. Persons interested in coming to Bloomington for research will be welcome, and assistance can be provided without any formalities, but guests are urged to communicate with us in advance to determine when and to what extent the Center and the Library may best be able to serve.

Furthermore, the published materials are available for interlibrary loan. In this manner, virtually every public or university library in the world becomes a regional Black music center. Information on interlibrary loan procedures can be secured at the reference desk in most libraries, or in Sarah K. Thompson's *Interlibrary Loan Procedure Manual* (Chicago: American Library Association, 1970). Please note that contractual arrangements may prevent the loaning or photocopying of special materials, including those items subsequently to be commercially published and that music for which composers' royalties have been requested.

The first two years of the Center were spent in two not unrelated areas: documentation and funding. The former is the Center's primary function. The second represents an effort to develop a financial base so that operations may continue and so that all projects may be completed without undue concern for future funding. The formats for documentation are designed so the information may satisfy multiple interests, thereby making the maximal potential of the research projects which are thought worthy of commercial publication. Royalties from such sales are then reinvested in the Center to care for areas of activity which the pre-structured budgets of various grants cannot allow. Some of these will include projects that will in turn produce additional revenue, and some will be in scholarship programs.

An additional source for income to the Center is in the area of donations. Several of the major publishing and recording companies regularly provide new issues for the collection, aware of the commercial advantages to them and the scarcity of foundation support for the acquisition of these materials. Large private record libraries of rare jazz recordings have come to us, as well as collections of special materials—not the least of which are the memorabilia of Philippa Duke Schuyler, donated by the pianist's friends, Mr. and Mrs. Joseph R. Myers, of Lexington, North Carolina.

An account for monetary donations was established in 1971, initiated by a gift from Professor Thomas A. Dorsey, a pioneer in gospel music. Those who followed him constitute the original members of the Patrons of the Black Music Center. Four classes of membership have accordingly been established: Affiliate Members ($50 per year), Associate Members ($100 per year), Benefactors ($200 per year), and Life Sponsors (one donation of $500). Donors are granted free registration to the annual summer seminars of the Center which are held on the Bloomington campus, during the period this membership is in effect.

The type of work in which the Center is engaged gives witness to our assumption that the use of existing educational channels will secure long-range benefits for society. The Center is not, however, directly involved in sponsoring instruction, nor in serving the interests of Indiana University to any greater extent than those of any other college or public school in any other state.

In support of educational programs and in addition to our major projects, we have provided extensive assistance to college and university administrators seeking to employ Black professors in music, and we have also played a role in the development of video tapes for college-level study in Black music history. Under consideration, subject to additional funding, is our interest in the production of recordings of music by Black composers, performed by outstanding Black instrumentalists and singers under the leadership of a Black conductor, so that this material may be used in teaching programs. We would like to determine the extent to which we might support recruitment and preliminary training programs for potential field research personnel for work in Africa through the cooperation of the International Library of African Music. We would also wish to develop methods whereby a recent graduate might substitute for a mature teacher who could then have the freedom to complete a research project, and we would like to play our role in the development of key personnel in those areas underpopulated by Blacks—such as music library work, musicology, music criticism, and college music administration.

In the area of documentation, we see the value of developing a national union catalog of books, scores, and of non-commercial recordings, which would register the location of special collections for interested scholars. Although the Center would be most happy to consider donations of entire libraries, it strongly supports that philosophy of keeping unified collections in one location, provided that this location will protect these materials in a professionally responsible manner and simultaneously permit their use by qualified personnel.

Time has permitted only the barest start toward one valuable project: that of supplying inmates of penal institutions with books, recordings, instruments, and concerts. With regard to this idea, I would urge all persons or organizations to conduct drives in various localities using the newspapers and other media to ask for donations of used instruments, such as saxophones and trumpets, to a central collecting agency for gifts to prisons or to nonprofit social action groups such as Chicago's Association for the Advancement of Creative Musicians. I offer this suggestion in a belief (which I admit to be naive) that music can provide moral enrichment and that if music is humanistically and selflessly approached and practiced, society can be the better.

In addition to providing a temporary or permanent depository for composers' manuscripts (ever so much better an idea than storage of the materials in attics or some cabinet—and how many composers, even of major stature, have written me of their losses!) we would like to help sponsor a contest for non-published works, including at least an informal performance and recording of selected works, with commercial publication of those compositions deemed outstanding by a panel of Black critics.

We seek also to encourage the publication of Black music, and its purchase, study, and performance. Not only the Black composers must be supported, but also those firms issuing their music. I was particularly delighted during a recent trip to New York, when I was invited by Diana Herman to visit the Joseph Patelson Music House on 56th Street. She and Catherine Malfitano had assembled a display of music by Black composers, available for sale, developed from the first appendix in *Black Music in Our Culture*. This is imaginative marketing based on the interests of the customer, or on what we may all hope (for whatever reasons) to be consumer interest. I am aware of only one publisher so far (the Edward B. Marks Music Corporation, which is not surprising) that has issued a special catalog of their publications of the works of Black composers. As I left Patelson's, Ms. Malfitano mentioned an interest in a similar exhibit of music by women composers, and I told her I would send a list of Black female composers so she could join the Fem Lib movement with one of its major progenitors.

We have also been active in assisting music and book publishers in their interests in Black music. Based on an article of mine which appeared in *Choice,* the Johnson Reprint Corporation is considering a series of major books which, perhaps for lack of support in the past, have gone out of print. And the Summy-Birchard Company, with whom I had corresponded while preparing the entry on Robert Nathaniel Dett for the supplementary volume of *Die Musik in Geschichte und Gegenwart,*[2] is reprinting the piano works of Dett which had unfortunately been allowed to go out of print.

Our work in sponsoring performance has been limited to special events, because of the expense which might be involved, diverting our funds from research. Even so, the first American performance of the

---

[2] Kassel: Bärenreiter-Verlag, forthcoming.

B flat violin sonata by Saint-Georges took place at a lecture-recital I gave in Boulder, as a guest of the Black Studies Program of the University of Colorado. On the same program was the première of Dave Baker's *Deliver My Soul,* a slightly idealized gospel tune for violin and piano. Both works were performed by Colorado's Paul Parmalee, piano, and by Indiana's Steven Shipps. Another première was Ulysses Kay's *Aulos,* for flute and chamber orchestra, which was performed by John Solum with an orchestra conducted by IU faculty member Wolfgang Vacano at a benefit concert for the Kincaid Memorial Scholarship Fund at Indiana University. The 1971 seminar included the American premières of the Saint-Georges C major string quartet, excellently performed by a student ensemble, and the Bridgetower song, *Henry,* by Bernadine Oliphint with Carol Stone as pianist. It is our intention to publish the works of Bridgetower and Saint-Georges.

In cooperation with the Voice of America, we produced a video tape (as well as a sound tape) of Dave Baker's *Black America,* both of which were used for national and international broadcasting and telecasting on the anniversary of Martin Luther King's death, in 1971. With the support of WTIU (Indiana University's educational television station), we have produced four half-hour video tapes on the spiritual and gospel in association with Rev. William Wiggins, Pearl Williams Jones, Leonard Goines, Hubert Walters, Louise Parker, John Patton, John Lovell, and Leila Blakey. The research of the Center proved a prime source for the information needed by National Educational Television for its special production on the Black composer, a part of the show "Vibrations."

In addition to the trip to Boulder, the Center has been represented at meetings and conferences in Iowa, Illinois, North Carolina, Florida, California, the District of Columbia, New Jersey, Georgia, Minnesota, Louisiana, South Carolina, and Tennessee, including Herndon Spillman's dedication recital for the new organ at Howard University's Andrew Rankin Chapel and a recital at Dillard University, both of which featured organ music by Black composers. Most *hors de série* was our support for an issue of commemorative postage stamps, honoring such figures as Charlie Christian, Charlie Parker, and Louis Armstrong (the only Black musician thus far on U.S. stamps is W. C. Handy).

Any additional work which the Center might undertake will be subject to funding which will support such a venture properly, provided that the project will not duplicate tangible and viable undertakings of other groups and scholars in communication with the Center. We do not feel enough money or time is available to reproduce each other's activities when there is so much work yet to do.

With the establishment of the Center, Dr. Anderson's *ad hoc* committee was transformed into the Honorary Advisory Committee of the Center, a group of off-campus musicians who accepted the responsibility of keeping us alert to the development and interests of the Black music communities, of assisting us in the channeling of personnel and resources, and of providing us with generally supportive assistance. The membership of that committee consists of the following persons, with Dr. Anderson serving as chairman: [3]

Thomas Jefferson Anderson, Jr. (Wincester, Mass.)
Leonard Bernstein (New York)
Kenneth Brown Billups (St. Louis)
John A. R. Blacking (Belfast)
James Brown (Cincinnati)
John Duncan (Montgomery)
Leonard Feist (New York)
Paul Glass (New York)
John Hammond (New York)
Natalie Hinderas (Philadephia)*
Ulysses Simpson Kay (New York)
Mrs. Martin Luther King, Jr. (Atlanta)
Undine Smith Moore (Petersburg)
Kurtz Myers (Denver)
Robert Shaw (Atlanta)
Hale Smith (New York)*
Pharaoh Sanders (New York)
Eileen Southern (New York)
James A. Standifer (Ann Arbor)*
Orrin Suthern (Lincoln University, Pa.)*
Sun Ra (Philadelphia)
Billy Taylor (New York)
Leon E. Thompson (New York)
Sir Michael Tippett (London)
Hugh Tracey (Roodepoort)

---

*Indicates those elected to the original *ad hoc* committee.
[3] Dr. Anderson, who was an ideal guide from the very start, felt that a new chairman should serve in 1972, when he assumed the position as head of the Music Department at Tufts University. The Honorary Advisory Committee elected Dr. Undine Moore as his replacement.

Wendell P. Whalum (Atlanta)
Olly Wilson (Berkeley)*
Don Lee White (Los Angeles)*

It would be audacious were we to suggest that all of our work is without precedence. That is not true. Even though every aspect of the Center is based on more than predominately Black advice, we feel it best to avoid as many areas as possible in which *total* Black participation is philosophically essential. As a result of these and other factors, our range of activities is limited (so there is room for other groups to continue or initiate their own projects); and our role is unquestionably supportive, free of interest conflicts or a desire merely to duplicate.

The future of the Center will depend on the moral, informational, and financial support it can merit from individuals, institutions, and foundations. It will also depend on the extent to which its subject is accepted in the teaching, performance, and research programs throughout this country and abroad. The 1972 seminar was dedicated to spirituals, blues, and gospel music. In cooperation with the University of Puerto Rico, plans are underway for a seminar to be held in the Caribbean (which may be followed by tours to Brazil and Africa in the future). The Center has been asked to host the first national Congress on Black Dance in 1973, under the supervision of the Modern Organization for Dance Evolvement.

Persons interested in securing information regarding the seminars and any future publications of the Black Music Center are invited to request that their names be added to our mailing list.

The present volume must acknowledge profound gratitude to many individuals who have assisted us in our embryonic years. Even though a few of the following names may be repeats from the dedicatory page, I unhestitatingly cite William B. Christ (Associate Dean, Indiana University School of Music), Jane G. Flener (former Assistant Director of the Indiana University Libraries), T. J. Anderson (friend and guide), Herbert McArthur (former Director of Education Programs, National Endowment for the Humanities), Louise Shepard (who transcribed the seminar sessions for this book as well as for *Black Music in Our Culture),* Thomas J. Ahrens (whose moral support has been of the greatest importance), Charles Ellison (whose philosophic contributions were of the first magnitude), Sharon B. Thompson (who unselfishly served the cause for four years and was, without a doubt, a key figure in every aspect of the work), and every one of the hundreds of correspondents who wrote for information and shared ideas with me—from

elementary school students to university administrators, and from established concert musicians to inner-city directors of church choirs.
Bless you all.

As *Black Music in Our Culture* was going to press, the establishment of the
Black Music Center was announced. Now, as the final draft of this manuscript
is being prepared, I must make the painful announcement that I have resigned
my position as Director of the Center at Indiana University. This decision was
based on a year of intense concerns and was a totally voluntary step on my part
for a complex network of reasons, not one of which relates to the degree of my
commitment. I have elected to leave this preface unchanged, despite that fact.

2. Introduction: Perspectives

As a guest of the College of the Virgin Islands in November of 1971, I was asked to serve on a panel with an assigned topic of the "Cultural limitations of calypso as pop music." This was an exceptionally provocative, stimulating, and controversial subject which, I regret, we did not explore in proper detail. My contribution consisted essentially in the statement that no manifestation of a culture is inferior if it satisfies the needs of the people of that culture, and it has no obligation to relate to other cultures. I know that seems sort of isolationist, but it was originally stimulated by the suggestion that the Caribbean has thus far failed to produce "another Beethoven."

Now Beethoven is fine, and it is true that he can speak for all men, not just Germans or Austrians and not just early nineteenth-century romantics. But I think it is simplistic to ignore the fact that he was basically a Germanic, nineteenth-century figure, and that he was one figure who rose up from his cultural milieu to give a synthesis and impetus to ideals present in the concepts of his contemporaries. I think it is potentially racist, in ignoring that, to perpetuate the myth that music is a "universal language." More important, it is sociologically and aesthetically dishonest to assume that any other cultural area or time has any kind of an obligation to transplant a musical power or spirit or quality from Europe. Despite my devotion to Beethoven (although I am neither German nor did I live in the last century), I cannot assume calypso music to be less valid in the Caribbean than Beethoven is (or was) in Vienna, and we must not be guilty of cultural imperialism.

I will return to these sessions in St. Thomas, but that panel topic serves as an illustration of something which can easily exist: a cultural inferiority complex. I suggested this to the islander who had assigned us the topic, and the validity of my suspicions were subsequently acknowledged, although he had not been fully aware of the sentiment's implications before, nor had his colleagues, seemingly. I was sensitive to the possibility of such a complex because it had been on my mind for some time that feelings of cultural inferiority may account, to some extent, for the resistance of White America to accept overtly the qualities of Black art, even though some aspects of this art had been absorbed into the aesthetic bloodstream of Anglo-America. It is this idea which I should like to explore in these introductory perspectives.

The relationship of the arts to the Anglo-American citizen (including those who were blanched in the melting pot) has not always been a comfortable one. Art in America has not been, or has not been recognized to be, as institutionally functional as it has been in other cultures. Because it does not appear to be an element of sociological importance, art to Whites has been largely either an imposition or, at best, an ornament. One could never make such a statement about Black art, and that is one of the characteristics to be outlined later. This basic contrast between (Black) functionalism and (White) non-functionalism has opened the way for White culture to become cloistered in the ivory tower, while Black culture has retained its unidealized acceptance of life and of the earth. Those American Whites who have not been inhibited by an anti-aesthetic puritanism, the pragmatism of a frontier society, or the traditions of these, have noted little of their own in the arts, particularly on the "elevated" level, and have been ashamed of their more useful expressions. With regard to music, the small percentage of Americans who attend concerts and operas with any degree of regularity is almost always nourished with music by non-Anglo Europeans, yet it is this which is considered a "cultural event." The percentage would be smaller, in fact, if the works represented the products of native talent. White Americans continue to believe that their own cultural strength rests in the extent to which they can prove themselves as good as European audiences and composers, still coasting on habits of thought which rejected the idea that an American with the name of Jones, Smith, or Davis could create or perform music of substance. It is not only racist traditions then which have led White America to overlook Quincy Jones, Hale Smith, or Miles Davis. We will see that even in the area of jazz, academic America waited until elements of this idiom were imported from Europe.

The enjoyment of the arts in the United States has often been thought a tedious task, so that "culture" has come to mean the "finer things" of life, rather than the *real* things essential to social continuity and expression, regardless of the economic or educational status of the participant. Such is the extent of an imposition on a people who have often seen themselves as culturally deprived, a term they invented to apply to those outside of their numerically dominant group.[1]

---

[1] The winter 1972 issue of *Journal of Research in Music Education* (v20n4) contains an article by Charles R. Reid entitled "Relative Effectiveness of Contrasted Music Teaching Styles for the Culturally Deprived." On page 485,

Antonín Dvořák came to the United States at the end of the last century, still burning with the ardor of Czech nationalism. He readily saw that America was trying to be German in its music, not American. But for one vote, the official language of the United States would have been German when the colonial period was ended, and until Woodrow Wilson and the First World War, this country was far more pro-German than pro-British. Until the Paris migrations of Boulanger students (both White and Black), German musical styles and education fairly well ruled the United States. Dvořák knew this, and he was also aware that this cultural inferiority complex and that racial prejudice prevented White America from acknowledging its distinct cultural heritage—in Black music. It is well known that, under Burleigh's direct stimulus, this Czech tried to awaken Whites to their Black potentials. The fact that the *New World Symphony* is more Czech than Black is irrelevant. (I do not wish to slight the American Indian in this consideration, but that element merits more space and thought than is presently available.)

Four Americans reacted to his suggestion. John Knowles Paine (1839–1906) spoke as a non-discriminating "liberal" when he said that "American music, more than any other, should be all-embracing and universal." Put to a test, his sentiments might easily have ended in favor of German music (in which he was carefully trained), which should be the measuring stick for other expressions. The academic traditionalist today might use the same words if his judgments were challenged by Black music. Benjamin J. Lang (1837–1909), who gave a Boston concert in honor of the Emancipation Proclamation, stated that it would "not be natural for a White man to write a symphony using real plantation melodies." Perhaps some of today's brothers would agree, particularly as this might be regarded as exploitation, yet was it any more natural for an American to write a symphony using Germanic materials? George W. Chadwick (1854–1931) bluntly said that in the light of "such Negro melodies as I have heard, I should be sorry to see [them] become the basis of an American school of composition." With all due respect, it must be admitted that he never quite found an alternative. Perhaps it was not modesty which caused Mrs.

---

the author confesses the problem of identifying his subjects in language that is distinctly educationese: "The difficulty of differentiating deprived from nondeprived students for experimental purposes necessitated fixing upon some arbitrary yet relatively appropriate criterion. Given the makeup of the experimental population, race was selected as that criterion. Negro students were designated culturally deprived; all other students were designated nondeprived." How fortuitous that some criterion could be selected to justify this study. Now that we know who is deprived, we discover who is cultural.

H. H. A. Beach (1867–1944) to say that "Negro melodies are the legitimate domain of a talented and sufficiently trained Negro composer."

What all this amounted to, of course, is the supposition that something actually had to be done to turn Black music into art, cast in a form which German-oriented audiences could understand. I am reminded of a comment heard at a Chicago meeting to the effect that someone needed to turn the ideas of Duke Ellington into a symphony, or the statement made at the Virgin Islands conference that a composer should convert calypso into opera. Should there be an individual who wishes to "elevate" steel band tunes or *Mood Indigo*—no, let's be fair: not elevate but transform—then he must have the freedom to do as he wishes. If he fails (and he would then be judged by European aesthetics) or not, he should be ready to be called an exploiter if he is White, or an Uncle Tom if he is Black.

Yet we must admit that cultural evolution is not much influenced by panel discussions or *a priori* philosophical musings.

Feelings of cultural inferiority are not solely the property of Anglo-Americans. In 1871 appeared an edition of *Music and Morals* by a British writer, H. R. Haweis. Within this book he tells us:

> There is one other branch of strictly popular music which seems to be considered beneath the attention of serious critics; but nothing popular should be held beneath the attention of thoughtful people—we allude to the Negro Melodists now best represented by the Christy Minstrels. About twenty years ago, a band of enthusiasts, some black by nature, others by art, invaded our shores, bringing with them what certainly were nigger bones and banjos, and what professed to be negro melodies. The sensation which they produced was legitimate, and their success was well deserved. The first melodies were no doubt curious and original; they were the offspring of the naturally musical organization of the negro as it came in contact with the forms of European melody. The negro mind, at work upon civilized music, produced the same kind of thing as the negro mind upon Christian theology. The product is not to be despised. The negro's religion is singularly childlike, plaintive, and emotional. It is also singularly distinct and characteristic. Both his religion and his music arise partly from his impulsive nature, and partly from his servile condition. The negro is more really musical than the Englishman. If he has a nation emerging into civilization, his music is national. Until very lately, as his people are one in colour, so were they in calamity, and singing often merrily with the tears wet upon his ebony cheek, no record of his joy or sorrow passed

unaccompanied by a cry of melody or a wail of plaintive and harmonious melancholy. If we could divest ourselves of prejudice, the songs that float down the Ohio river are one in feeling and character with the songs of the Hebrew captives by the waters of Babylon. We find in them the same tale of bereavement and separation, the same irreparable sorrow, the same simple faith and childlike adoration, the same wild tenderness and passionate sweetness, like music in the night. As might have been supposed, the parody of all this, gone through at St. James' Hall, does not convey much of the spirit of genuine negro melody, and the manufacture of national music carried on briskly by sham niggers in England is as much like the original article as a penny woodcut is like a line engraving. Still, such as it is, the entertainment is popular, and yet bears some impress of its peculiar and romantic origin. The scent of roses may be said to hang round it still. We cherish no malignant feeling toward those amiable gentlemen at St. James' Hall, whose ingenious fancy has painted them so much blacker than they really are, and who not unfrequently betray their lily-white nationality through a thin though sudorific disguise; we admit both their popularity and their skill; but we are bound to say that we miss even in such pretty tunes as *Beautiful Star,* the distinctive charm and original pathos which characterized *Mary Blane* and *Lucy Neal.*[2]

We may all wish to react to certain implications and statements in this quotation. He errs in assuming European melody aided so much in the birth of this music, but he notes the distinction not just between European and Black-American music, but between that music written or sung by Blacks from that of their less gifted imitators. When he urges critics to give attention to popular music, he anticipates ideas of scholars such as Charles Keil. He is an intellectual victim of prejudice when he suggests Blacks are primitive, and he expresses feelings of cultural inferiority when he sees the Blacks as being more musical than the British.

If we are to credit Rev. Haweis with critical acumen, we must assume the performance of such a tune as *Mary Blane* provided substantially more quality than the music itself, but performance by Black musicians has often had more to it than the music would suggest, and some of this must have rubbed off on the White minstrels. We acknowledge, by the way, that the *Christy Minstrels* was a White troupe and that the composer of *Mary Blane* (which may have been William Bennett,

---

[2] Haweis, Hugh R., *Music and Morals* (New York: Harper & Brothers, 1871, pp. 429–31.

George Barker, Charles White, or yet another figure) is not known to have been Black.

His reference to *Mary Blane* encourages me to reprint this song in that version held by the Black Music Center. The title page of our copy identifies it as a "new edition" [3] of "The Favorite Negro Song / Mary Blane / As Sung by the / Ethiopian Serenaders / Christy's Minstrels and Campbell's Minstrels / Arranged with / Chorus & Accompaniments / for the / piano forte." The inner title page states that the song is given "as sung by the Ethiopian Serenaders at the St. James Theatre London, and Palmos Opera House New York."

_____
[3] See G. L. Kittredge. "Note on the Song of 'Mary Blane,'" in *Journal of American Folklore* 39 (April 1926): 200–207.

2

While in de woods I go at night
A hunting for some game
A nigger came to my old hut
And stole my Mary Blane
Long times gwan gwan by it grieb[d] me much
To tink no tidings came
I hunt de woods both night and day
To find poor Mary Blane.

CHORUS

3
I often ask[d] for Mary Blane
My Massa he did scold
And said you saucy nigger boy
If you must know she's sold
If dats de case she cannot live
Thro'-out a weary life
Oh let me die and lay me by
My poor heart broken wife.

CHORUS

By its musical style, this simple song would never suggest the Black-American spirit, despite the simple syncopations (which result from, or are stimulated by, the English text). Perhaps in some performances more was expressed than is indicated, yet such a song did stimulate British interest in American music, a stimulus which may have begun with the minstrels and which appears destined to continue past the current jazz and blues figures. The appreciation and support for these various types of Black music in England has been noted by John Hammond in *Black Music in Our Culture* [4] and is bibliographically manifest in *The Black-American Musical Heritage,*[5] perhaps suggesting a degree of cultural inferiority feelings on the part of the British, in favor of Afro-American music (as was subjectively confirmed by an English musician who recently visited my office).

If we look at American musicology (which has a great potential, not yet fully used, for influencing sociological and educational attitudes), we will find additional evidence of this thesis. In "Black-American Music Viewed from Europe," [6] I speculated on the probability that American musicology is *Musikwissenschaft,* that the American does not hesitate to teach about Bach and the Lutheran choral groups which helped nurture his style, that we are encouraged to study about Haydn and the *Ländler,* but not to transpose these ideas into the American musical experience. How much attention is given the New England hymnody before the music of Ives is discussed, and how much does the American music student know of social dancing in advance of studying Copland? As a preface to the songs of Schubert, "historically important" composers of *Lieder* from Berlin or Vienna are given

[4] Kent: Kent State University Press, 1970, p. 51.
[5] The second edition, revised and enlarged, is forthcoming.
[6] In *Your Musical Cue* 6 (December 1969/January 1970): 22–24.

attention, but how much note is made of Bernstein's roots in Gershwin, James P. Johnson, or Noble Sissle. As a matter of fact, academics may tend to ignore Bernstein's *Mass* because of its social values and style, and many American music teachers have refused to see the substance of *Porgy and Bess*. That's a long way from a juxtaposing Chopin waltzes and Joplin rags. And it will be the established musicologist who will equate Joplin's *Treemonisha* with Hiller's *Der Teufel ist los?* It might not be too difficult to find American dissertations on medieval French manuscripts, but where is the dissertation on Duke Ellington?

I am not belittling either the subjects or techniques of German musicology. What I am saying is that, were Black-American music native to the country/culture which initated musicology, these topics would receive serious consideration. To a large and significant extent, they are anyway, despite the fact that Black music is not indigenous to Germany. There are studies of genuine quality on jazz and the blues coming from German scholars. What is the American counterpart of the Institut für Jazzforschung at the Akademie für Musik and Dartstellende Kunst in Linz? Closest might be the Institute for Jazz Studies at Rutgers University, Indiana University's Black Music Center, or the projects in American and Black-American music at the University of Missouri, Brooklyn College, Howard University, and Virginia State College. Token offerings of a public relations jazz band or mention of Louis Armstrong or Nina Simone in a freshman, music literature class do not make it.

It appears that musicologists will have to bow to the anthropologists, sociologists, and ethnomusicologists who, with others, have accepted the challenge from Black music. The subject demands their viewpoints, but I think the time has come that one being trained in music research must study these ethnic areas as well, or we will only continue to cloister musicology toward that "unusually large degree of esotericism" cited by Alexander Ringer.[7]

Having secured my Ph.D. in musicology, I am aware of those factors apart from Black music which might give musicologists moments of paranoia, and I'd not like to encourage a protest movement to add to their problems. I would nonetheless wish to alert that profession to the possibility of cultural inferiority symptoms which, when coupled with sporadic interests in "quality," lay the groundwork for academic racism and social irrelevancy. Starting with the freshman year of a college student, the patterns of his historical and aesthetic perspectives

---

[7] Quoted in *Black Music in Our Culture,* p. 28.

on music are largely formed by musicologists. If that student is an education major, he may perpetuate these patterns in his contacts with a much larger population; it is not just the graduate musicology major who needs to be concerned. And very much the same argument can be posed to the music theorists: Can we not use *Ah Done Done,* as well as *Es ist genug* for analysis?

Educators have not always thought about who it is they are educating, or for what purpose. We ignore the fact that at least 25,462,891 of us are non-White (of this total, based on the 1970 Census, something under ninety percent is Black). We compartmentalize music into traditionally segregated areas,[8] each seeking to establish its own identity and curriculum, despite the fact that many of those students who major in these areas are qualified only to perpetuate the teaching of their majors (and employers, alas, think along the same lines). We are not always relating teaching to job opportunities. How many schools provide both the subject knowledge and skills to enter some aspect of the music industries, as an example? What school has surveyed the entire professional world of music, consulted with specialists in these various fields, evaluated the potential job market, and then developed a curriculum which may provide an interested student with training for actual positions—other than those which advance their own cause within the classroom. I wonder if college administrators, who might know quite well the implications of *prerequisites,* are as alert to the *requisites* of a music editor, a concert manager, or an acoustical engineer. Does he have some distress about graduating another senior class of piano majors, not one member of which may ever earn a living playing in the styles he was taught?

If I may introduce yet another comment to this network of challenges, I would acknowledge that education must teach skills, but it must also help the student relate these skills and data to others. The study of any subject which becomes an end in itself is not being considered with sufficient profundity. We may find the music of Bach tremendously exciting. We may love to work with the performance problems he poses, and we may thrill to his architectural inventiveness, but the end of Bach studies is not to write esoteric treatises in increasingly specialized areas. The study should lead us to a better understanding of mankind, not Neopolitan sixths. If our work does not end with a richer appreciation of all the cultural elements which helped produce Bach's genius, we will not know the significance of his greatness. We would

---

[8] Hale Smith refers to this in *Black Music in Our Culture,* p. 23.

then be tempted to move on to the next "great man," and overlook the fact that Bach was a man who managed to idealize factors within his own environment and achieve a synthesis (not an improvement) of aspects of the baroque, German, Lutheran, and European spirit. If we cannot move from Neopolitan sixths to music, and from music to men, we are playing the role of a humanities dropout. If we segregate and departmentalize every element within our art, we violate the art itself. It seems to me that curricula and departmental structures were established before the subject of music was considered, that those who developed these patterns were educational philosophers without the subject information which their decisions required. American music education now needs visionaries like Dean Michael Hammond at SUNY's Purchase campus, or Mel Powell at the California Institute for the Arts, who pattern philosophies on realities.

That structure has worked against the acceptance of Black music in the university because this repertoire has few works which are *only* music, few which can be abused (as we have done to European music) as ends in themselves. I am speaking now of blues and jazz—genres which are expressions of the people, uttered in their behalf by a performer who is one of them. There is a Black man's burden also in music education, and as with so many implications of the entire revolutionary movement, the acceptance of this burden will bring benefits to things we have only partially understood in the past, and we will come to know that "soulciology" is the message.

I am concerned also about the matter of concert repertoire. The Office of Education has published a booklet [9] which, by implication, poses some real challenges. Although the photos of the audience give more than token Black representation, despite the complaints registered (pages 37–38) by ethnic groups about the racial makeup of the orchestras, regardless of the fact that the orchestras reporting are often from cities with particularly large Black populations, there is listed not one work by a Black composer which was performed at the children's concerts.

A slightly better picture is provided in the report from Broadcast Music, Inc.,[10] which surveyed the programs of 5,877 concerts, given by 582 American orchestras. The only premières for that season of works by Blacks were the *Reverie and Rondo* and *Theater Set,* both by Ulysses

[9] *Schools and Symphony Orchestras; A Summary of Selected Youth Concert Activities* (Washington: U. S. Government Printing Office, 1971), 99 pp.
[10] *BMI Orchestral Program Survey, 1968–69 Season* (New York: Broadcast Music, Inc., in cooperation with the American Symphony Orchestra League, n.d.).

Kay. Among the 87 most frequently performed works from the twentieth century, there appears not one Black composer (although there are many White composers cited with works very definitely written under Black influences). There were, however, 68 performances of compositions by 12 Black composers:

Anderson, T. J.: *Squares*	3 performances
Cordero, Roque: *Mensaje Funebre*	1
Cunningham, Arthur: *Concentrics*	1
Dett, R. Nathaniel: *Juba Dance*	3
——— *The Ordering of Moses*	1
Hampton, Lionel: *King David Suite*	2
Handy, W. C.: *St. Louis Blues*	10
Kay, Ulysses: *Of New Horizons*	2
——— *Reverie and Rondo*	2
——— *Scherzi Musicali*	3
——— *Serenade for Orchestra*	1
——— *Sinfonia in E*	1
——— *Six Dances for Strings*	2
——— *Theater Set*	4
Nelson, Oliver: *Complex City*	1
——— *Concerto for Xylophone*	1
——— *Study in 5/4*	1
St. Georges: *Symphonie Concertante in G*	1
Smith, Hale: *Contours*	7
Still, William G.: *Afro-American Symphony*	13
——— *Blues,* from *Lenox Avenue*	4
——— *Old California*	3

In "A Course of Study for High School Band," [11] an unidentified compiler developed a chart of band repertoire, listed by historical periods (of sorts), which was suggested for a three-year band program. The only text accompanying the chart comprised the following statements: "Perhaps, if time does not permit all compositions in all categories would be used. One or two readings should suffice since perfection is not the aim. Rather acquaintance with the style and period." The compiler's contribution evidently escaped the eye of the editor and, as we will see, miraculously avoided the trash can of the editorial board.

---

[11] In *The School Musician* [Joliet] 43 (October 1971): 53. The spelling errors have not been corrected in the quotations which follow.

The band director, seeking to acquaint his musicians with a variety of musical styles, learns that the baroque period existed from 1675 to 1775, that the classical period extended from 1720 to 1800, and that "Nate Romantic Nationalism" was in force from 1860 to 1950, during which time "Sibeluis" composed *Finlandia,* but the composer of "Theme from Piano Concerto No. 2" is not identified. That style known as "Modernism" contains works or arrangements thereof by Shostakovich, Bartok, Bernstein, "Prokofreff," and Gershwin (including his *"Porgey" and Bess*). The diet for the "Contemporary" style is exemplified with music by Grundman, Gillis, Giovanni, Nelhybel, Reed, Williams, Creston, and the *"Devertiments"* of Persichetti. It is probably just as well no Black composer was included.

At a recent meeting of executives from major national music organizations appeared an alert and well-informed panel that discussed "Who is listening to serious music and why not?" The subject was considered from the viewpoints of the radio broadcaster, the recording industry, and the concert manager. Even though the term is not felicitous for either Mozart or Cecil Taylor, we can grasp the basic orientation it required. Had the audience been Black (it was not), we would easily find a critic who would have called them "Black bourgeoisie." One reviewer of *Black Music in Our Culture* stuck this label on our panelists who were not talking about jazz. Perhaps I am being equally guilty when I seek to label the "serious" music discussants as "classical music chauvinists." I don't do this with disrespect for them or the music they were professionally concerned with, but I can't look at youth music as being some kind of a "counter culture," and I would be more concerned with the repertoire offered in the concert halls of the inner city for those living nearby than I would be about transporting self-exiled suburbanites back into town for a few hours every once in a while to hear what they regard as "their" music. In a like manner, I lament those foundations which seek to perpetuate "serious" music to the exclusion of what other audiences would like to hear. Although the predominately Black audience at the Atlanta première of Joplin's *Treemonisha* was as beautiful a one as I have ever seen at an opera, I'd like to see operas and concerts given which could be freely attended by persons who did not have or were not interested in fine clothes. When we realize that *Aida* or *Tristan* need not be performed amidst flashbulbs which illuminate dignitaries in tuxedos and furs, we will begin to find what music is really about. When we have richer governmental and private subsidy of concerts— particularly those whose production is expensive—less wealthy citizens might relax their suspicions and find live music is really fun (but we sure better not scare anyone away by calling it "serious"). I refuse to believe that anyone from the inner city with the slightest appreciation of television, for example, could not be won over by *Aida,* but I do not say this in the thought that people *have* to like opera. I'd also like to see the carriage trade, stripped down a bit, at a jazz concert or listening to a good gospel chorus. That kind of ecumenism has been advanced by Dave Baker in *Black America* and his several instrumental concertos, and by Leonard Bernstein in his *Mass.* This is the area which should secure attention from the foundations, from concert planners, and concerned citizen societies.

Such projects will bring up the question of quality. Whenever we hear a reference to quality vis-à-vis Black music, I hope we will be sensitive to the implications of academic racism, hidden by the good old American tradition of euphemistic subterfuge and double talk by which unpopular causes are advanced. I enthusiastically acknowledge the subjective validity of evaluation, and I know that we all search for those factors which enrich our lives and which stimulate us to the goals we seek. But, in connection with campus aesthetics, "quality" implies that the academic community has already defined the term and that the subjects it considers and the way these subjects are approached have already been determined.

We might all agree that Beethoven's melodies are less beautiful than those of Schubert. It is possible that Beethoven could not write really good tunes, full blown and complete unto themselves, but he did not need to. His melodic lines and fragments are merely materials for a much larger structure. It does not matter if any of us could improvise a melody which we might regard as superior to those Beethoven struggled over in the laboratories of his notebooks. His use of these themes surpasses the incompleteness of their ideas. To assume that Beethoven should write good melodies because he was a good composer is as fallacious as to suspect Mozart was a great pianist because he could play with the keyboard hidden by a handkerchief. In order to evaluate Beethoven's creativity, one must see the melodies in their context. What we have here is the relationship of a detail to a master plan, to borrow a phrase from Pharaoh Sanders (which would doubtless have been accepted by Beethoven). Once we have passed from consideration of the melody and the many other elements which go to make up any one of Beethoven's works, we should be stimulated to relate the composition to the romantic movement; from the culture of the tune, to that of the piece, to that of the man, to that of his society. When that path can be followed all the way, we have a perspective of the forest.

A parallel exists with Black music. However much we might like a given element within the culture, we cannot evaluate it until we see it in its context. What other attitude will get us away from the pseudo-aesthetic philosophies which we have made serve us for so long? I'm not saying we must juxtapose Aretha Franklin with Hugo Wolf or Ned Rorem. We must see her heritage, observe how she expresses it, and know the place of her contributions to her audience. We already know that Liszt's *Faust Symphony* is functionally different from Schubert's *Heidenröslein,* though they both provide evidence for the definition of musical romanticism. We know William Grant Still's *Afro-American Symphony* differs from Carman Moore's *Drum Major,* but they both express Black-American culture and may be accepted in this role. White academics will not believe I am right when I state that a rejection of jazz or blues on the pretense of "quality" is tantamount to the rejection of Black culture on the basis that *it* lacks "quality." We cannot approach a whole culture, especially not our own in terms of history or heritage, with preconceptions about what quality means. We must take man as he is, and his artifacts as they exist, and know that a work of art has an obligation only to serve the people for which it was created. No musician need have a commitment to museum visitors of generations yet to come, not as his foremost aim. The contrary is true, in fact, isn't it: It is the museum which has the obligation. Most musicians may claim to be in the business first of all to earn a living, although few will deny a more secure living can be earned in other pursuits. Forgetting other factors for the time, his success in reaching that goal depends on the extent to which he represents his society or culture. We must therefore be careful not to apply standards of a different culture as a means of condemning a whole group of people. This is an argument for Black aestheticians, for Black teachers, for Black administrators, for Black performers, or for non-Black participants who have graduated from the ranks of liberalism.

I was delighted to read a statement of Ralph Ortiz, founder of the Museum del Bario, for Puerto Rican art:

> By the process of its collection and display, culture is now so depersonalized that it can no longer transform or humanize anyone. Just as our automobiles cannot transport us without ravaging the air we breath, a positive value is turned by technological and moral failures into a liability. The artist contributes to this

cultural crisis by compromising the human values implicit in the art process. One way he has done so is by supporting the notion that fine art is a higher form of culture than so-called folk art— that the gratuitous objects produced for a consumer society are more important than an art intimately bound up with an authentic social structure which humanizes one in the pursuit of happiness. This exclusive view is further confirmed by the artist's alliance with the gallery, museum and educational institutions. All these rationalize inflated philosophic and money values for art with oppressive elitist notions of quality.[12]

We have not yet left the consideration of a cultural inferiority complex which, combined with aggressive or disguised racism, has resulted in efforts to suppress products and attitudes not reflecting a relationship with (often misunderstood) European standards. If we seek to explore new perspectives, however, it is not only the thoughts and practices of Euro-America which might be challenged. This was brought home to me particularly by the Virgin Island conference.

My initial participation at these meetings came after one speaker innocently observed that the Caribbean had not yet produced a composer with the (Western-) worldwide impact of Bach, Mozart, or Beethoven. He is quite right in this remark, and it is a statement which could be applied to other geographic and cultural areas as well. How unfortunate is this? My brief contribution was a statement that I did not feel the islanders should have undue concern, because a culture is responsible only to those in whose lives it plays a part. The Black students understood that implicit in this remark was my firm belief that a Negro spiritual, an Indian raga, or a Caribbean calypso is not to be equated with a Mozart opera, a Bach cantata, or a Beethoven piano sonata because each of these plays its individual and unique role within its society. While I am profoundly convinced of the merits within European contexts of Mozart's music, we must acknowledge that judgments transposed from one culture to another are totally fallacious.

For this reason I cautioned the islanders against supporting any belief that an individual should apologize for his own heritage. There is no room in culture or the humanities for racism, but there is all the latitude in the world to admit the validity of more than one culture and to be sensitive to its uniqueness. This is what the study of the humanities is all about.

Despite that speaker's observation, I signalled the creative output of

---

12 In "Culture and the People," *Art in America,* May/June 1971, p. 27.

the Chevalier de Saint-Georges, from Guadeloupe, and of Amadeo Roldán, from Cuba. I had no reason to think these names were already known to those at this conference. I should not have neglected to mention Joseph White, another Afro-Cuban, whose violin concerto was at that moment being readied for a revival by Paul Glass, of Brooklyn College. These are only three Black figures from the Caribbean who, if they might not equal Beethoven (but why should they?) were nonetheless of substance.

I amplified my remarks during the panel discussion a few days later, when the topic was on the "cultural limitations" of calypso. I did not fully grasp why calypso was not described as popular in the panel's topic; it was certainly evident that the students had an allegiance to calypso as ardent as the stateside Black's fidelity to soul music. To make it more popular, I wondered, did they wish to export it? If so, for reasons which were financial or cultural? I called their attention to the fact that exporting or exploiting calypso would produce modifications through acculturation, that it would become different functionally and structurally.

I was stimulated to speculate on the contrast between secular-generated calypso and the church-generated music of Blacks in the United States, but I lacked enough information to attempt an understanding of any possible implications. In the process of mentioning this, I used the expression *Black experience*. It was used with as much objective expertise as might be the case when I speak of eighteenth-century rationalism. I have no subjective knowledge of either, and any such claims would have been sheer foolishness and an offense to the ears and eyes of those to whom I spoke. Being not insincere, uneducated, or insensitive, I am alert to the basic characteristics of these terms, nonetheless. I had hoped that the general remarks I made would provide the basis for an exciting panel discussion. What followed was exciting, but had as little to do with the topic as with what I said. A member of the panel, whose contributions to music have not been in the least insignificant, avoided the assigned topic completely and inverted the meaning of my comments. He felt I was on the verge of proclaiming myself a specialist in Caribbean music, that I felt the Afro-Caribbeans should "keep their place" and not try to "elevate" themselves.

I cite this matter only as an example of two basic errors in thinking: Some of us (especially educators) will fight to the end to justify our professions, and Black is no more consistently beautiful than it is right. If we have dedicated our lives to the concept of the symphony orchestra or the Ph.D. degree, we react very strongly in the face of any challenges. Our actions and our words betray a less than dispassionate dedication: The symphony orchestra represents "culture" and the doctorate is the "terminal degree." In order to become "cultured," one must know those works whose future is perpetuated within the institution and, in order to become educated, one must adhere to the program of topics and skills on which an institution and the education profession has established a foundation for its continuation. It really is true that sometimes these traditions are self-perpetuating and do not have any validity to those who are not playing the game. I suggest, then, that the panelist felt his role as a composer was being viewed as meaningless. It was not, but (alas) the rest of the world does not always recognize our priorities in the same order.

The matter of Black involvement in philosophic decisions regarding Black life is absolutely essential. To deny this is naive (and to state it smacks of dreary liberal rhetoric). If we are going to do a computer analysis of melodic style in the blues, however, the culture of the programmer is far less important than his skills. If we are to make an evaluation of the blues, however, the table is turned: Unless an outside view is thought really important, the critique simply must come from one whose perspective makes him deeply sensitive to the nuances and implications of the texts and the performance practice, even though that approach might be facilitated by the research of a non-Black programmer. Ethics of personal relations aside, the cause of any minority interest often must involve coalitions: We must know that being Black *might* give one very special and critical insights, but skills are not necessarily an accompaniment, nor is it impossible that a non-Black might be without acumen in substantive or philosophical areas. It is particularly important, then, that outside ideas be evaluated logically and that one not assume that a thought from a Black must always be regarded as right (particularly if it is advanced in the manner of a White pseudo-liberal or the spirit of a demogogic racist). The reader may gather that I am being critical of a specific instance, but that is only an exemplar of realities we must all face.

The next evening I spoke alone, calmly outlining the function of the Black Music Center. The antagonist from the previous night was there and, when I finished, he shook my hand. I thought then of the problems this gentleman had experienced and regretted they had stimulated an antagonism toward one he did not understand or know, but I was delighted to feel the warmth of his clasp. This was not the time to refer to a statement he had made earlier, regarding his conducting Spanish musicians in Spain, in the performance of Spanish music, but I knew that if I tried to teach a Black group to sing spirituals, no matter how expert a conductor I wish I were, the reception would not be warm.

It was not immediately understood when I told the islanders that I was not ready to apologize for my heritage because, if I were forced to do this, their turn would come. In just a moment, they all understood what I meant. Perhaps stateside Blacks would have grasped the implications faster, because American society made their parents apologize.

How twisted can become man's thinking and how perverse his actions when pride in one's own culture cannot be admitted or accepted, when we cannot see the manners by which these cultures differ and that this fact, with others, gives mankind his definition. But we must know that we have yet to prove ourselves worthy of our individual heritages, and there is a long way to go before we can benefit from our corporate existence. A sense of perspective may never be secured by the provincial or the isolationist, and perspective is not the Black man's burden alone.

3. Black Music in the Pre-college Curriculum

Marian Brown, Pearl Williams Jones, and Robert H. Klotman

● Marian Tally Brown is presently on the humanities faculty of Jacksonville's Florida Junior College. She secured her baccalaureate from Bennett College and holds a master's degree from Indiana University. At the time of our 1971 seminar, she was on the faculty of the University of Maryland. As a specialist on Black culture and music, she has been workshop consultant and guest lecturer on various campuses, including Queens College, the University of Wisconsin at Milwaukee, Indiana University, and the State of University of New York at Brockport. Her paper on "The Music of the Black Church" was read before the 1972 annual meeting of the National Association for the Study of Negro Life and History. This charming young lady is the wife of William A. Brown, professor of voice at the University of North Florida and distinguished concert tenor.

Pearl Williams Jones, as she indicates in her discussion, has returned to teaching after an interval and is now on the faculty of Overbrook High School in Philadelphia. Her formal role for this seminar consisted of participation on the pre-college curriculum panel, although at the final dinner we imposed on her to sing some gospel music—an area in which she is an acknowledged specialist.

Dr. Klotman is chairman of the Department of Music Education at Indiana University and a member of the Black Music Committee. Prior to his initial appointment to the IU faculty in 1969, he had been music supervisor for the Detroit and Cleveland public schools. He has long been active and interested in the music of Black Americans and holds honors and citations from many organizations, including the National Association of Negro Musicians.

MARIAN BROWN: The *function* of music as an art form does not vary from pre-college, college, and graduate curricula. It is the usage of the function which changes. This usage is determined by the teacher's personal philosophy of education and how he sees the role of music within the humanities, how he sees the academic demands of the school and the needs of the community. Most significant are the needs of today's children, which brings us directly to the issue of Black music in any curriculum. We all know how we've short-changed ourselves and our students by not representing the totality of the cultural heritage of man, how we've talked humanism while practicing dehumanization.

Music emerging from the Black experience is a distinct musical idiom with its own traditions and performance techniques. Academically it can stand objective scrutiny, yet its inclusion into any curriculum exceeds the purely musical. To ask who is in need of such a curriculum, might be an academic question to some, but the ramifications of any course that might aid the Black child in personal and racial discovery are far reaching, and here we're talking about linking the child to his culture, in more than a superficial way, by using the contributions of Blacks to show that we have aided in the growth and building of America despite our oppression.

The American way of life, with its Anglo-Saxon ethnocentricity (to borrow a phrase from Dave Baker), has netted the psychological trauma of inferiority bred into Blackness. Consequently, we cannot overstress the need for building positive self-concepts.

Let's look at one aspect of the Black experience: the Black church, a very exciting entity and seed bed for the development of many of our outstanding commercial artists. You have but to visit a store-front or rural church to witness the talent, technical skill, and spontaneous creativity alive in that setting. Yet, because of our Euro-Germanic conditioning, we have solidified our prejudices against everything outside this mold, and consequently, we contribute to the students' attitude of indifference to learning and lack of racial pride by perpetuating an atmosphere in the classroom which has no place for this facet of our heritage. So when you get a seven- or eight-year old in your classroom who is singing in the gospel idiom like Aretha Franklin or Lou Rawls, don't tell him that he's singing inaccurately because you are hung up on the concept that a young child's voice is "ethereal and flute-like." Just remember that he's authentically reproducing one of the many contemporary performance techniques.

The greatest response many of us may have will come from our students. They don't talk music like we do; they *live* it. And we must get interested enough to seek ways to communicate with them, for we can no longer hide within the sanctity of the once-called "ivory tower." As teachers, we must be personally committed to what we're doing. Whites cannot vindicate the four-hundred-year-old actions of their forefathers, but their presence in the classroom should indicate that desire.

In addition, being Black is not enough. Sporting that dashiki and that Afro will not give us any special insight. We must be able to be articulate. We have to get historical with our students. Don't begin and stop with the spiritual that's a "spontaneous outburst of religious fervor," but tell them that protest did not begin with the Civil Rights movement, that the slave songs are filled with metaphor and protest and that many of the slave songs, as well as many of our commercial hits today, parallel the African songs of recrimination. Most of all, stress the fact which Henry Pleasants has stated, that as far as music is concerned, America became new only as the African contribution became conspicuous. What distinguishes America's indigenous music today in the purely technical area is the explicit beat and the musician's swinging relation to that beat. And this "new" element is African. This is the heritage of our students, and they need to know it. We have to provide models for them to emulate. This seems quite a bit for us to do within any curriculum, because there is so much remedial work to care for. There is a tremendous task before us. To ignore it is only to perpetuate further the deep-rooted deficiency within our societal matrix, but to acknowledge it is to commit ourselves to unceasing work until the job is done.

JONES: I'm glad Marian went first because I would like to tell you about a kind of fulfillment or realization of some of the concepts she set forth so beautifully. I want to share with you some of the innovations we are attempting at Overbrook High School in Philadelphia.

I returned to teaching in the fall of 1968, after having taken a short vacation while I raised my children. I guess I was really not prepared for what I experienced that September. First of all, Philadelphia—maybe like many large urban communities in America—is a city that is undergoing a tremendous transition. The students in 1968 had led a protest against the Board of Education. It was one in which many students experienced violence. Among the things which the students were demanding was relevance of the school art programs to the Black student. I was very challenged in my return to this atmosphere because, like many of you, I came from a middle-class home with traditional training in music, and it was a kind of assault on or affront to all my background and training to be confronted by these students who were demanding what they wanted to learn. But I must say that an artistic revolution occurred in me that is still going on, and one of the greatest things in my own personal musical development started at that time.

At Overbrook High School, supposedly the largest high school in the state of Pennsylvania, we have about 5,000 students. About a decade or so ago, it was ninety percent Jewish and ten percent everything else. By about four or five years ago, it had become eighty percent Black, with the remainder Jewish and Caucasian. Our special music program is just in its third year and is not yet proven, but it is something exciting and dynamic which is slowly growing and developing into shape. In the near future we look forward to the crystallization of many of the innovative ideas with which we are now experimenting. Three of these innovations I shall describe to you.

The general music program is for students from the ninth grade up who need a minor subject for their schedules or who are working for extra credit. They are not interested in lectures about people from the past; they are vitally concerned with their own times, with the music of the present. It's a cultural revolution for the traditionally oriented musician, but not for the students. I had to learn all over again how to communicate with young people, and I did this by having the students actually take over the class. The students were responsible for preparing the lessons, bringing in their own recordings, and explaining the nature of the music. I must say the results were fascinating. This past year we made an analysis of *Jesus Christ Superstar* and studied the *Missa Luba* and *Porgy and Bess*—all diverse yet interrelated musical expressions. The students prepared reports on psychedelic music and its implications on our society and their concepts of life. When we went into string music, we compared Ravi Shankar, Wes Montgomery, and Andreas Segovia. Without even mentioning Aretha Franklin or James Brown, these are areas which interest Black students. I'm not using any text because there isn't one. The students make up the program with day-to-day flexibility, and there's a tremendous sense of excitement and achievement because they are running it. They know what they're talking about and they really enjoy it. Educators in the pre-college curriculum will know that the students are not interested in singing as we had been doing. In fact, even in assemblies our students refuse to sing *The Star Spangled Banner* (or to stand for the salute to the flag), but they are enthusiastic about singing *Lift Ev'ry Voice*. Music that is related to the student's own experience—the things which give recognition to their cultural heritage—is very much a vital part of our innovative curriculum in general music.

Secondly, there was a course instituted this year called "Bach and

Rock." It is a five-period-a-week major subject, without prerequisites. The subject deals with music as a social, political, and cultural aspect of modern society. The teacher engaged in instructing this course has indicated that it is exceptionally stimulating.

Third, and perhaps most important, is the Music Magnet Program. This brings students from all over Philadelphia to our school, regardless of the district in which they live. They are interested in majoring in music in college, in becoming performers and teachers. This course includes the initial ninth- and tenth-grade work in developmental music, with a stress on the basic elements of music. The fact that these are predominately Black students doesn't mean they do not need a concrete foundation in the elements of music because, regardless of the area in which they go, they certainly need basic tools in order to handle their art proficiently. They know this, so we aren't faced with the reaction to the fundamentals we would meet if we were to teach these basics in the general music program. In the tenth grade, we move into first-year harmony, seeking methods less dull than those we all had when we were taking harmony and theory in school. We are trying to introduce new methods by having the students compose their own music, discovering harmony this way. Many Black students are able to do things harmonically by ear before they ever recognize what they are doing on paper, and this is a most exciting way to discover harmony. We also have an advanced course in harmony for the seniors where the student is exposed to historical traditions. And there are also concerts by our musical organizations and visits with these groups by exciting musical personalities—such as David Amram, who was with our band, and Dr. Elaine Brown of the Singing City, who has often been with our choir.

All of these kids, no matter what program they are with, secure a broad perspective of the big world of music. They are as equally adept with *Carmina Burana* as with music by Thomas Dorsey. There is no conflict in their minds; they are not hung up in the ivory towers of "classical" music. We have a madrigal group, a stage band, a rock band, the orchestra, concert band, concert choir, and my own special pet project, the Overbrook Singers.

This last group came into being about three years ago, following the student interest in ethnic heritage. The Philadelphia students are fortunate in having such a wide variety of this heritage in a city of gospel music. In fact, I'd say that Philadelphia is perhaps one of the main centers for gospel music at the present time. Many of the great gospel performers come from Philadelphia. Well, about twenty-five students got together and organized the first gospel choir at high school level in Philadelphia. There has been a number which developed subsequently, of course, even in the colleges. But this group was organized by the students themselves. Two young gentlemen, both 17 years old, write all of the original music for the chorus; only one of them is in the music program. This group has brought great distinction to our school and is a source of genuine pride to all the students, providing them with a sense of recognition for their musical heritage.

Those of you teaching in predominately Black high schools should not be discouraged. When the students are able to do something, let them do it. They know what they are doing. And don't worry about standards of excellence because they will know when they are nearing their goals. My role has been that of a sponsor with moral support to encourage them to give what they have inside.

KLOTMAN: Too often we thing of Black music as being only for Black students. My contention is that this concern applies to the entire school system, to all who go to school. In some areas it is even more important for White students to be exposed to the Black humanities.

A second matter that requires clarification is that we are not rejecting the great European traditions because no one can claim that the White Western tradition has not made superb contributions to society. But this is not the *only* tradition in this country's rich heritage! We must not confine our attention to only one aspect of what is ours. There are four elements in the music curriculum for our concern: pre-Western music, youth music, contemporary music, and ethnic music. The Black contribution has musical elements in all of these categories.

Every child brings something of himself into the classroom, something of his own background and heritage. No teacher whose background might be different from the child's has the right to destroy or undermine his or her cultural identity. Those who have controlled the classroom have based their teaching on their own background and ideologies for years, to the detriment of those children who have something different to offer. Every teacher must discover what each child has to offer, to enhance it, to nurture it, to develop it, and to bring it to the fore so that the student has a positive self-identification and a cultural image which is better in focus with himself as a result of his education.

When I was Director of Music for the Detroit schools, we found it impossible to find a single basic music series with a positive Black image. This occurred as recently as 1966, and seventy percent of the

Detroit students are Black—so we're *not* talking about minority groups! The book order involved a $200,000 purchase, and the publishers were quite concerned when we began rejecting every series with the same complaint. How interesting to note that economics can change philosophy! We told the publishers about our concerns and finally settled on four series, each of which made necessary adjustments. We took out things like *Dixie* and put in *We Shall Overcome,* and we asked for a positive male image in the music of Black children. Every demand was met. We also asked that this not be a special Detroit edition, but that these changes be made for national distribution. One publisher had even issued one series for the North, and one for the South.

We also compiled our own song book, to be issued quite soon by the Marks Music Corporation as *Afro-America Sings.*[1] We solicited compositions from many Black composers so the students could see the contemporary writings of their people. Many of the Motown writers contributed. We also published our own *Bibliography and Index of Black Music.* Those of you without material should develop your own. Don't sit back in depair! Before I show you an example of one of our homemade products, let me point out a few books you should have. One is *Echoes of Africa,*[2] a song book by Beatrice Landeck, published by the Marks Music Corporation. You should also know Vada Butcher's *Development of Materials for a One-year Course in African Music for the General Undergraduate Student.*[3] This is extremely valuable and can be used in high school.

Now, I'd like to show you a kalimba which was made by one of our junior high school students in Detroit. You can buy the slats and various materials, and have the shop cut out the strips of metal which are needed. If you want to teach children about the elements of tuning, why not use instruments from their own heritage, and let the students make them themselves? Give them the metal and the wood, let them assemble the parts and make their own scales. By loosening a screw here, the metal strip can be lengthened or shortened to change the pitch. So we can teach them all the fundamental things we have

---

[1] Published by the Department of Music Education, The Detroit Public Schools (5057 Woodward Avenue, Detroit, Michigan 48202) in 1971. The foreword is by William Koerper, and the volume (xvi, 182pp.) was prepared under the direction of Ollie McFarland.

[2] This was originally published in 1961. The second edition appeared in 1969, issued by David McKay in New York.

[3] Washington: Howard University College of Fine Arts, 1970. The contribution to this anthology by Pearl Williams-Jones is generally regarded as a major study on gospel music.

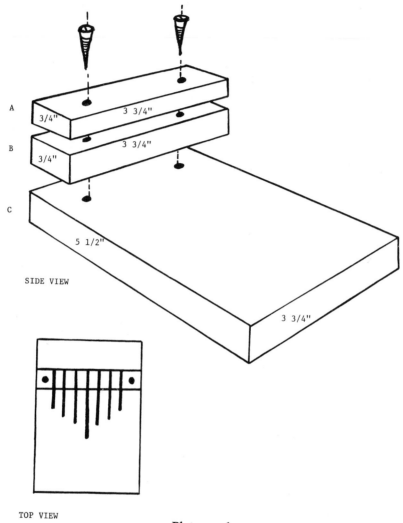

Plate no. 1

Drawing by Bryn Boepple. Materials needed: Wood, screws, metal or bamboo strips, shoe polish, and sandpaper. Directions: Sand all pieces of wood thoroughly, then assemble as shown in the side view. Arrange keys made from metal or bamboo strips between wooden blocks A and B, spaced as illustrated in the top view. Screw the three pieces of wood together and stain with shoe polish.

been talking about for years—concepts of pitch, tone, timbre, and the rest—but let them have the empirical involvement through discovery, on their terms. All of these ideas contribute to the child's feeling for himself and encourage him to express his identity in a creatively educational manner.

And if you need published or recorded materials, there are some good things available. There's a marvelous recording, *We Live in the City,* published by Presser. It is the work of an Indiana University theory graduate, Alfred Balkin, now at Western Michigan University. Within the Latin-rock idiom, he has written pieces based on actual life in the city: the policeman, construction, traffic, crowds. He has taken normal experiences of urban "kids" and turned them into entertaining, "learning" songs. Dorothy Ashby has a piece, *The John R. Blues.* Now John R. is a street that runs right through the heart of Detroit. As soon as the kids hear this piece, they say, "Oh yeah, that's right around the corner!" It has special meaning for them, and it is a beautiful song. When people want to know what we mean by relevance, it is something the kids can relate to, something that has meaning at a particular time to a society.

QUESTION: Regarding the student who plans to go to college, not necessarily as a music major, what are the pre-college objectives?

BROWN: You have to make your own, working within the latitude of your school's academic objectives, but you need to give the student what you feel he should have. You and the student could sit down and formulate objectives, but I think a good idea might be to consider comprehensive musicianship—not in terms of training a person to do everything, but with the view in mind of interaction and correlation, getting away from the compartmentalization concepts of the past. We're still talking about listening, creating, analyzing, and interpreting, but we have to emphasize the totality of man's cultural heritage. That is it in a nutshell. We will continue to acknowledge the worth of European music, but when we are talking of the Black child, we have to be free to move *past* the area of music and into the sociological aspects of developing as an individual.

KLOTMAN: The most important thing our students can learn in a liberal education is that this is a pluralistic society, made up of people with different concepts of beauty. The different attitudes and behavioral patterns acceptable in different societies define what humanity is. We must know that music served different functions in various ways to many people.

BROWN: Black music is so personalized. If only we can teach without turning the student off. When they come into the classroom, they are essentially creative. We must stop and find out their resources before we begin imposing on them. Visit the Black church with your student and see him improvising, spontaneously creating. We can never teach him to do this is class, never in the way he is doing it because he is living it. We are *talking* about something but he is *living* it. This is the beauty of it all! You simply must take him where he is—and I know we're trying to create horizons and this is fine—but don't destroy what he already has. Just add to it.

KLOTMAN: Perhaps most of you have seen *Up Against the Wall,* a film made for educational television in which the pianist Lorin Hollander sits down and "raps" with high school music students. One thing really hit me: a young man who was totally rejecting his music class, who asked why he was bound by musical notation. He said he had sounds in his head, but his teacher would not let him express them. After this, he and Hollander sat down and improvised. Unfortunately, this film is not readily available.

QUESTION: I was never so impressed with anything in my life. It would be perfect for children to see. It was a beautiful film with a great message.

BROWN: It took place at Edison High School in Philadelphia and was prepared for educational television. It may be publically available before long, and I agree that it is a valuable document.

KLOTMAN: There's another excellent film, *Discovering the Music of Africa,* in color with splendid illustrations of instruments. It was produced at UCLA with Ghanaian narrators, but with American students demonstrating performance on the various instruments.

QUESTION: Doesn't the enlightened educator have problems trying to get his administration to see the light?

KLOTMAN: Usually he has many problems. Administrators are governed by the games of numbers and finances, and it is not easy to get them even temporarily diverted from this pattern of thinking.

Let me give you an example. We set up five troubadour harp centers in the inner-city schools of Detroit. Children came there with their parents (an idea we borrowed from Mr. Suzuki), and the entire project eventually proved really quite good and secured national attention. But it all started when I went into the Associate Superintendent's office and told him, "I want to start five harp centers in the inner city." He looked at me and said, "You're crazy! Who ever heard of harp centers? Why harp, of all things?" I asked him what would be the last thing he would expect to find in inner-city schools. "Harp centers!" he laughed. "Right," I said. He told me to go ahead.

What I'm getting at is the need to sell the administrators on innovation. You must convince them that it is unique and that it will contribute something to the children—not that it is an irrelevant dream emanating from your own ambitions. Tell them your children are entitled to the same advantages as those who live in the suburbs.

JONES: We've had wonderful cooperation from our administration, and they respect the fact that ours is an innovative program. When we know a junior high student is coming to us for the Music Magnet program, his music schedule is set up before the academic subjects are scheduled. He has to belong to one of the major musical organizations, take harmony, and so on, so these are set first. The general music classes are offered throughout the day; there are no scheduling problems here. Our school is on a dual shift, by the way. The eleventh and twelfth graders come from 7:30 to 12:15, and the ninth and tenth graders are in school from 12:15 to 4:55. This means we have to schedule the choir and orchestras in the middle of the day.

KLOTMAN: Cass Technical High School, in downtown Detroit, has a special music program which is attended by up to five percent of the students in the city, and it also operates on a dual shift.

QUESTION: Can you tell us about instrumental instruction in the schools?

JONES: We have five on our faculty who teach various orchestral instruments. We have practice rooms, and students may take lessons in school. Those who need basic piano training are sent to the Settlement Music School. We have a full-time string teacher, and the band director has time within his roster for private teaching.

BROWN: I am not a teacher in the inner city of Baltimore; my experience with the Baltimore School System has been through the student teachers. Many elementary school classrooms in Baltimore have electronic organs. Students go to those organs with earphones when their schedule permits, sometimes getting together to improvise. One fourthgrade class even developed a trio on one organ: one student played the pedals, one the great, and one the swell.

JONES: For some years, we've had a bell choir. After the students learned about improvisation being an African retention in our music, they began improvising on a melody with the bells. We also developed a bongo drum ensemble which has performed with the Baltimore Symphony Orchestra.

KLOTMAN: This matter of improvisation reminds me of a big question discussed in Zambia where I was visiting just over a week ago. The purpose of the conference was to discuss music education in Africa. On the matter of improvisation, many people said that they could not teach music in the schools unless they transcribed it. "But if we write it down," they said, "we are destroying the beautiful element of improvisation."

Going back to the matter of instrumental music, Cass has an extremely strong instrumental program. Even though the choir program is good, it is in instrumental music that the school made its musical reputation. In an effort to spread music educational opportunities throughout the city, we set up pre-school violin centers. At last count, 120 students were enrolled. Northwestern High School, right in the heart of downtown Detroit, had a string ensemble which has played some of Dave Baker's jazz pieces, things Dave wrote to encourage young people in string playing, and they're really terrific. He's got five out now with William Lewis & Son, and an album of ten more should be out before long. William Lewis & Son, string importers and makers in Chicago, have developed amplified string instruments.

QUESTION: My small community lacks the financial resources of Philadelphia or Detroit, so we have to fill in our instrumental faculty on a part-time basis, bringing in persons from nearby locales.

KLOTMAN: I think you're making a very good point. We must not be totally dependent on that which seems immediately available and forget resources around us. When we started our jazz program in Detroit, the easiest thing to do—and the best—was to go to the professional players with Motown and other people who might not have all been "certified" for teaching.

QUESTION: What about general music for the pre-school Black child?

BROWN: The Martin Luther King Recreation Center in Baltimore comes to my mind right away. This building has been secured in the inner-city area, and neighborhood youngsters come every evening to work with volunteer teachers in music—choral or instrumental—dance, in almost any field. Youngsters respond more readily to things requiring physical action, so there are songs and dances, and chances for the children to accompany each other with bongo drums or even the tops of wash tubs.

QUESTION: Nursery rhyme songs alienate the child. Can we find a substitute, something good for the Black pre-schooler, perhaps with gospel roots?

BROWN: Certainly, but I wouldn't wait until someone else has come up with it. Nursery texts can be changed, or you could use the material found on the recording *African Story Songs,*[4] with some modifications.

QUESTION: Like it or not, we have been reared in this Western society, and there's no way we can escape nursery rhymes or *Sesame Street,* and it would be almost as difficult for the child to avoid some contact with "classical" music. As a teacher, I've had to acknowledge these facts, but I've also known I didn't want to stay at these points. I've had to go past them, to use them for my own purposes. The projects for my children involved making our own stories, drawings for the wall which would illustrate them, acting them out in dance, making up our own songs about them, and then—as a climax—making instruments for the project. This was not an effort to avoid assimilation, but an effort to go past it. This approach was tested about two years later when I worked in Washington for the Summer Education Program with primary students, not all of whom were academically advanced. Fifth-grade students were at times working at the second-grade level. But they knew what they wanted, and they did not want to stay with

---

[4] University of Washington Press, 1969.

nursery rhymes or *Sesame Street*. They were already there, and they wanted to go further.

QUESTION: The International Children's School in Los Angeles teaches children from pre-school ages up to the third grade. They have already finished a program in African culture, working under the guidance of a young man from Nigeria. They did not learn African songs. They learned African *children's* songs, and the teacher taught them how to play on the instruments of his country. This summer they will be working with the music of northern and southern India. They will become particularly sensitive to the cultural ranges of the world's citizens, but through the guidance of people from these cultures, not from dilletantes.

KLOTMAN: An excellent point. This is a good time to get on the bandwagon. It seems that everyone has become an expert in Black literature and music. Permit me to caution you to examine materials for their authenticity.

HAILSTORK: When I was in high school, I was allowed to write for the band and orchestra, and this was a valuable experience for me. To what extent are high school students encouraged to compose, and what are the chances this music might be heard?

JONES: We are slowly developing composers. The two I mentioned earlier are both children of gospel song writers, and their works are constantly being performed. The local band has a couple of fellows who write original material. We've not had as much success in traditional music because our students are often deficient in these particular skills, but they are given encouragement to write whatever they wish and we are happy to provide individual guidance when it is needed.

KLOTMAN: This reminds me of the work being done by Lena McLin at the Kenwood High School in Chicago. She has her students work together, even in the area of opera composition. They accept what they like and reject the rest, but they end up with a work of their own creation. We have a marvelous opportunity to provide creative experiences, and Mrs. McLin's work is an excellent example.

Regarding the pre-school question, we should mention the Children's Museum, which is part of the Detroit public schools. The person in charge of music is Barbara Wilson. The collection of African instruments she has gathered can be played by the children, and the kids love to experiment with the rattles, the marimba, and the other instruments there. These experiments raise questions in their minds about timbre and pitch, and help them identify with their cultural heritage.

DE LERMA: What is going to happen when these students get to college? Will the curriculum be ready for them? Note, I'm not asking if they will be ready for the curriculum.

KLOTMAN: The college is changing too, but not very fast. I am chairman of the Teacher Education Commission of the Music Educators' National Conference and, if any of you have read the report in the October 1970 issue of the *Music Educators Journal,* you will see the amount of emphasis being given to new areas. The college structures with all the committees and such can move slowly, and it takes time to grasp all the implications of change. Here at Indiana University we are aware that we must modify some traditions, but the high schools have been remiss in giving a potential music student the kind of preparatory training he needs for college. If he decided in his junior year to consider a college education in music, his school should provide him with a special curriculum to give him the skills he will need.

BROWN: One thing we have to admit is that Black music is not a fad. It's not going to blow over. The music can stand on its own feet and doesn't have to be proven; it can withstand analysis and scrutiny, but we have to face the battle. Even if we don't win everything, things will never be the way they were before we started fighting.

KLOTMAN: Right. And I'd like to say that there is nothing in a music school curriculum which can't be taught through Black music.

I mentioned changes taking place in college structures. One thing which has bothered me, which we are changing, is the sole requirement for admissions to the music education program that the applicant be able to play a recital.

WILLIAM BROWN: Are you objecting to the requirement in performance?

KLOTMAN: Not at all. I am disturbed that this is the *sole* requirement —spelled *sole,* by the way. I'm not against the recital itself. In fact, I feel every music educator should be able to perform and be able to present a recital. There is no question about that qualification, but it should not be the only one.

I'd also like to see certain specifications in the recital requirement. When I was in school, we had to perform at least one contemporary work. A balance—something which reflects the pluralistic nature of our society—should be sought in recital and concert programs, but there are requirements we should ask of potential teachers beyond musical ones. If you hate children, for example, teaching is not for you, no matter how well you play.

BAKER: Bob, you mentioned the need to structure recital requirements and attitudes along the lines of interest of the student. I'm not sure what all the answers are, but I know the whole world is out there, and I don't think somebody who is White owns all the music written by Beethoven. But we have to admit the validity of individual needs. The recital that might be adequate for one player—indeed, desirable— would be anathema to another. I'm rejecting categorically this notion of setting up molds, and that's why we're rebelling. All along, people have been saying, "It doesn't make any difference what you need or anything else. This is what you have to do." College bulletins shouldn't say all players have to learn exactly this piece, or that all players must play this on a recital. This is ridiculous. You might say that all recitalists should achieve the level of such a work; that makes sense. But I get very uptight when I hear all the students of one teacher working on the same composition.

● Evolving through this seminar was a greater awareness of the extent to which Black music directs its attention on people. This is true, certainly, with that music which is supported by the people themselves, but it is also evidenced by many philosophical attitudes held by composers and—as shown here—by educators. The educational program is designed to serve individual needs, not the program itself. The teaching seeks to build on the student's own potential, rather than to brush aside his previous experiences for the foundation of a totally different structure which the institution might deem valid for its subject. Certainly there are basic skills which might be essential to education, but ghetto English is a language which can serve inner-city citizens in their social roles, and student preference for *Lift Ev'ry Voice* (which, unlike the *Star-Spangled Banner*, was conceived vocally from the start) does not make them less members of this country.

With even the basic linguistic or musical skills will come disadvantages. Black music, like much of the world's non-European music, is essentially part of an oral tradition. If the music is not notated, cultural changes mitigate against its preservation but, with the introduction of notation into one's musical education, there may a corresponding loss of aural facility. This has not been true in the past (witness the cases of Bach, Mozart, and Beethoven), but the academic scene today tends to suppress "playing by ear" (excepting in jazz studies) with the feeling that the printed note tells all, even though no respectable teacher will admit this. That performer who can improvise, who is not bound to print for all of his information, can have a much better grasp of harmony and might regain that sensitivity of hearing which should have been his all along. Furthermore, one who has been so liberated may more easily find the spirit of the music to which Mrs. Jones refers.

The extent of personal, individual involvement in Black musical education gives emphasis to creativity, not revelation. The student is stimulated to discover his own potentials, not to fit his being into a preconceived mold. By extension, all history is forced to have relevance for the present and not to be an end in itself.

Dr. Klotman mentioned that Blacks were not in the minority in the Detroit school system. Urban school teachers perhaps need not be reminded that 10.5 million of the nation's 22.3 million Blacks live in fifty major cities. The 1970 census revealed the following percentages of Blacks within the population of these cities:

71.1% in Washington, D. C.
71.0% in Compton, California
69.1% in East St. Louis, Illinois
54.2% in Newark, New Jersey
52.8% in Gary, Indiana
51.3% in Atlanta, Georgia
46.4% in Baltimore, Maryland
45.0% in New Orleans, Louisiana
44.9% in Savannah, Georgia
43.7% in Detroit, Michigan
42.0% in Birmingham, Alabama
42.0% in Richmond, Virginia
40.9% in St. Louis, Missouri

Statistics such as these pose obligations to the educational systems, but the implications may go much further. Of these cities, for example, several have professional orchestras: Washington, Newark, Atlanta, Baltimore, New Orleans, Detroit, Richmond, and St. Louis. How many of these orchestras contain within their ranks even a portion of the city's Black population? How many perform concerts for the school children which represent Black creativity on their programs? How many seek the support of the inner-city citizens, and how many book Black soloists for the season? It should be immediately added that such Black conductors as Henry Lewis, Paul Freeman, Denis de Costeau, and Coleridge-Taylor Perkinson have made major contributions in this area, but on a national basis this is only a start.

A second example might be in the area of membership on the state arts councils. These bodies exist in every state, and they have the potentials to fund various projects in the arts which can support most manifestations of Black culture. It is extraordinarily possible for a panel that is either totally or "essentially" White to perpetuate a tradition which ignores minority cultures.

Many other examples of the problem can be cited without any effort, particularly within established channels. If proper attention is not given to the development of Black talent on Black terms in the school systems, the established channels may never be challenged. Without this challenge, they will be destined toward further elitism and additional irrelevancy, and they will be unable to serve the causes for which they were established—educational, judicial, cultural, economic, whatever. The extent to which educators can develop students with a greater sense of social commitment—within the multi-cultural context of this country —is a challenge inherent in the specific points raised by our panelists. In the end, it cannot help but be involved in the teaching of that person who is leading a Black chorus in Palestrina, or a White chorus in a gospel tune, who is discussing mariachi music or songs from the Appalachians. The school teacher is thereby forced to look beyond roll calls and traditional subjects and teaching techniques, to show a degree of that alertness evidenced by James Standifer and Barbara Reeder in the "classroom experiences" outlined in their *Source Book of African and Afro-American Materials for Music Educators* (Washington: Contemporary Music Project of the Music Educators National Conference, 1972). It is an extraordinary responsibility, but an equally splendid stimulus to build for goals which reach past the present semester.

4. Black Music in the Undergraduate Curriculum

Johnnie V. Lee, Portia K. Maultsby, Undine S. Moore,

and John A. Taylor

● Johnnie V. Lee is a graduate of Bishop College in her native Texas, where she majored in Greek and piano. She secured her master's degree from the American Conservatory and has taken additional work at the New England Conservatory, Eastman School of Music, and Northwestern University. She has been on the faculty of Florida A. & M. for most of her teaching career and counts among her students John Carter, Julian "Cannonball," and Nat Adderley. Her gentle and noble ways have endeared her to all with whom she comes in contact.

Dr. Undine S. Moore, an emeritus professor from the Virginia State College in Petersburg, was codirector with Altona Johns of the project "The Black Man in American Music." She is an honor graduate of Fisk University (where she was recipient of the first Juilliard Scholarship), and has her master's degree from Columbia University's Teachers' College. Other study has been undertaken at the Manhattan School of Music and the Eastman School of Music. Her choral music is published by M. Witmark and H. W. Gray. She is one of the great ladies in American music and has, as former students, Leon Thompson, John A. Taylor, and Billy Taylor. Particularly during the past few years, she has been a frequent guest on many major American campuses. Her research has taken her to Europe and Africa, and she has a particular interest in interdisciplinary aspects of the humanities. In 1972, the Honorary Advisory Committee of the Black Music Center elected Mrs. Moore to the post of committee chairman.

Portia Maultsby, who has been active in the Southeast and Midwest for several years as leader of a soul band, is a member of the Indiana University faculty and has participated in the Seminars of the Black Music Center since their inception, even while completing her doctoral work in ethnomusicology under the guidance of Lois Anderson at the University of Wisconsin. Since joining Indiana University in 1971, she has continued to prove herself a campus leader and a young lady of exceptional scholastic and personal merits.

John Taylor was a most valued member of the Black Music Center staff during our first year, when he was completing doctoral course work in music education at Indiana University, on leave from his position with the Hampton Institute. I was delighted to serve on his graduate committee and observe how easily he sailed through his qualifying examinations. We are all convinced that the future of this profoundly perceptive and brilliant young man will be of major importance to American musical education.

TAYLOR: In *Curriculum Development; Theory and Practice,* Hilda Taba writes that "a curriculum usually contains a statement of aims and specific objectives; it indicates some selection and organization of content; it either implies or manifests certain patterns of learning and teaching, whether because the objectives demand them or because the content organization requires them. Finally, it includes a program of evaluation of the outcomes." [1]

Curricula differ according to the emphasis given to each of these elements, according to the manner in which these elements are related and according to the basis on which decisions are made. The criteria for these decisions are derived from a study of the factors which influence curriculum choices. In our society these factors are the learner, the learning process, cultural demands, and content of the disciplines. With these matters in mind, our panelists will speak from their own experiences and philosophies.

MOORE: Evelyn Waugh once said a writer should never tell his readers where he is going for fear he may never get there; [2] but I will take the risk and say that all I wish to talk about is somehow based on the philosophy of a poem by Langston Hughes which we all know: the "Epilogue" to his *Weary Blues.*[3] It takes a brave or foolhardy person to say to whom a poet speaks. This poem seems addressed to a particular audience, but I invite you, this audience, to consider it as addressed to you.

---

[1] New York: Harcourt, Brace and World, 1962, p. 10. Appreciation is expressed to those Indiana University students and faculty who assisted in identifying sources for the footnotes of this chapter: Dr. Anthony Shipps, Clyde R. Rose, Earl Shay, and Gene Hunn.

[2] I am indebted to Daniel Bell for this introductory remark about Waugh.

[3] Copyright 1926 by Alfred A. Knopf, Inc. and renewed 1954 by Langston Hughes. Reprinted from *The Weary Blues,* by Langston Hughes, by permission of the publisher.

I too, sing America
I am the darker brother
They send me to eat in the kitchen
When company comes,
But I laugh,
And eat well,
And grow Strong.

Tomorrow,
I'll sit at the table
When company comes.
Nobody'll dare
Say to me,
Eat in the kitchen,
Then.
Besides, they'll see how beautiful I am
And be ashamed—
I, too, am America.

The subject assigned this panel has many ramifications—maybe enough to demand a lifetime for answers. I found myself involved in all sorts of questions: What should be the chief aims and hopes of an education in music? What responsibility should the music educator assume for aiding students in understanding their own culture—perhaps using it as a bridge to understanding other—even alien—cultures? What relation does the teacher's understanding of the cultural heritage of the student have to the teaching-learning process? As humanists, do we agree with Norman Cousins that "the new education . . . must teach man the most difficult lesson of all—to look at someone anywhere in the world and be able to see the image of himself?"

In a certain, somewhat specific sense—whether related to performance, history, literature, listening, or composition—one important, direct goal of an education in music has for a considerable time been accepted as related to the *understanding and mastery of the basic literature in the field*. When those of us in this room look at the phrase, understanding and mastery of the basic literature in the field according to what we have been taught, what we are teaching, what we have read in textbooks, what we have heard at concerts, that phrase will bring to mind little, if anything, that is Black. This is a paradox. For anyone living in 1971 cannot turn on the television, the radio, or go to a bank or a supermarket, or ride a bus without hearing something that is of African or Afro-American derivation, even though commercialized and often corrupted. Furthermore, with regard to the so-called, more serious contributions, the creativity and influence of the blues and of jazz are recognized by authorities almost everywhere. According to E. Jaques-Dalcroze, the well-known Swiss exponent of eurythmics writing in 1930 in his book, *Eurythmics, Art, and Education*:

> It cannot be denied that Negro rhythms have had a salutary influence upon the development of our sense of rhythm. Twenty years ago *our* children were incapable of singing syncopation in the right time. Freedom of jazz bands, extraordinary vivacity and variety of their cadences, their picturesque turns and twists, their wealth of accentuation and fanciful counterpoint; all of these have certainly infused new blood into music rhythm.[4]

The truth of this statement by Dalcroze was forcibly brought to my attention just last week when I went to a mass sung by a group of nuns. I had gone to hear Gregorian chant, but as I took my seat a bit late, three sisters rose: two with guitars and one with a string bass to accompany a piece, "Shout from the Highest Mountain." The two hundred sisters assembled, having been little exposed to the Negro rhythms to which Dalcroze referred, did indeed have the same difficulty with the syncopations which he described. The directing nun stopped the procedures, "Ah, just a minute sisters! Let's practice that syncopation and see if we can feel that rhythm a little better. Perhaps a bit faster."

In his book *Music and Imagination*, Aaron Copland tells us:

> Most commentators are agreed that the source of our rhythmic habits of mind are partly African and partly Spanish. Since the Iberian Peninsula was itself a melting pot of many races, with a strong admixture of Arab culture from Africa, the Iberian and African influences are most certainly interrelated. . . . As time goes on, it becomes more and more difficult to disengage the African from the Iberian influence. We speak of Afro-Cuban, Afro-Brazilian, Afro-American rhythms in an attempt to circumvent this difficulty. Since Spain and Portugal have, by themselves, produced nothing like the rhythmic developments of the Western countries, it is only natural to conclude that we owe the vitality and interest of our rhythms in large measure to the Negro in his new environment. It is impossible to imagine what American music would have been like if the slave trade had never been instituted in North and South America. The slave

---

[4] London: Chatto and Windus, 1930, p. 226.

ships brought a precious cargo of wonderfully gifted musicians, with an instinctive feeling for the most complex rhythmic pulsations. . . . Oriental musics contain subtle cross-rhythms of polyrhythmic implication, but we of the Americas learned our rhythmic lessons largely from the Negro. Put thus baldly it may be said, with some justice perhaps, that I am oversimplifying. But even if I overstate the case the fact remains that the rhythmic life in the scores of Roy Harris, William Schuman, Marc Blitzstein, and a host of other representative American composers is indubitably linked to Negroid sources of rhythm.[5]

But in spite of these fine tributes and those of discerning persons, such as Thomas Jefferson and Benjamin Franklin and Fanny Kemble in the Colonial days, there are two places where the music of Blacks is not found: in textbooks, and in theory classes and college music courses in general.

We referred earlier to the commonly accepted goal of developing in students an understanding and mastery of the basic literature in the field. How shall we go about making this phrase include Black music? By the same process we use with all literature: We perform; we have our students perform; we listen; we analyze Black music; we study the lives of Black musicians, including those James Weldon Johnson referred to as "Black Unknown Bards." "In a humanistic sense this study becomes truly meaningful and educative when it is used to illuminate the oppressive character of the slave system; the historical obstacles in making possibilities for study for careers in music for Blacks; the hostility shown to Blacks of rare talent." [6]

The good teacher of literature and materials can scarcely avoid listening to music with the teacher's ear. The opening of John Work's "At a Certain Church" from *Scuppernong Suite* always reminds me that when you want to clinch the dissonance of the major seventh, don't forget this piece.

---

[5] New York: New American Library, 1952.
[6] Doxey A. Wilkerson, "Negro Culture: Heritage and Weapon," *Masses and Mainstream* [New York], August 1942.

Music example 1:

I file away in my mind the codetta of Dett's *Juba* for use with beginners learning IV six-four. Within the pianistic figuration there is that clear movement: two voices to the upper neighbor and back, the chord occurring where the bass is the middle of three repeated notes.

Dett's "Night" should make perfect fifths unforgettable.

Music example 2:

Coleridge-Taylor's *Hiawatha* hammers away at the Augmented Dominant- C_7 $C+_7$ F major.

The teacher of music literature and materials will constantly be collecting his own anthology of Black works and examples for his classes. He will not desert Bach, Beethoven, Brahms, and Mozart. But the music of Blacks in the Hinderas album,[7] for example, is made of the same elements: rhythm, melody, harmony, tone color, texture. The basic principles of organization—repetition, contrast, variation, unity, balance, dominance—are observable in all art works. In compact fashion, what I am saying is that no matter what you teach, use some illustrations from the Black literature—the Black idiom.

To continue, for example, if you are teaching seventh chord qualities, perhaps you might have used the opening measures of Debussy's "Maid with the Flaxen Hair" because they illustrate the small seventh chord so well. You could at the same time scarcely find a more poignant example of the major large seventh chord than William Grant Still's *Summerland*. Perhaps you are teaching the song forms; The Mendelssohn *Songs Without Words* are often quoted for such examples as three part form, introductions, extensions, codettas, elisions. The suites of Dett, the pieces of John Work, Florence Price, and countless others, do these things beautifully. A nice question for self-study listeners might be to decide whether *Magnolias* is song form and trio or first rondo form. Or suppose you are teaching sonata-allegro form, is there any reason why George Walker and Howard Swanson might not be included? Or if you are directing attention to melodic contour and the relation of the text to the music in a song setting, is there any reason why one might not use a piece like *Four Winds* by Cecil Cohen? Or if one wishes to investigate how much wit can be expressed tonally, there is no reason to leave out "Easter Monday Swagger" by Thomas Kerr. Mixed meters are, of course, found in Stravinsky, but they are also found in John Carter's *Cantata*.

The first time I heard Olly Wilson's *Cetus,* which won first prize in the First International Contest for electronic music, I filed away in my mind the fact that it was a beautiful example of arch form. Interestingly enough, a group of quite unsophisticated students in a Black humanities course commented independently on this structure and demonstrated it with an appropriate movement of the hand to suggest an arch.

Or, suppose we are dealing with the modes, it takes our Baptist, Methodist and Holiness church students (Black and White) a little longer to internalize the modes in Gregorian chant, but they will not forget the Dorian mode in *Run to Jesus,* the spiritual which Frederick Douglas said first gave him the idea of running away from slavery.

---

[7] Dr. Moore refers to the recording of piano music by Black composers, performed by Natalie Hinderas and issued by Desto Records (DST-7102/3).

Run to Jesus
Shun the danger
I don't expect to stay
Much longer here

Music example 3:

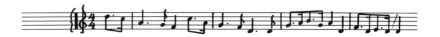

Sometimes we are reminded that much romantic music of Blacks seems dated now. We do not hear that comment very often except in relation to Blacks. It is as if a deliberate effort were made to forget that every piece must be listened to in its own context. Mozart is not expected to sound like Stravinsky, and Tschaikowsky still holds his own on concert programs, especially in Virginia where I live.

Within the space of a few measures of Altona Johns' *Barcarolle* on the melody "No Hiding Place," one meets an extension in the form of a ground motive, several secondary dominants, exchange of mode, and borrowed chords. It is good for first year students. I'm skipping about—but I'm thinking now of the teaching of compositional devices. Exact and modified repetition, sequence, imitation. Time does not permit me to play the multitude of examples which students find so stimulating, but let me note once again how a whole contrasting section evolves from a single motif in Still's *Summerland*.

If taught from this music, such things will linger in the mind. Teachers should know that we remember with our *hearts* as well as our brains. Blacks and Whites alike respond, as the Americans they both are, to the inherent aesthetic qualities of this music. A Black student who hears a beautiful passage written by a Black man has an appeal to his intuitive sense to support his intellect. So unsentimental a man as Charles de Gaulle recognized the place of this intuition. As recorded by C. L. Sulzberger, he wrote: "Bergson made me understand the philosophy of action. He saw how necessary it is to analyze questions in search of truth. *But intellect alone cannot act . . . Bergson showed me that action comes from the . . . combined application of intellect and instinct working together.*"

In a certain sense, all the music of Blacks referred to thus far, will soon have little trouble entering the classroom. But how about the blues—W. C. Handy, B. B. King, and Aretha—Dr. Dorsey and gospel, the various jazzes?

The blues and the forms from the past which have emerged and mingled must be brought into the classroom. The blues are an authentic poetic form, a rhymed couplet with the first line repeated. When I speak of this couplet, I remember my days in sophomore literature dealing with the heroic couplet of Dryden and Pope:

> Be not the first by whom the new is tried,
> Nor yet the last to lay the old aside.

The classic blues are often written in iambic pentameter. We might pause to point out that this iambic line is common in English literature. Shakespeare used it in practically all his poems except the songs. Milton wrote iambic verse in *Paradise Lost*. Pope used it for the *Rape of the Lock;* Wordsworth used it in *Tintern Abbey,* Coleridge in the *Ancient Mariner,* and Keats in his sonnets.[8] The classic blues have that compactness and often subtlety of meaning characteristic of good poetry. The Black speech, not a substitute for standard English, is nonetheless a beautiful language of its own. What can the Existentialists add to:

> Sometimes I feel like nothin;
> Something th'owed away.

Of course, it is possible to use blues for an emotional bath, but students should have an opportunity to observe such matters as the unique twelve bar form, the special scale structure, the peculiar emphasis on the subdominant, the non-tempered scale and its expressiveness in the sliding voices, the non-Western vocal timbre, the pianistic adaptations caused by tempered scale.

I asked students why they throught blues were not played in the classroom. After hacking the answer out in little pieces, we finally got an admission that blues are about SEX. We listened to B. B. King sing, "You're Still My Woman Now." There is a marvelous ostinato and codetta where the haunting line is repeated over and over. The theme of this is, of course, the *constancy of love* and the ultimate meaning is the same as Shakespeare's sonnet:

---

[8] This summary appears in "The Humanities," Virginia Union University, Richmond, Virginia.

> Let me not to the marriage
>   of true minds admit impediments,
> Love is not love which alters
>   when it alteration finds
>   or bends with the remover to remove.
> Oh no! It is an ever fixed
>   mark that looks on tempests and
> Is not shaken . . .

In other words, without even discussing really erotic poetry, college anthologies are full of poems that deal with love-sex. Sometimes, I think we deliberately try not to understand in other lyric poetry what offends us in the blues. Marlowe's Passionate Shepherd writes:

> Come live with me and be my love
> And we will *all* the pleasures prove [Italics supplied]

And Shelley writes explicitly:

> The fountains mingle with the rivers
> and the rivers with the ocean,
> The winds of heaven mix forever
> with a sweet emotion,
> Nothing in the world is single
> all things by a law divine
> in one another's being mingle,
> Why not I with thine?

We cannot logically accept these and then exclude the blues on the basis of sex.

We cannot exclude the blues on the basis of loudness. Think of some Wagner, some Mahler, some Tschaikowsky!

Why should we exclude the blues for emotionalism? Yeats, that poet of poets, writes:

> God guard me from the
> Thoughts men think in the mind alone.
> He that sings a lasting song
> Thinks in a marrow bone
>
>   . . .
>
> I pray—for fashion's word is out
> And prayer comes round again—
> That I may seem, though I die old,
> A foolish, passionate man.

The blues are earthy, often lusty. I have told several groups that it occurs to me that Bessie Smith, Aretha Franklin, and Billie Holiday would have had a perfectly fine conversation with Chaucer's Good Wife of Bath on the way to Canterbury. Remember where we start rejecting Bessie and loving the Good Wife, that Chaucer says of the Good Wife:

> Bold was her face and fair and red in hue . . .
> Five men in turn had taken her to wife
> Omitting other youthful company—
> But let that pass for now—
> She was a good fellow;
> A ready tongue was hers . . .
> All remedies of love she knew by name
> For she had all the tricks of that old game.

If any teacher succeeded in exhausting the technical musical elements and organization of the blues, the jazzes, gospel, or the related musical ideas, though not central, yet peripheral; if the relationships to other poetic expression were fully explored, if the various philosophies revealing the knowledge of the human condition were fully explored, who could complain of shallowness and lack of worth in blues study? Who could justly say that these musics are unworthy of academic consideration?

Let us listen to blues, gospel, jazz with our own ears, our minds and hearts and not with our inherited, unthought prejudices. Of course, these musics must be accepted with the same principle of selection operating eleswhere. There is *no* genre on which everything is of equal value, but we must rid ourselves of the feeling that these musics are low and unworthy because of the social status of some of their creators. Social status has absolutely nothing to do with aesthetic value. The blues are an original creation, something which never existed before. Let me repeat, these blues are an original creation, something that never existed before on earth. We may do well to remember what Arnold Schönberg wrote on this subject in his essay *Style and Idea,* when he himself had been criticized:

> To understand the very nature of creation one must acknowledge that there was no light before the Lord said, "Let there be light." And since there was not yet light, the Lord's omniscience embraced a vision of it which only his omnipotence could call forth.

We poor human beings, when we refer to one of the better minds among us as a creator, should never forget what a creator is in reality.

A creator has a vision of something which has not existed before this vision.

When you feel an attack of contempt coming on about gospel, ask your students, or perhaps take out your own pencil, to notate "Sing Alleluia! Sing for the Baby Jesus Christ is Born" by Earl Mumford and the Camden High School Choir. Let the students observe the limitations of Western notation in rhythm and pitch while they struggle with the beautiful complexities of the Black heritage as expressed in this gospel Nativity.

Both Blacks and Whites must be given an understanding of this music since it is now embedded in American culture—perhaps in world culture. All groups need to understand its worth. Learning is facilitated, and teaching is made joyful when the basic literature is in some measure a part of the student's heritage or his life. The sense of dignity, of pride, releases the student, and he creates more freely in all his idioms because of this release. This point of view so well established in Sylvia Ashton Warner's book, *Teacher,* now a classic in its field, has since been validated by numerous other studies in the psychology of learning.

If we do not accept the challenge offered by Black music as part of our teaching material, we will soon find ourselves in a situation, as I did recently, where three integrated music classes, performing Black music, had not one student, Black or White, who knew that the idiom was basically Black. What an opportunity for increased dignity, respect, and admiration was lost in this school, set in one of the last strongholds of the Confederacy. I was impressed with the manner in which the Catholic Church has been leading in the acceptance and use of the Black idiom. As an example, at the mass I referred to earlier, a sister seated next to me moved over to share her hymnal—the piece around which the service was centered was "Let us Break Bread Together." It was listed simply as traditional. There is a growing tendency to do this; not so with traditional French songs, German songs— "Bring a Torch," "O Tannenbaum." Maybe we could get a movement going to preserve the expression *Traditional Spirituals* so that coming generations in America would know the Black source of what they love and often admire.

Entirely apart from these spiritual matters, Black music must be taught because it is, in fact and truth, a part of the story of America. Black people are everywhere, and any study of any facet of American life and/or thought which ignores them is incomplete and thus automatically unscholarly. One hears a great deal of concern expressed that course materials related to the Black idiom will be lacking in depth. One hears very little criticism on the shallowness of a piano teacher who teaches the Bartok *Suite Opus 14* without having the student understand that the thematic basis of the work is African. A scholarly approach to the study of Charles Ives' *First Piano Sonata* could not leave the student without some recognition of the meaning of the note included by the publishers: "Ives is yet thinking more directly in traditional forms: two scherzi (and quite properly they are ragtime.)" Does the student then learn anything about ragtime to make his conception more valid? Or later, to quote again, related to this Ives work: "The fourth movement, however, (a second scherzo) is concerned with that often astonishing Americanism, the jazzful worship." "The jazzful worship"—the phrase invites some further study for the serious teacher and student. Neglecting to have a serious student explore these terms is like teaching history, literature, or philosophy courses where students deal only with excerpts and secondary sources. It is not respectable scholarship.

If you will look at the small list of music in the Black idiom by non-Black composers which we passed out to you this may serve as a clue, a confirmation of the influence of Blacks. The works do not prove anything because the jazz and ragtime idioms have been much better handled by others for whom the Black idiom is not a second language. Indeed, in my humanities classes, students are often unsophisticated enough to be quite irreverent about such names as Stravinsky, Debussy, Milhaud. They find a work like the Ravel *Piano Concerto in G* or the blues in Milhaud's *Creation du Monde* merely amusing.

On a lighter note, it is quite possible that some of us, having taught these works somewhat unthoughtfully, may find ourselves in a fairly happy state. Like Molière's *Bourgeois Gentilhomme,* who was delighted to learn on his way up the social ladder that he had been speaking prose all his life, we may note that, without knowing it, we have been dealing with the Black idiom all the time.

I hope that I have dealt with some of the questions posed by the planning committee of the seminar related to Black music in theory and humanities courses. Let me append a sort of *credo* which will mention briefly some of the most important of these questions submitted by the seminar which I may have omitted.

I believe Black music is a necessary study for Blacks and Whites. I believe that it should be integrated in the curriculum where it is appropriate, i.e. where it belongs. I agree with all my students whom I have polled that since art is long and academic semesters are short, Black music must be taught, also, separately where there will be time to compensate for the omissions of the past. As the students say, "When the time runs out, you know what is going to be left out—Black music." In time this may not be necessary, but in the words of Warren Burger, "Because of the racism of the past, it may be necessary for a time to follow unusual, awkward, even bizarre arrangements."

QUESTION: Can the teaching, performance, and/or study of Black music provide American society with a distinctly humanizing experience?

MOORE: Yes. It should focus attention on the treatment of Blacks in America, particularly illustrating the manner in which the Black idiom and the Black musician have been excluded from textbooks, from recognition, from financial gain, in spite of the fact that the idiom almost completely dominates the culture. Besides, the difficulties and tragic conditions surrounding the lives of Black musicians lend themselves especially well to an understanding of the human condition. Humanities courses are by definition involved with philosophy. The unknown Black who sang *Sometimes I Feel like a Motherless Child* knew what it meant to be a stranger, alienated, three hundred years before Camus wrote *L'Etranger*. Billie Holiday's life is a revelation of the myth of Sisyphus. And, even such spirituals as, "I got shoes, you got shoes; I got a robe, you got a robe," often listened to as laughable and comic, are actually heartbreaking; to think that a human being should so long for these ordinary essentials of life—a pair of shoes, a garment, something to eat, a crown, i.e., a small symbol of some measure of dignity and power!

QUESTION: What unique challenge might be posed by Black music to a student of music theory in distinction from those traditionally offered in theory classes?

MOORE: The challenge of analyzing and dissecting styles which include the unique use of melody, rhythm, harmony, tone color, texture, design, and the non-tempered scale. For example, Black music offers the opportunity to come to grips with more complex rhythm, with varied scale structures, with improvisation in a set style, with chord structure, etc. and with the deliberate use of voices and instruments to create a non-European Sound; a special type of contrapuntal texture. The several Black musics, spirituals, gospel, jazz, have their individual stylistic characteristics as definable as the Bach chorale style. The process of keen and disciplined musical mind. It is a good area for research.

QUESTION: Should history or literature be taught in a chronological approach and, if so, what effect does this have on Black music?

MOORE: Teachers differ in their opinions. I personally believe these courses profit from beginning with that music which is most a part of the student's experience. Black music will take its place, if properly taught, either way. Chronologically—starting with the ancient nations—the influence of Africa will assume great importance. As racism declines, as the written trade records in Arabic and other languages come to be more widely known to supplement the oral traditions, it will be accepted that most European instruments had their origin in Africa. The early prevalence of contrapuntal texture will also be observed there. Dr. Halim el-Dabh, musician, linguist, philosopher, associated with African Studies in Music at Howard University and guest professor at Kent State University, has done much work in this field.

QUESTION: Is the first goal one of knowing one's self, then one's society, then the contemporary period, and only then history in general?

MOORE: It is impossible for an individual to know himself apart from the society and the environment in which he lives. Knowing one's self involves knowing where one came from, where one is; thus knowing oneself cannot be separated from the past or what is contemporary.

QUESTION: Can the music of another culture or time be taught in a manner that will prove a meaningful experience?

MOORE: The answer is obvious. The only music which Americans, Black and White, have studied seriously up until now is chiefly

European music of another time and place. We have all found it meaningful.

QUESTION: Are these questions valid or should education aim for skills?

MOORE: Where skill alone is the aim, the term *education* is not proper— dancing elephants, performing monkeys have had a skill developed. We speak of them as *trained, not educated.* True education always involves more than skill—i.e., it involves insight and understanding.

And finally, on the matter of research and researchers, the European tradition approaches the study of music history and literature most often through the individual composer. The music of Blacks which has thus far most influenced the world is a *people's* music. While a search for the individual Black composer is certainly long overdue, it should be recognized that an approach to the contribution of Blacks solely in the European tradition loads the dice against recognition of the most original contributions made by Blacks. The method of study should be adapted to the situation, otherwise the failure to locate a second Mozart among Blacks may make certain persons undervalue the unique creations of the Black people. In other words, the White European tradition of studying music chiefly in the context of the individual musician, if continued, will be a part of the philosophy "white is right," and may do as much harm musically as it has done socially. Indeed, attention focused on the Black composer as an individual must always be given in a broader context, otherwise, in the hands of the racist or the unscrupulous, it may be only one more example of using a so-called objective device (such as IQ tests) in such a manner as to conceal areas of great superiority while demonstrating, by so-called objectivity, an area which Whites can comfortingly designate as inferior.

I do not mean to be abrasive, but I wish to point out that Blacks, from the less polite to the Dawsons, Stills, the John Carters, the Kays, the T. J. Andersons, and others, may be said to have achieved already a measure of the noble aims of art so well described by Joseph Conrad:

> To arrest for the space of a breath, the hands busy about the work of the earth, and compel men entranced by the sight of distant goals to glance for a moment at the surrounding vision of form and color; of sunshine and shadows; to make them pause for a look, for a sigh, for a smile—such is the aim,

difficult and evanescent, and reserved only for a very few to achieve.

But sometimes, by the deserving and the fortunately, even that task is accomplished. And when it is accomplished—behold!—all the truth of life is there; a moment of vision, a sigh, a smile —and the return to an eternal rest.

LEE: In the music department at Florida A & M, we have a choral and an instrumental program, both carrying the option of the B.A. degree (for future performers) or a B.S. degree (for those interested in teaching). The course in Afro-American music is offered particularly for these music majors, but also as an elective for non-music majors. Although I need to provide the majors with specific information, I must be careful to consider the background of the other students. The course is based on the syllabus which was mentioned in *Black Music in Our Culture*.[9] Through the years of my work in Tallahassee, I have found students who were tremendously talented, who could express themselves in a Black music way, but who had shortcomings in their educational background—especially theory.

I'm quite concerned that my students learn through participation, and I know that they are concerned with ideas which they bring to the campus from their own lives. We talk about a combo which might have performed the previous evening, about recordings they own, and about musical experiences from their past. I encourage them to perform also. Those gals with that low guttural type voice can swing blues like everything, and the fellows in a jam session create I don't know how many things, very few of which can be notated. They must all be allowed to do this, but our role is to show them how these activities relate to their musical education.

They need the discipline of theory so they can understand what is in their imagination, and they must know that a knowledge of theory is important so we can, for example, register on paper our musical heritage. At the same time, we know that theory is not an end in itself. Music must get across the idea of living in harmony and peace, not hating any race or any person. The teacher must try his best to prepare his students for that great challenge out there, a challenge which is greater today because of those sentiments, which are growing, that see us in a positive manner.

I am proud to acknowledge a close teacher-student relationship with John Carter, pianist and composer, who has been Composer-in-Residence

---

9 Kent, Ohio: The Kent State University Press, 1970.

of the National Symphony Orchestra. The youngster had an amazing memory; the Liszt rhapsodies, etudes and *Mazeppa* presented no problems at all. In addition to John, there was Julian ("Cannonball") and Nat Adderley, who would boost the pride of any former teacher. I gave these brothers their first piano lessons. I remember Nat was always a great one with the cornet and trumpet when he was in college, even though he wasn't a music major. When Julian was a little boy, he always tried to hide when he saw me coming to give him piano lessons. I had him later as a theory student.

My hope for these students and all the others I have had the good fortune to teach is that they will be guided by the principles I have tried to instill: respect for human dignity, a continuing search to satisfy the human need for communication, and a realization that it is their music which will generate that pride which gives them their identity.

MAULTSBY: There are six questions which I feel should be answered by one developing a course in Afro-American music:

1. What are the prevailing attitudes of Black students and music departments concerning Afro-American music? In many of the major universities and colleges of the nation, Black students in particular are questioning the relevancy of established university courses and programs. They seek means that will provide an understanding of the methods for dealing with internal problems. Most important, Black students are questioning the silent, yet prevailing, attitude that consideration of aspects of the Black experience need not be included in the curriculum. This omission implies that the Black experience is subordinate to the Anglo-Saxon tradition. Yet, in reality, the history of Black Americans becomes a valid element in referring to the social, political, economic, and musical development of the United States. Afro-American music is the major form of indigenous American cultural expression, yet this music has never been considered to any degree as being as "high" or "cultivated" as Western music.

The music of any culture reflects the attitudes and life styles of the people. All forms of musical expression must therefore be viewed in the proper context. Too often indigenous musical forms are compared with unrelated traditions and cultures. It would be unrealistic to try to understand Korean music on the basis of information on Indonesian music; it would be fallacious to compare gagaku (court) music in Japan with kubuki (theater) music because, although both are Japanese, the functions of imperial life are different from those of the middle-class merchant. The folk music of Europe cannot be equated with that of the composers. Although Bach's cantatas are now performed in concert, they were written for the church and should be viewed in that context. By the same token, Afro-American religious music before the Civil War reflects the hopes, desires, and dreams of the slaves. The music after the war expresses something else and therefore, even when examining the music of this particular cultural tradition, we must be alert to the manners by which two manifestations might differ socially. Too often the structural components of Afro-American music are compared with Western music. We see, for example, unconventional harmonic motion, unconventional melodic patterns, or unusual scale structures which don't conform to Western absolutes. If the music is viewed in its original context, the harmonic and melodic structure may prove to be quite conventional. I haven't quite accepted the idea of Henry Krehbiel, presented in *Afro-American Folk Songs,*[10] that a certain percentage of the songs are pentatonic, so many are major, and such. In the concept of Western harmony, it may appear that a certain scale degree has been omitted. This omission might be not at all true in terms of that music itself if consideration is given to the fact that certain scale degrees were never part of the original scale structure. Rather than try to compare, interpret, analyze and criticize Afro-American music as if it were totally Western and European, we must examine it as a part of its own culture.

I offer these points in partial reply to my question, indicating that Afro-American music *is* distinct and must be treated in this manner. This presupposes that the institution is willing to consider course work in the area.

2. What is the role of Black music in the university curriculum? Many music departments have special courses on the history of the symphony or of chamber music. They are sometimes open to non-music majors. Why should Black music be a topic that is more lightly regarded? A class in Black music should have the same objectives as any other: to stimulate an interest, to provide an opportunity for a deeper understanding of the nature of music, and to give students a chance to learn techniques of research. The contemporary accounts, the importance of early editions, the concepts of analysis and evaluation, the significance of developing a historical perspective—these factors are essential to traditional musicological discipline and apply with equal validity in the study of Black music. If we can train someone

---

[10] New York: F. Ungar Publishing Co., 1962.

to be a scholar with the use of only European music, can it not be done just as well with European and Afro-American music?

3. Can Black-American music be effectively covered within a chronologically structured course on Western music? We know it will end up being for the most part neglected. How can we deal with idioms such as the blues, when we can't get to the twentieth-century avant-garde Black composers, jazz figures, or even contemporary White-American composers? The way Western music history is taught today, we divide the subject in two parts, placing the eighteenth century at the end of the first half or the start of the second. Where in this pattern would you place slave music, as only one example?

I'm impressed with the program here at Indiana University, with Dave Baker's four three-credit courses on Black music history. This way, you can cover the subject, but it takes time. I'd like to see more schools offering such courses and, rather than telling the student how many credits in Western music he must have, the administration should simply urge the student to take some work in Black music. When we have that flexibility, the opportunity for adequate curricular coverage will be presented, and the interests of individual students will be better served—and that is what, I'm sure, all of us on the panel have defined as an educational goal.

4. How can the works of Black composers be included in the teaching of music theory? Until my appointment at Indiana University, I was a teaching assistant at the University of Wisconsin, working with freshman and sophomore theory. When I saw the students sometimes had trouble, I asked myself how I could expect them to understand secondary dominants, for example, if the music I used for illustrations was unknown to them. They might understand harmonic ideas, but the musical language seemed artificial to their own lives. You can find Neopolitan sixths in Bach, but Black and White composers of popular music know that chord too. So I dug up some new examples, from literature the students knew and when I gave the ear-training test, very few failed—if, in fact, any did. Professor Moore made an excellent point about this approach.

5. What new approaches and concepts relating to Afro-American music should be considered by music administrators? I feel there *must* be more emphasis on improvisation. Students often come to me and say, "Show me how to do this; show me how to do that." I say, "It's simple. Just start on the black keys and do your thing." You know, anything played on the black keys is going to be right! But then they want to explore more and complain that what they have done isn't soulful

enough, so then we have to move into more complex areas of basic chord structures.

We must also incorporate within the university setting more ensembles which relate to Black music. Many schools have jazz bands. I think the schools need to know there are other types of Black music, that a soul band might be a good musical experience, even for someone who doesn't read music (which does not mean he's culturally deprived). What's wrong with a gospel choir, as one finds in some Black high schools? And I think music majors should be expected to play in one ensemble whose music is in the Black idiom, especially those who might be subsequently engaged in teaching or performance. And I think the reason for that belief are evident: How can a White music educator deal effectively with an integrated class unless he himself is familiar with the Black tradition? I spoke with one choral conductor whose high school group had just performed a program which included Bach and a medley based on music of the Supremes. He told me he had actually played with Black bands to learn the techniques so he could become a better teacher, because his college degree program had offered no opportunity for this experience.

In teaching aspects of performance, the college should carry things further. Blacks have been victims in recording (and in publishing) which resulted from their not being aware of the legal details. If we teach the history, we need performance experience; if we have a performing group, we must teach about the music industries—about the details of the copyright law, about the fine print in standard contracts, about the total meaning of singing with a booking agency, and how to go about getting music or a book published. It is important that our teaching programs see real-life possibilities in their full implications.

6. Can Afro-American music be viewed independently of its history? No, Black culture must be seen in its totality so that, in this area as well, we see the music in the context of the culture. We cannot talk about spirituals unless we talk about slavery, we cannot talk about blues unless we talk about the effects of "emancipation," and we can't talk about gospel songs unless we talk about Black churches.

● "There are perhaps other ways for a musician to exist besides the ones we grew up with, and other systems for producing musicians of the next generation. Maybe we should rethink the entire process of educating young musicians? —usually we start them on eighteenth-century harmony and counterpoint, although the twenty-first is just around the corner." So writes the

British composer, Peter Racine Fricker, in "Music in America, A Personal View" (in *Soundings,* no. 2, 1971/2, pp. 4–5).

It is, in truth, the most horrible type of academic philosophy which regiments minds, rather than expanding them. Certainly a student in music must know the concepts of what has been termed "Palestrina" counterpoint, and that which passes for "Bach" counterpoint (either of these is normally taught from texts, rather than scores); he also needs to know that Josquin and Monteverdi fit into such and such a place in music history, but all is total folly if that student is not turned on to *L'Orfeo* or *Tu Pauperum Refugium.* I've lamented before that the academic teachers in our colleges approach music as if it were sex education: All is physiological. That won't work for either subject, and Black music will not permit it. We should never have let it happen to Dufay or Lasso, but try it with Bessie Smith or Charlie Parker!

The curriculum was developed, along with majors and degrees, without the benefit of Black music. In those courses which have integrated the two implied cultures, European music should have been approached more in the area of the humanities. When the time comes that every administrator will require his theorists and musicologists to be as conversant with Duke Ellington as with Robert Schumann, these subjects will not become ends in themselves and they will be drawn back into the humanities. Students will then be encouraged to see the human element in all cultures, and to know his own heritage and his relationship to it. This may be part of the heart of the matter to which Undine Moore was speaking.

Black music, as with many major aspects of Black life, can be a liberating experience. We've had too many performers (even since the Swingle Singers) who can't swing with Bach, whose approach to Mozart is rigidly museum-like, who see Baroque ornamentation as a musically sterile musicologist (and never listened to Aretha). We've had too many academics who lecture and grade according to the gospel of St. X (insert the name of the author of virtually any textbook on music history) thus perpetuating that kind of scholastic impotence which sees musicology's role as harmonious with these words from the *Harvard Dictionary of Music*: "Briefly, musicology is generally thought to include everything that is not clearly in the domain of 'practical' or 'applied' music, i.e., composition and performance." Nonsense! Anyone who is to be entrusted with the education of our students in music should approach his teaching from the standpoint of the end result: sound. And that must be allied to human expression. Perhaps in hyperbole, I'd like to require our theorists and musicologists to give one recital or concert per year, and that the program must include a proper representation of ethnically Black music. We would then not spend so much time committing the *formes fixes* to memory or be at such a loss when it comes to the question of *how* to make music, or what music really means in terms of humanity. That teacher whose instruction does not improve society should request of his degree-granting institution that he be reprogrammed. Black music, which has never been a party to these travesties, will be an essential element.

Undine Moore's philosophy will be part of this. She has quite specifically stated that education must be an emotional experience, and despite the depth of her education, her perspectives have become even more profound. Those who know, as she does, the beauty and validity of the Afro-American language and who have been deeply moved by the corporate involvement of the Black church, will have no doubts about the quality of the Black musical experience and the significance of its importance to humanistic education. Those who are sensitive to these matters will no doubt find the distance back to James Meredith and Rosa Parks isn't too great on some campuses.

5. The Composer and His Relationship to Society

T. J. Anderson, David N. Baker, John Carter,
John E. Price, and Herndon Spillman

● T. J. Anderson, who served as chairman of the Black Music Center's Honorary Advisory Committee from 1969 until he resigned in 1972, is presently head of the Music Department at Tufts University. Previous appointments include Morehouse College, Tennessee State University, and Langston University, with a two-year intermission from teaching as composer-in-residence of the Atlanta Symphony Orchestra. His music has been performed and recorded in the United States and Europe, and his reconstruction of the score to Scott Joplin's *Treemonisha* provided the 1971–1972 opera season with a major première.

David Baker, Associate Director of the Black Music Center, is a well-known figure in the jazz world and a specialist in Black music history. In addition to his teaching and performance, he is a frequent contributor to *Down Beat* and appears often as consultant and speaker on various campuses. His interest in music is not totally limited to jazz; he has proven himself a substantial figure in non-jazz composition, although this second idiom is never far from its Black roots.

John Carter is a highly energetic and gifted young composer, whose spiritual-based song cycle, *Cantata*, must be one of the most popular works of Black composers in that repertoire. He has served as composer-in-residence to the National Symphony Orchestra and been engaged in teaching as well as tours as pianist, frequently accompanying the gifted young Black tenor, William Brown.

John E. Price is on the faculty of Miami's Florida Memorial College and was previously active in Missouri and Oklahoma. He is a composer with an exceptionally large catalog of chamber, vocal, and orchestral music.

Herndon Spillman, who was the Center's Assistant to the Director during its initial year, is an extraordinarily gifted organist who left his post with the Center for private study in Paris with Marice Duruflé. While he was with us, he presented three all-Black organ recitals: one for the 1971 seminar, one at Dillard University (his undergraduate alma mater, where he worked under the distinguished musician, Frederick D. Hall), and the dedicatory recital for the new organ at the Rankin Chapel at Howard University.

SPILLMAN: The Black composer today belongs to a multi-racial society and may, as a result, wish to decide which race it is he will address if it appears he cannot speak to all at the same time.

CARTER: The role of a Black composer differs from that of a White composer since we live in a predominately segregated society. Obviously Black experience is different from White experience. This was covered by the composers' panel in *Black Music in Our Culture*. Because you are a composer, you are not removed from your race.

PRICE: I think that the Black composer is the same kind of entity within our society as the White composer except that, because he is Black, he somehow comes out being different or is made to believe that he is different.

CARTER: Well, society's reaction to him is certainly different.

ANDERSON: I think any Black artist is a collective individual. Stokely Carmichael, in a lecture at Fisk University, made an interesting analogy. He said a White businessman was looking at Blacks catch a bus one morning. He saw maids, gardeners, handymen, and other laborers and he said to himself, "Niggers." Then he was a group of college students from Meharry Medical College, Tennessee State and Fisk, with their blue jeans, tennis shoes, and sweat shirts with the college names written across the front of them, and he said, "educated niggers." I think the point is very important. What we are trying to say is that all Black people are basically linked together. For survival needs, there is an interdependence of all Blacks on each other. We, as Black people, have to think in terms of collective liberation. If a Black artist addresses himself to the plight of Black people (and that's what any artist does, he identifies with his own humanity), he is saying that we are not free until all Black people are free.

SPILLMAN: Then, in this part of the twentieth century, the Black composer is definitely identifying with his own people?

ANDERSON: Yes. He has no choice. He can't identify with the Whites; I mean, he's not White.

SPILLMAN: Do you feel this has been true from the start of the century? I think of Coleridge-Taylor or Florence Price.

CARTER: That's a very important point you are suggesting. When you say *White* and *Black* you are referring primarily to social conditions in *this* century. Coleridge-Taylor was a Black British composer. I don't think he went through social circumstances which would identify him as strongly with his race had he been an American. Black should be thought of *primarily* in terms of this country and a few others, such as Rhodesia or South Africa. It doesn't mean the same in all countries.

BAKER: Conditions change, too. When you mention Florence Price, you're talking about a completely different set of social, economic, and political conditions. If she chose to write Western concert music, one set of imperatives was brought to bear. Now we live in a pluralistic style culture, and now we know it. I'm sure she wrote out of her experience, but she had to aim her music consciously for a public which would support it. That public was interested in Stock and the Chicago Symphony Orchestra, and she knew it when she wrote for them.

ANDERSON: Black people are basically an emotional people. We have been able to unite the body with the mind. Whites tend to be less emotional in general. Certainly there are exceptions, but Black people generally will relate their physical beings into their mental state. It's common to see a man cry in the Black church. I have a friend, a White professor (some of my best friends are White professors, incidentally) on the faculty of Mehary Medical College. While he was there, the dean of the college died. He went to the funeral and was surprised to see the president of the college cry when he spoke about the dean. My friend told me he couldn't conceive of this happening in a White school. There is a life style, totally different, in Black humanism. This is the kind of humanism which should reach the "main" society.

BAKER: A technological society often finds itself in the kind of situation that happened with the assassination of President Kennedy. Jackie Kennedy was lauded for the way she reacted to the death of someone she loved very deeply. The papers talked about how super cool she was because she didn't cry. What has that got to do with anything? The normal reaction would be hysteria, but society had turned things around so that a value judgment was made because she didn't respond in public in a natural manner. T. J. is right. Because Blacks have not been absorbed into the mainstream, we can usually retain the right to react emotionally. You know, if you're Black and you're getting ready to go out to a dance, your grandmother or mother says, "Don't act like a nigger now!" That means don't laugh if you're tickled. When I go to a concert that gets to me, I react! If I hear something I dig, I respond.

CARTER: I don't agree that Blacks are emotional and Whites are not. Black society generally accepts certain kinds of behavior, and it may happen that these standards are different from those of the Europeans. It is considered very correct for Mrs. Kennedy to hide any visible sign of emotion, but this could be abnormal for a ghetto woman whose husband had been killed. Different societies chose different values. In some societies, as Ruth Benedict points out in *Patterns of Culture,* it is appropriate to be cool, nonchalant, and undemonstrative; exactly the opposite is true in other societies. I don't know why Black society has apparently decided that emotional behavior is acceptable and why White European society has decided that it is not, but I think it is making things too simple to say that Blacks are emotional and Whites aren't.

BAKER: Yes, but don't you think that cultural patterns are, as with music theory, *ex post facto?* Things arise out of a set of conditions, not with people adhering to these patterns, but by people formulating them.

ANDERSON: If we take the concept of emotion and extend it, we could say we are a spiritual people. I'm not talking about the church, messiahs, organized religion, or prophets. I'm talking about a spiritual base within the Black community. If you read Lorraine Hansbury, Richard Wright, or Ralph Ellison, you will find the hero has a humanistic spirit which transcends all of this violence and oppression. This is the *thing* that makes us survive. One could certainly say the treatment of Indians in this country has been as oppressive as that of the Blacks, but Indian culture has not been able to survive in the same manner as Black culture.

CARTER: Indians were not assimilated with the Whites to any great extent. They were pushed off by themselves, or real integration took place through miscegenation. Blacks were slaves, and they at least participated to that extent in society. It just may be that this was a more favorable condition for cultural survival. But the conditions of oppression were not the same for both groups.

ANDERSON: Certainly economically true, because it was not favorable to enslave Indians for work. What I'm trying to say, however, is that the condition of any ethnic group within the total majority reflects on its ability to survive and adapt to the outside forces which govern its condition.

PRICE: In the latter part of the 1950s we coined a word: *soul*. I think this is emotionalism against non-emotionalism, and I don't think it began in the twentieth century either. We got into trouble with the Europeans by using so many percussion instruments. Lots of strings were all right, but percussions. . . .

BAKER: I think the percussion thing is symptomatic of something bigger. Our focal thrust was rhythm, as opposed to harmony and melody. One thing common to all African-derived music is this propensity for intricate rhythm.

PRICE: Yes, but I am thinking of the so-called Holy Roller Church. There's always some sort of drum there, or cymbals, and everybody says "He's got the spirit, he's got soul!" And if you take the drums away, we clap.

DE LERMA: You are speaking of emotionalism. Might you not ally this with spontaneity? It seems to me, even on pretty much of an international scale, that Black music always permits the performer and the listener to improvise, to react on the spur of the moment.

SPILLMAN: May we hear now from the composers on their reaction to an obligation to write for the ghetto citizen?

ANDERSON: I'm thinking about the famous Black ballad, John Henry, which says "Man ain't nothin' but a man." If you haven't lived in the ghetto and don't know what it's about, no matter how sympathetic you might be, you ain't there. I think any composer should be where he is. You have to relate to those things with which you've had experience. When people come up to me and say, 'You music sounds like Webern; it's disjunct," I tell them "Dizzy Gillespie's *Salt Peanuts* is disjunct. The source of inspiration can come from a number of places. What I try to do as an artist is put it together. If someone says I got this from Mahalia Jackson, and this from Beethoven, that's all right. Every musician can choose his own ancestors. The thing that makes Beethoven's Ninth Symphony so great is that it deals with humanity—not just Germans or Austrians. The blues are not just for Black people; they are for any oppressed person, Jewish, Arabic, or whatever. This is what art does.

Now, when you speak of ghettos, there are all kinds: the platinum ghetto where the White folks live, the Black ghetto. . . . Being Black, I am emotionally involved in the plight of Black people; and that means I'm concerned about the ghetto, but it doesn't mean I go down there and stand on the corner and hear the wine bottles rattle and say, "Ah, that's what I want to get in my music." The artist has to transform the obvious into the universal, in his own way.

BAKER: People come up to me and ask if what I've written is jazz. I can't try to divest my music of those things which make me, and it doesn't matter if I write a twelve-tone composition or not. I learned the language of the ghetto as a native tongue, as my first language, and it's still with me. But that doesn't negate the need for learning something about craft and skill. Like I've already said: Beethoven belongs to everybody. All I want to think about is what I've got to say first, and then I determine the medium in which it is best expressed, and then I worry about form.

CARTER: The typical ghetto inhabitant, who might be making $75 a week, is not interested in symphonies. He's interested in improving his life, and art resides with leisure. I've heard people who come up and say they speak for the ghetto. Well, the ghetto is unconcerned with them.

SPILLMAN: But what about television, or the radio. You don't mean the people in the ghetto don't listen to music, do you?

CARTER: No, but they want an immediate catharsis. And, after all, even the majority of the Whites are not concerned with symphonies. Why should Black artists think they can have any significant impact by writing classical music on the life of a ghetto citizen? People who are poor need money, not symphonies.

BAKER: I agree. I won't make any argument for the symphony orchestra but, by the same token, I wouldn't want to get hung up on the notion which so many Black students have now. So many times I hear a cat say, "I'm not interested in learning anything about Duke Ellington, or William Grant Still, John Carter, T. J. Anderson, or John Price. I'm only interested in survival." He means a course in political science or Black nationalism, without realizing that when you're talking about survival, you're also talking about the survival of your culture. If the student doesn't see that his culture sets him apart from a lower animal, he's got a world of trouble.

Now, if classical music reaches the ghetto, that's very, very beautiful, and I think it is possible to acquaint people with some other kind of music than what they always listen to. I know there's a difference between Isaac Hayes and Dizzy Gillespie or Cannonball Adderley, and I know which of them the ghetto dudes would dig first. When you get into the more esoteric and specialized kinds of music, you're not talking about the same kind of thing at all but, if we're going to be honest, we *do* write out of our experiences and we have something in common with all men.

CARTER: A Rockefeller Foundation Study found that less than three percent of the population is involved with art music in America.

ANDERSON: But when you define art as being symphonies and ballets, you miss the boat. So-called primitive people have been dancing for years, and that's art. Black women have been singing over washtubs, and that's art. When you say that a string quartet is the ultimate in terms of sophistication, I say that's bunk. Anything that recreates the human experience is artistic and has meaning. We don't have documentation on primitive dance perhaps, but art goes on. It continues because it's a human expression, and the contrast between the primitive and the "cultured" is not as great as one might think. We must expand our concept of what art is so we have a gamut which relates to all aspects of society.

BAKER: I get kind of tight when cats come up to me and ask, "Man, do you relate to the ghetto?" Like if you don't sound like Aretha Franklin and you ain't doing this kind of thing, you don't count. I figure it this way: The Man has had us in jail for many years, and I ain't gonna turn around and let some Black dude put me back!

QUESTION: As a teacher in a largely Black high school, I feel that you composers are image builders. What do you feel you should do to reach these people, my students?

ANDERSON: I think that point is very important. However, I think that the artist has to be very careful that he doesn't become overly involved in deciding who his audience is going to be, in deciding how to reach particular groups or making himself available to masses of people. What I'm saying is that the artistic process is an individual thing. After the product is finished, it's available. I don't think we must expect all artists to spend time running up and down the road making speeches and shaking hands.

This brings me to the question of Black studies—that pacification program for Black students in White schools which, I think, is an insult. Now certainly, what Dr. de Lerma has done here at Indiana University with the Black Music Center is fantastic and marvelous. Eileen Southern's book is a monumental contribution. The work by Undine Moore and Altona Johns at Virginia State College is certainly highly significant. These are favorable points. The other day I was in Wendell Whalum's office at Morehouse, when he received a telephone call from someone who wanted to arrange an interview for help in her Black studies program. Wendell, who is one of the great descendants of the Black oral tradition, asked her what were her qualifications. She said, "I'm Black." Now this is ridiculous! "I'm Black; therefore, I can teach Black studies." I went to one school where the Black students wanted a Black teacher. The institution could not find one so they agreed to let the Black students teach Black studies to themselves and gave them academic credit for it. This is vicious! You may have an "arrange-ment" this way, but you don't end up with an education. Another example: a state-supported university had a group of Black youths traveling throughout the country, singing gospel songs in the name of the school. No faculty representative was with them or responsible for their performance, and they sounded like it.

This isn't Black studies. It has nothing to do with Black studies. This is the Black pacification. "We'll let them do their thing as long as they stay out of our way." This may be an easy decision for White administrators (who will then be free to stay on their traditional course), but it is detrimental to our cause.

A recent study showed that only three percent of the matriculating population in White schools was Black. By this, we know there is no sincere involvement in the education of Black youth. And just because they matriculate, that doesn't mean they graduate. People have to come constantly to symposia such as these held by the Black Music Center and really begin to look closer at the things that are going under the name of Black studies so we can get some sense of standards. All this is by way of saying that the perpetuation of images is a job of the educators. The job of the artist is to create.

BOSTIC: May I say something about this thing of image? My main bag is performance. I give at least fifteen concerts a year in Washington, in the schools. I am a "formally structured" musician, and that's what I am and what I believe in. When I play in the inner-city schools, I do not turn my program around in favor of rock or jazz. I don't like it when a Black person decides that all Black children must be constantly exposed to rock, jazz, or gospel. They must have the chance to hear other music. Education is a constant process of growth. We should not decide that every Black child has to like rock, or that every Black musician must be into soul music.

CARTER: If our students are not going to have the same opportunities the four of us have had, our image is a fraud, and we can be the agents for that pacification TJ mentioned. We are all aware that this is one of the oldest tricks of the government: A Black is appointed to the Supreme Court, for example, and this is supposed to pacify the man in the ghetto. That appointment doesn't change his life one bit and, until you involve the *mass* of Blacks in some sort of program which *will* change basic conditions, it is all a fraud.

BAKER: Maybe our problem is semantic. *Image* conjures up a lot of things. Maybe it's more just making them aware of what accomplishments are taking place on all levels, without making any judgments. Let them know that if they aspire to this, it's possible because somebody made it. But the word *image* sounds like you're deifying someone.

CARTER: But because one person has succeeded, don't think the door is open.

LEE: I think the composer's greatest obligation is that he be free from isolation in a ghetto or in any other kind of world. He must express *himself* and, as Dave said, he must have that freedom.

BAKER: There's no other way. I don't think there is an alternative.

ANDERSON: Yes, I agree. I'm trained as a musician and, therefore, I react as a musician. If I lived in the ghetto, I'd get a gun instead of a pen. I can work with a pen, and I know what it means (if I had a gun, I'd probably shoot *myself*). My job is to write. I don't care what part of me is White and what part is Black. Other people can decide that. If they say, "He's a real Black man," that's all right. If they say I'm an "oreo," that's all right too. Just let me keep on doing my thing. A creator is judged in the final analysis by what he has put down on paper.

TIBBS: It seems we are gearing ourselves to the upper crust of music. When I think of music, I think of the whole spectrum. Mention was made that ghetto residents don't have time to listen to music. I think they do, and that it is a very important part of their lives. There is a distinction, I feel, between entertainment and art, and I consider B. B. King entertainment. In other words, art generally presupposes some prior knowledge. If you don't know anything about music, you don't get anything out of a Beethoven symphony, but you don't have to know anything about music to get something from B. B. King. I don't think this distinction should be blurred.

CARTER: It's important in life to recognize distinctions so we don't fall into all sorts of disaster.

ANDERSON: Some like steak, some like ham.

BAKER: Chitt'lin's.

ANDERSON: Teachers cannot say to their students, "You're Black, so you're going to listen to B. B. King; I know you dig this stuff." Present the whole spectrum, and don't suggest for a minute that the kids should move *up* from ghetto music to Beethoven. I don't think we have been suggesting that. We might misstate our case at times, but we don't think in those terms. Ulysses Kay told me his mother-in-law came in the room one day. The radio was playing the Beethoven Ninth, and she didn't know anything about music, but she told him, "Son, you know that man said what he had to say!" It is true this is perhaps exceptional and that most people need some kind of background before they can understand ideas expressed in a different style. We all know that. Last night we heard the Crispus Attucks chorus from Indianapolis, and that group was really turned on. Educators all over the United States are looking for an experience like that for their students, music which can excite people. This is where the composers are losing the battle: We're concerned with the three percent.

CARTER: We're living in an era of mass entertainment which didn't exist seventy-five years ago. It is big business, and it is in the hands of the money makers. They are not really interested in entertaining the masses. They take them as they find them, pander to their tastes at that level, and leave them as they were before. This has happened in television and other areas. Until the business situation changes, I don't know how any other change is possible.

ELLISON: I think it's very important for us not to wait for an outside factor—White people in this instance—to come to our music and, at their convenience, prove it to be legitimate. We are capable of saying that B. B. King is just as beautiful as Mahler on our own.

BAKER: We have been put in the bag of waiting for White people to approve of our art forms before we accept them. We saw this happen in the blues. You know how you hid your B.B. King and Muddy Waters records under the bed when the White friends came over but, the minute it became fashionable to dig B.B. King, the scene changed, you dig? Now let's not say that art and entertainment need be mutually exclusive. There is some entertainment that is just entertainment, but you're talking about art when you mention B.B. King or Elmo James. Okay, it *does* sell, but don't let that mean it is something other than good. It is art *and* entertainment.

And when we write music, I don't think you want us to cheapen our work by writing down to people. One of the functions of an educational institution is to provide an on-going growth, like Miss Bostic said. That means we stimulate acculturation. I don't feel I've got to go to some other dude. I mean, why don't I train him to dig what I dig, since I already dig what he digs?

HARRIS: What does the panel see to be the role of the educator. There seems to be a dichotomy of goals here.

BAKER: The primary function of the educator and the system is to produce acculturation.

HARRIS: To what degree should the composer and educator work hand in hand?

ANDERSON: I don't think the composer should be concerned. This may sound like we're divorcing ourselves from education—but I have devoted a lifetime to teaching and I enjoy it—but the interpretation of what we do is up to the theorists and educators. For us to create, then turn around and interpret, then turn around and tell you how to teach, is too much.

HARRIS: Yet much music is beyond the comprehension of the majority. What should we try to achieve in public school music? Naturally, we want them to be able to consume some of that three percent, or do we? Do we aim for that kind of erudition?

ANDERSON: Well, Beethoven was *erudite* and Boccherini was *popular*. We shouldn't get into nebulous terms. Positions and evaluations of artists constantly change. My attitude toward Joplin is not the same as it was thirty years ago. We see him now as one of the most important creators of his generation, certainly comparable to Schönberg. Yet most people knew nothing about Joplin when he was alive—other than as a composer of rags. Because art lives, a constant evaluation is taking place, and a whole shift in terms of aesthetic consideration is more than possible. There were problems performing Webern when he was alive, but I heard a high school chorus perform his first cantata, opus 29, ten years ago.

TAYLOR: If we had taught our students to perceive the elements of music in their broadest applications, not basing our examples on a small spectrum, we would be in a different situation now. Our problem today with Black, popular, and youth music is that we educators are brainwashed. We can't get out of our own bag and see that we are dealing with the very same materials of music with all of this, only that they are being treated in a different fashion.

QUESTION: Opera is the particular thing I love. I know we can get kids who never heard opera to enjoy it. I've seen an all girl class sincerely weep in *Traviata* when Violetta was going through her thing, because this was a woman's woman. I've seen it with *Aida,* which also has the matter of race. But it can be done! We can work in positive and active terms, and we can get the music of you composers on the panel to our kids. We can show them that this is good too, that you are giving something to our community, just as B.B. King is doing. We need to make it "in." Let's just *say* it is "in" and forget about labels.

BAKER: Right! Buy the music and learn it, then play it for your kids. Don't let anybody tell you there ain't nothing in Black music but gospel and rhythm and blues. A well-known singer told me this, and I bristled. I told her, "Lady, like you know you're going to have to re-evaluate that. I can't handle that at all!" We've just got to represent the *entire* spectrum of work in music by Blacks, by performers and composers. You don't have to draw the line at *any* place. Play it *all!*

DE LERMA: Last winter I was at a meeting of the National Catholic Music Educators Association, chairing a panel with several major figures. The audience appeared to be rather conservative (I missed the Berrigans, but they were busy). The panel's sentiments were moving in the direction of letting composers fall by the wayside so that more attention could be given to the music of the people. Well, there was what appeared to be a healthy militant sitting there among all those H.R.C. brothers and sisters. He was reacting to some of the ideas non-verbally and, when he raised his hand, I thought to myself, "Okay, here goes the roof!" Quite the contrary. He wanted to advance the cause of Bach, Brahms, and Beethoven. Our good friend, Eileen Southern was on the panel, and she surprised me when she responded that she didn't think it was necesary to like Bach, that the best we educators could hope for was to help our students like *music* more. Now that was great, because she was advancing the cause of music as a human experience and, if you don't see music in that role, you aren't ready for Bach or B. B. King.

CARTER: But there is another point, and it relates to what T. J. said about Black studies and pacification. I taught one year at a school that was 99.44 percent Black. The whole question there was "is it relevant?" That means, "Do I already know about it?" Education exists to expand your horizons. The students at this school were interested in a gospel choir. Almost any ten-year-old kid in the ghetto can pop his fingers. He knows that, and he's got it. When you become educated, you learn something you *don't* know. That doesn't mean you have to put aside what you already have, but you are born in provincialism. You are heir to the life of a certain block, a certain city, certain experiences. From then on, you must constantly try to understand things further from you and your point of origin, and to relate yourself to the world.

BAKER: And that answers the question about the role of the educator!

I'd like to inject another thing here. When we are teaching about the Black composer—about John Carter, for example—do we write to him, or do we rely on the experts? When we go for the experts, do we find someone who is able to view the subject from the Black perspective? Even though I have a few reservations about her book, Eileen Southern has a plus, because she's writing out of a Black experience.

QUESTION: Are any of your works recorded?

BAKER: Well, what ain't recorded is available on tape I bet, if you ask. I think I'm speaking for all of us. Of course it may be nine months before you hear from some of us, but we like the attention. And if people are interested, a demand is created. If the record companies know there is a market out there, they'll put those things out. People like John Hammond can be reached. Desto Records has managed, and they ain't got as much money as Columbia.

CARTER: You know, Desto is a very small outfit, like a one-room office, and Columbia is an organization of immense power. They are up to their ears in popular music.

BAKER: But they have areas they can use as tax write-offs. I'd be one. I can be helpful to them!

ANDERSON: I don't want charity.

THOMPSON: May I suggest that we all buy the CRI recording of TJ's *Chamber Symphony* if, somehow, this has been overlooked. Such sales may encourage the release of his *Squares* or *Intervals*.

● Basic to this discussion was the assumption that Black music has distinct qualities which encourage, or require, a different aesthetic. Within the aesthetic latitude (whose limits are to be defined *after* the art works are examined) is the age-old Black concept of social responsibility. No one could state that this aspect is *always* or *must* always be considered by the Black composer, if that person has a broad concept of Black musical history (e.g., Bridgetower and Saint-Georges were not musically concerned with particular social issues, nor were their White contemporaries), but it is a factor far more frequently encountered in Black music than in the White music which lacks Black influence. It is by no means a matter in "art" music alone. In fact, it may be of substantially greater importance in the works and performances of John Coltrane, Pharaoh Sanders, Sun Ra, and Richard Abrams.

We must understand that there is a difference between being a Black citizen and being a composer whose works exhibit Black traditions. I certainly don't feel those creators who use the sonata form, whose descriptive works have no programmatic relationship to African traditions, or those who avoid blue notes are traitors to their race. Such a statement would deny the right of an individual to his individuality, or require that he fit certain standards of membership. It is quite possible for one to have a firm and active allegiance to Black society, and to compose electronic or serial music as if he were a German, although some more given to *a priori* philosophy than to music might not agree. Dave has hit upon this idea several times, and clarifies the issue again with the statement that "things arise out of a set of conditions, not with people adhering to these patterns but by people formulating them." It also is a perpetuation of a myth, one to which many White academics subscribe, that European music lacks social relevance. If the Black movement operates with the same limited logic which justified the birth of the movement, it will fail to rectify historical errors. The energy is then not used to its full potential if it stops short of its implications, and the more immediate goals will be only temporarily satisfied. In effect, we do not need a liberal revolution; we need a radical one.

Lest someone think I'm speaking of stockpiling hydrogen bombs rather than rifles, let me offer an idea of what I mean by these words. The conservative is either unaware of a problem, or feels it is unimportant, or thinks it is rooted in subversion and should be treated accordingly. The liberal secures personal satisfaction from treating problems which do not relate to him directly, but tends to be more concerned about symptoms of the problems than their causes. The radical is aware of the problem and is willing to seek solutions, starting with the fundamental issues. The extent to which the latter may resort to non-traditional methods of change doubtless relate to the extent to which social conditions have deprived him of any remedy.

Under no circumstances do I feel the Black movement should be only a vehicle for social change in other areas, but it is inevitable and wholesome that other groups would take strength from the extraordinary courage manifested by students, housewives, laborers, and professors who fought and protested for Black rights in the 1960s, and it would be ideal if—on the heels of Black, Brown, Yellow, and Red freedom (if those ethnic groups will permit this chromatic classification)—the civic, economic, and amatory rights of *individuals* could be won. It would also be ideal if the implications of these freedoms would be grasped in all areas, including a more humanistic approach to earlier European musical figures and a less emotionless approach to the teaching of young musicians.

But as for the right of a Black musician to be active in music as his education and talents direct him, nothing is more direct and liberated than Dave's refusal to "let some Black dude put me back" in jail.

6. The Black Composer Discusses His Music

T. J. Anderson, David N. Baker, John Carter,
and John E. Price

● It has been stated more than one time that a composer is not the best person to speak about his music. This certainly may be true in some cases, for various reasons, but it has just as frequently been observed that the composer's words can be of great importance—although no one's words can be more important than the music itself.

ANDERSON: In January of 1965, the *Washington Post* published an article by Carl Shapiro, the critic-poet from Nebraska, which stated that "a great poet has been living in our midst for decades and is almost totally unknown." That same year, in the August *Saturday Review,* Robert Donald Spector wrote, "Tolson has been almost entirely ignored. At 65, he has won few honors, received attention from only a handful of critics and poets, and yet *The Harlem Gallery,* like his earlier work, *Libretto for the Republic of Liberia,* marks him as one of America's great poets."

Those of us who knew MB certainly knew this to be true. While he did not enjoy many honors during his life (he died in 1966), he might be best described as a regional poet: The impact of this man in the Southwest, on the students, was monumental. He was the product of a family which was deeply rooted in religion; his father was a minister. The flair for drama flows through his poetry, as well as his daily being. Langston Hughes best described what I am talking about when he said that "Tolson was a great talker, and there was only one Tolson."

He did receive a few awards. The first was for *Dark Symphony,* which won the National Poetry Contest conducted by the American Negro Exposition in Chicago, in 1940. Four years later, he published his first book, *Rendezvous with America.* His psychological poem, *E & OE,* which was awarded the 1951 Hokin prize, created a tremendous excitement among poets. In 1947, he had the honor of becoming the Poet Laureate of Liberia, a distinction which he really enjoyed. It would have been interesting to see this man, then serving four years as mayor of the all-Black community of Langston in Oklahoma, when he went to a small country service to put on the Poet Laureate medal. It was bigger than his tie, and he was very proud of it.

He coached the Dustbowl Players at Langston, and he taught a full load of subjects in English (and those of you who have been teachers in Black institutions know exactly what I'm talking about when I say a "full load"). He carried on his creative work continuously, yet still had time to coach a debate team and to teach.

In my *Variations,* use is made of extracts from *The Harlem Gallery* and the *Libretto for the Republic of Liberia.* Tolson described *The Harlem Gallery* as "an odyssey of man from the primitive to the sophisticated, carrying out the function of portrait in mural, and covering the period in the history of the Negro people from 1619 to the present." The text itself deals with several things: the concept of colonialism, of religion, of sex, of Black life and history:

> In Africa, in Asia, on the Bay of the Barricades, alarm birds
> Alarm birds bedevil the Great White World.
> Berindian's ass——not Balaam's——
> between no oats and hay.

This particular passage has reference to the great revolution of the Third World to create a new and more humane order, for which we all hope. Biblical scholars will know that Baalam's ass knew what to do, but Berindian's ass did not.

The concept of colonialism comes forth clearly in a passage like this:

> Bola boa lies gorged to the hinges of his jaws,
> eyeless, yet with eyes in the interlude of peace.

Tolson was greatly influenced by the French symbolists. In this quotation, the snake represents the capitalist nations. The rape of Africa over the centuries by the colonial powers has never been satisfied. The continual exploitation of our people goes on even today where the resources of the earth are constantly drained, only to replenish the luxury of Europe. The alliance between the United States and South Africa is clear to all of us, and these are the things that Tolson was greatly concerned with. As the capitalist nations continued to rape Africa, Tolson envisioned intervals of peace as being only temporary conditions between the continuous grabbing.

We see the concept of sex in

Come back, Baby, come back——I need your gravy.

The rhythm is definitely blues. Those of us raised on Billy Eckstine's "Jelly, jelly" know that jelly, just like gravy, is a symbol of male potency. In the line, "Jelly Roll killed my pappy and ran my mammy stone blind," we see the essense of blues, the communication of the earthy, yet the total involvement of life.

One might also analyze the text by the cadential passage within the *Tolson Variations.* There are small sections in which metaphysical African proverbs are used, somewhat like witticisms with pungent meanings, as "the White man solves between white sheets his Black problems." Problem functions in a dual manner. "Where would the rich cream be without skim milk? . . . The eye can cross the river in a flood." These things happen continuously in the *Variations,* serving as transitions from one section to another.

Composers traditionally set texts by treating the concepts of a particular poem. I wanted to become more involved with MB than that. For years, he tried to get me to do his *Dark Symphony.* It has been set by several composers and is a popular text with musicians, but my music tends to be angular and I was interested in another level. I therefore extracted sections which were more meaningful to my daily relationship with him. As a result, the text does not run in a continuous manner; it jumps from one thing to another. The emphasis is on the subconscious, not on reality; on psychological moods, rather than messages.

When I was interviewed by Dr. de Lerma for the Black Music Center's score bibliography, I gave him a statement I had prepared for a German encyclopedia: "My works show the adaptation of pluralistic values, whose range reflects the influence of primitive music, jazz, post-Webern and avant-garde styles. I feel it is the duty of the composer to make audible the inaudible and, thus, link some part of mankind. The compositions do not represent any one style or school of composition, but seek a continuous arrangement of sound in a given time-and-place context. Its only meaning grows out of my experience with humanity and, therefore, manifests a genetic state of flux."

I continue to hold to this concept. In the *Tolson Variations* we see it manifest in metrical ambiguities, shifts and conflicts of rhythmic relationships which relate to the text, occurring quite frequently. Repetition is used as a unifying device, and only represents a pattern. Transitions always function in anticipation of a musical event. The work could be described as organic, in that it has metrical contradictions, uniform patterns, cross rhythms, and a symmetrical arrangement of beats. Figurations are sometimes redundant, fluctuating and then reassuring themselves in confirmation. The work is polythematic, with many homophonic overlaps. The music, as the text, is influenced by Negro life, which is its source for inspiration. The whole last section is a chaconne, which goes by very fast, and at the end there is a statement of the blues which had been the harmonic basis for the fast section that preceded. Individualized thought of instrumental color combinations is very important, with the voice functioning as an instrument. Great attention was given to hypnotic images. The work makes use of internal space, inexactness and interweavings of flux, and never uses anticipatory action in obtrusive projection.

I consider myself very fortunate to have known MB. He told me once that Thomas Hardy had the ability to create all his novels based on the concept of faith, and he talked to me constantly about the importance of the artistry of circumstance. Being in any situation, the artist can conceive the relationship of the situation to his own personal life, and this is most important so that we address ourselves to fundamental values.

The concept of a humane art is not only the concern of Black writers. In 1960, at the Princeton Seminar for Advanced Musical Studies, Roger Sessions warned the White musicians that the danger of dehumanization is real, saying that the individual should resist with all his energies any attempt at dehumanizing the art itself. The purpose of the art is to assist the development of a new humanity. The artist must be convinced that this is his goal. I am certainly thankful that MB revealed this to me.[1]

QUESTION: Please tell about your decisions in the area of the text, the form, and the instrumentation.

ANDERSON: In my earlier works, form was not a problem. I knew what sonata form was, and that took care of certain things. As I began to write more atonal music, the sonata concept died. Most contemporary composers have had that experience. In order for any piece to live for me, it has to create its own form as the piece evolves. When I start a

---

[1] *Variations on a Theme by M. B. Tolson* has been recorded for Nonesuch Records (The Contemporary Chamber Ensemble; Arthur Weisberg, conductor; Jan de Gaetani, soprano) and should be in print in 1973.

work, some formal idea may be in my mind but, as I get involved with the composition, the piece dictates to me and I try to be as responsive to the material as possible from then on.

I read quite a bit of poetry. There are certain poets whose poems I could never set, however. Even though I like a poet, I have the problem of my own stylistic identity to maintain. If it is not a marriage in which the two go hand in hand, it won't work. I was fortunate that the later works of Tolson, rather than his early works, were those to which I related.

The instrumentation makes use predominately of a jazz ensemble because the "come back, baby" section at the end really is blues. And *The Harlem Gallery* is rooted in life in Harlem (it would then be hard for me to write a string quartet), so I used jazz instruments. They function in various ways, in reference to jazz; wide vibrato and jazz mixes occur in the piece, yet they also function in classical traditions.

QUESTION: How do you account for the violin and cello?

ANDERSON: Strange as it might seem to some, these have been jazz instruments. A lot of people think of them only in classical terms, but early jazz bands had violins and cellos also.

QUESTION: Your title is enigmatic. *Variations on a Theme by M. B. Tolson?*

ANDERSON: Most people ask where the theme is. Those who do not know Tolson was a poet, assume he was a musician. The *theme* has to do with humanity. It is about Black life, about suffering. It's involved with our heritage of African experiences and those on the American continent, but the theme can have implications for Whites as well as Blacks. That's why I chose *Variations,* because the theme is really diverse in its concept of humanity.

QUESTION: What are the religious contexts?

ANDERSON: One constantly finds allusions in Tolson's work to religious concepts, to things which happen in the Bible. Then too, perspective which Tolson possessed is fantastic. Read the poems and you will see how complex it is. One writer said "Tolson out-pounds Pound!" He does, without question. It's unfortunate he could not be around today to witness the evolution of the Black Power Movement. He was involved in this at the end of his life but, by dying in 1966, he missed the boom period, so to speak. The tragedy is that, had Tolson been a White poet, every college English department would be reading his poems; there's no question in my mind about that! But he was constantly ignored, rarely honored, rarely praised—in his own country. But *we* have his poetry. No matter what they say about Robert Frost (and I like Frost) or Keats or the English tradition they want to perpetuate, you cannot get around the fact that Tolson is one of the most significant creative writers of this century. I would suggest that you read *The Harlem Gallery* and *The Ode to the Republic of Liberia,* which were his last and most mature works. He had planned to write four volumes in *The Harlem Gallery Series,* but he did not live long enough.

BAKER: *Black America* is a cantata, for want of a better term. It is a theater piece for jazz band, rock rhythm section, a choir of cellos and basses, chorus, three soprano soloists, narrators, and miscellaneous percussion. The work was originally written on the assasination of Martin Luther King. As so many other composers, Black and White, felt moved to do on the moment of that senseless murder, I tried to portray through music my indignation and my grief. The work has undergone modification. Certain formal things have been changed so that it has become a stronger musical statement than it was originally.

I started writing it the night of the assassination. From then to the night of the first performance was less than a month. Although it had an emotional impact at the première, it was not as articulate as it could have been. The work has since been performed four times in Bloomington alone. The instrumentation, the poetry, and the basic thrust have changed in the process.

The opening poem is by Stanley Warren, who teaches at Indiana University/Purdue University in Indianapolis. This narrative depicts the plight of the Black man in Africa and on until what's happening today, although in different terms than Tolson. Other poets are Langston Hughes, with his eternal optimism, and Claude McKay, whose poem (*If We Must Die*) is the antithesis of the work of Hughes. I also used poetry by another very, very talented man from Indianapolis, a jazz pianist originally from Tennessee: Carl Hines, who taught at Crispus Attucks, my alma mater.

While I was writing the work, White people were having meetings with us and coming out with eulogies. The minute things seemed to cool off and they found we weren't going to burn down the country, my writing took a different approach. I was already convinced all of the talking had been so much screaming in the wind, and I knew I wanted to do something to keep things active. Dr. King was often acerbic and abrasive, but he was filled with hope that things would work out. In Carl Hines' poem, "Now That He Is Safely Dead (Martin Luther King)," the hopelessness of the whole thing is summed up, and I've used this text at the end of the work. So the texts vascillate between the optimism of Dr. King and Langston Hughes, and the harsh realities depicted by Claude McKay in his "If We Must Die" and the preachments of Malcolm X.

The work is in four sections. The first is called "The Wretched of the Earth; Missionaries, Money, Marines." You recognize the philosophy Malcolm espoused when he said that the United States moved with the political, capitalistic attitude that said if we can't win people over through our "good will," we will try it with money and, if that doesn't work, we send the Marines. We've seen this happen over and over again, not just in Vietnam. This first section talks about the blues. After a long, declamatory poem, the jazz band comes in with the blues and then, on top of that, we get another layer of sound: first, the singers with *Wade in the Water* in another key (setting up a kind of controlled conflict here, harmonically, rhythmically and—I hope— philosophically). On top of all that, the choir and brass come in with *Sometimes I Feel Like a Motherless Child.* People have said this reminds them of Charles Ives, but I think of these layers of sound are like the strata and substrata of rhythm and melody you find in African music. The blues soon takes on another aspect (and it's been running along all of this time): One by one, these other elements are removed, so you end up with the blues again and, as far as I'm concerned, the blues is home. So I'm also making a statement that you always come back to the blues, I don't care where you've been. When I'm talking about spiritual music, or gospel music, when I'm talking about any of these roots, it's the blues that's pervasive.

The second section is "Kaleidoscope," and here I tried to point up the vastness of the Black experience by pointing up geographical regions, such as the Caribbean, 125th Street, the Southern Church, and such. On one hand, you've got the band doing these Latin things and, on the other, a rhythm-and-blues thing is reflecting *I Got a Woman Way Over Town.* Here I've set up the open-and-shut-door effect. One of the musical elements is constant and, against that, there is another element which I can cut off any place in the phrase.

The last two sections deal primarily with poetry and the whole philosophy that undergirds the kind of tumultuous situation, including the dichotomy between Dr. King and Malcolm. For somebody that's really got it all together, you know, we can see there's no real conflict at all. The only question is one of method and the speed at which social, political, and economic change will take place.

The work is through-composed, with *Leit Motives* (forgive the Western terms). I make liberal use of transformation with the spirituals, and the one which is carried through the work is *Sometimes I Feel Like a Motherless Child*. The words and music of this depict the hopelessness I was after. *Wade in the Water* also figures prominently. Many other themes, not really spirituals, have spiritual characteristics: a simple line that's to the point, and somewhat the same basic structure. Needless to say, the work is very heavily rhythmic, because that's the kind of bag the jazz musician comes from, you know. The strings are used as jazz instruments (and TJ has already pointed out there is a precedent for this) as well as in the manner which might have been used by someone like Dr. Still for a spiritual setting.

The third section is an ostinato that is very long, where it's really jazz music, but all these divergent influences are used. And the last section starts with Dr. King's "I have a dream." Against this I've tried to create a mood something like the Dr. Jesus section of *Porgy and Bess,* where you have these interjections, a call-and-response treatment with the preacher (Dr. King) doing his thing while the jazz band interjects all of these "Amens" and "Right on, brothers!" only I use music, not words. This is gradually overlapped with the soprano who sings *I Dream a World Where No Other Will Scorn,* accompanied with a jazz thing. All of a sudden, the poetry recedes and there is a string quartet (in this case, four cellos) and a soprano singing from the twenty-second Psalm, *Thou Dost Lay Me in the Dust of Death.* Christ used these words from the Psalm of David when he was being crucified. Against this the speaker is saying, "If we must die, let us nobly die . . . pressed to the wall, but fighting back." At the moment I was writing this, I thought this dichotomy would ultimately be resolved. This leads into another setting from Langston Hughes: *Give Me a Song of Hope,* but all of this changes with that block-buster by Carl Hines which tears down any notions, and the choir ends with the entire group on *Sometimes I Feel Like a Motherless Child.*

CARTER: *Cantata* is based on a few well-known spirituals. I was always curious that Black composers rarely concerned themselves with this music. They've been arranged, but Black composers have not cared for their folk music as have Chopin or Bartók, for example. Even the arrangements seem timid, and have always been brief. This is not the way you hear them when the choruses sing them; the arrangement may look as if the performance would last only two minutes, but the chorus sings for five. This is what I decided to do with this material, with one movement for each of the five spirituals. The first, for piano alone, is the *Prelude.* Second is a rondo, based on *Peter, Go Ring Them Bells. Sometimes I Feel Like a Motherless Child* is third, as an air, and then comes *Let Us Break Bread Together.* The last movement is a toccata, *Ride on, King Jesus.* The first performance was given by Leontyne Price, at Constitution Hall.

LEE: John is a very outgoing person with ideas on many things—a very alert mind—but he is modest about his own music. I think we should mention that he performed his piano concerto with the Baltimore Symphony, and wrote the second movement within a month. He is also, you see, a concert pianist, and a very excellent one. He also has accompanied William Brown, the tenor, on his tours.

CARTER: Your teachers always like you.

OLIPHINT: In working on the *Cantata,* I found it very approachable. But now, I've had discussions with people about how to sing spirituals. How do you feel about this in your work? Should we approach it in the classical manner, as if it were Mozart or Bach? That is what I've done.

CARTER: Frankly, I don't want to meddle with the artist, like there's the score and the artist has to recreate the music. You know, when you look at the music and come to your conclusions, you'll find others will treat it differently. And why shouldn't they, as long as the general indications are observed? I've heard you sing, and I know anything you decide to do will be fine.

QUESTION: How do you manage to indicate exactly what you want in the score, and you did change the spiritual tunes, didn't you?

CARTER: Almost any composer has got to leave latitude for the artist's interpretation. No matter what he wants to do, the notation has its limitations. As for the melodies, a lot of spirituals are pentatonic, and twelve minutes of five-note melodies might not be too interesting so I've not hesitated to alter the melodies. It is interesting that the concert singers usually perform the music straight, unchanged, while all sorts of nuances and subtleties arise spontaneously from the choral groups, and arrangements have never captured these.

PRICE: I wrote my second piano sonata in 1958, looking for something in terms of African music. I selected five notes—B flat, C, B, E flat and G flat—and worked with these notes and their transpositions throughout the whole piece, with the accompaniment changing and appearing in various shapes. You hear the same thing through the entire piece, and I feel this is African, because—as with African music—it may appear that the same thing is happening continuously, but it really is not. It changes and transforms itself without your understanding exactly what's taking place. This is particularly applicable to the first movement. The second movement is based on a 13/4 meter, and is a long climax. The last movement is a rondo, not totally unrelated to rag music. It has an ostinato passage which begins very quickly with intermittent passages which flow into the last portion. It is here that the rag idea appears.

    ● TJ's devotion to the works of Tolson made me realize the sensitivity he showed to the stimulus available to him at Langston University. It is easy for those of us at large schools or who live in large cities to become rather chauvinistic about our situation when it can be measured by some fashion or another against conditions of others. One's perspective is always sharpened when visiting a smaller campus, for example, where we can find other intellects (sometimes better ones) and new perspectives. TJ could easily have wished he had a faculty post further south, say at the University of Oklahoma, or further east, for example at the University of Illinois. But he was nurtured by his stay at Langston and, as a result, gave us a strong and powerful new composition. Even had Tolson not been the great poet TJ recognized, even if Tolson had been unknown to him, TJ would have found strength within his immediate environs (and, no doubt, he did find more than Tolson). This may relate to that Black characteristic of "inspired intensity" which TJ termed at our 1969 seminar to apply to that spirit which finds expression, no matter what the obstacle—sort of like keep on keeping on.
    The performance of Dave's *Black America* took place that evening. It was the second time this work had been performed

at our seminars and, I'll admit, it might have been a little selfish of me to urge him to repeat it. I knew we didn't have the budget to bring back those former students who had been soloists in the earlier performances (and Dave cited several whose participation was essential), but I also knew that the performance would take place at the same time many high school students would be attending Indiana University's annual summer music clinics, so I approached the Indiana State Arts Commission for that money needed for the production, assuring the Commission that the performance would be open to the public. The money was graciously provided, and the hall was filled with seminar registrants, high school students, faculty, townspeople, college students, and visitors. With the patronage of the Black Music Center, this work had been videotaped a few months earlier by the Voice of America and the campus WFIU Radio-Television Department. For that recording, Dave elected to add a large gospel chorus, and the choir was retained for the seminar performance. This really was the best performance yet.

If there is a Black soprano who has not sung John Carter's *Cantata*, there is still time. I wish we had a recording of Leontyne Price's première (or, even, of a subsequent performance), but John was very pleased with the performance of Bernadine Oliphint and Carol Stone—both of whom, it turned out, are Indiana University graduates now teaching in Nashville. In fact, this team (which has since been engaged in touring) proved to be one of the highlights of all our seminars.

John Price performed his own second piano sonata, proving himself a really excellent pianist as well as composer. He had been kind enough to accept a very late invitation and took time off from his teaching duties to join us. At last report, not one of his works was commercially available but, if those works of his I have heard are indicative (and this piano sonata is certainly a fine and very effective emotional expression), the time is ripe for a publisher and many performers to devote attention to his work.

7. The Social Role of Jazz

Richard Abrams, David N. Baker, and Charles Ellison

● Joining Dave Baker on this panel is Richard Abrams, from the Association for the Advancement of Creative Musicians, and Charles Ellison, a former staff member of the Black Music Center. The work of Abrams is certainly known to those who have followed the AACM in Chicago and in Paris. He is a gifted and perceptive musician, whose talents are immediately reinvested in social betterment. "Chas," who had a peripheral association with AACM during his Chicago days, is Dave Baker's trumpeter. His calm and cool manner betrays an incisive and sensitive intellect of a broad latitude, which is firmly rooted in basic philosophic convictions.

ELLISON: LeRoi Jones has proposed that the most creative music, the most valid contribution in general of any people, will be an exact reflection of the socio-political, economic, and psychological status of that people at a given time. I want to concentrate on the social status of the people, extending it beyond the obvious manifestations into the individual aspects of social conditions as they relate to us as individuals. I think that with John Coltrane's *A Love Supreme, Ascension Meditations* and the albums that followed, with the general projection of Coltrane's charisma, many Black people who had previously been only marginally interested in Black music, in their own personal life style, and conditions in general, changed their life styles immensely. The reason for this rests in the tremendous spiritual reservoir which is found in Coltrane's music and that of his various disciples. When I was in high school, people started listening to Coltrane and liked what he was doing but, beyond that, they began to get into his spiritual philosophy and the philosophy of the life style in general. They saw that what he was projecting was very valuable, that it was a model which required us to follow and made us change our attitudes and manner of thinking. It was an event analogous to the Black man who had not been particularly conscious politically before coming under the influence of Malcolm X, or before discovering the political and social validity of the things W. E. B. DuBois had to say. Coltrane's music made us reevaluate ourselves, see ourselves more objectively, more clearly, and place ourselves in a position within society.

With the event of a personal feeling of ethnic-nationalistic consciousness, there is a highly enthusiastic devotion which comes along as part of this new awareness, almost like an over-reaction. The political or musical message has to be lived with for a while, because it is impossible in most cases to understand the total impact of the implications. You have to deal with it from where you are and to the extent you understand it at that particular moment. As you get into it, you begin to grow and see more, your horizons expand, and the growth continues. I've seen junkies, hustlers, and people who had been taking advantage of their own brothers who came under the influence of Coltrane or Malcolm, who were changed accordingly.

Coltrane's music is a guideline in terms of consciousness that leads our people into something very spiritual and cosmic. In essence, it transcends the immediate needs and talks of Utopia, of real brotherhood.

Leon Thomas, another very beautiful musician, collaborated with Pharoah Sanders in *The Creator Has a Master Plan.* I see Coltrane's music as a continuation of the spirit of King Oliver, continued by Albert Ayler and Archie Shepp, and all of this as part of that master plan—not only the musical master plan, but in terms of shaping the soul of an individual.

When Coltrane's messages reaches a person, he is obviously affected. He begins to reject actions and thoughts detrimental to mankind and starts to direct his energies toward the betterment of human conditions. When a whole mass of individual people thinks this way, the social strength of music is very obvious. I'm not saying that Coltrane's music in the only answer, but it is part of the overall plan, a plan which includes DuBois, Malcolm, and Martin Luther King. And it certainly includes Wayne Shorter and Miles Davis.

If you really understand the music of Coltrane and his disciples, your life will change. The kind of thing he was into before he died was not concerned with traditional form, or the framework of "jazz." It is the music which Pharoah Sanders terms high energy, where the vibrations (the music) are self defining. It's highly emotional music, and it brings you closer to the Creator and the marrow of being itself.

The effects of Miles Davis is entirely different. From the general time of Coltrane's *A Love Supreme,* we see evidence of his whole spiritual religious sense. On the other hand, Miles Davis has always been extremely individualistic, as if to say "I really don't need nobody; I do my own thing." That philosophy is important because it plants the seed for another Miles to keep pushing. His ideas reflect what we as a people have had to go through since being brought here in chains. The music of Miles is very strong and defiant, but it can be subtle, it can be bittersweet, it can be swinging, and it reflects his own strength. In terms of the overall plan, it is just as valid as Coltrane's music because it takes all kinds of individuals to mold a strong and durable body in the final analysis.

Horace Silver and Cannonball have covered the whole spectrum of music, including the foot-tapping, finger-popping music in a club situation that brings people together. I'm thinking of Cannonball's things, those actually written by Joe Zawinul, a White pianist: *Mercy, Mercy* and *Why Am I Treated so Bad?* And, before that, Bobby Timmon's *This Here and That There*—things that were gospel influenced, which have an immediate appeal to people. And there is often a social message in this music, too.

Charlie Mingus was a pioneer in the use of ethnic and gospel influence, as in *The Faubus Fables,* and things like Slide Hampton's *Sister Salvation.*

All of these different kinds of expressions influence the attitude of people, from the foot-tapping thing to the music of Shepp and of the AACM, groups which overwhelm you, sometimes scare you, sometimes embrace you. All of this music ties together and leads us to a true self-evaluation, and molds us into a unit.

ABRAMS: I think we should strike the word *jazz,* not in hostility, but because most terms for Black music were given by Whites. If we check their decisions in light of the time the terms were assigned, we would find social and spiritual considerations which influenced these words.

As far as this country is concerned, Black music is revolution: social, spiritual, and physical revolution. When you say "United States," you are saying "revolution." When you say "Black music," you are saying "nature," which is parallel with what you call balance. It's not the only balance in the land, but it's on the bottom rung of the ladder, and the natural tendency is that this balance is much greater. There has never been a name given this music by its major innovators, so when we're talking about the social role of jazz, we're talking about the social role of music.

We have to include all kinds of music, including Black people playing Black music on television. From this you can pick up a truthful vibratory-type decision for yourself about what is taking place and why, and the impact of that decision usually brings you to a certain

Yet he said that we are brainwashed to believe with the masses that type of truth. It has nothing to do with anyone else or someone else's decision about what took place.

Anybody can play jazz—you hear it all the time—even Tom Jones. When we talk about Black music, that's something different.

BAKER: While listening to these two brothers speak, I was reflecting on the interviews we conducted just before the Center was started. I thought of Tom McIntosh, a very spiritual cat, a trombonist, now doing some scoring on the West Coast. He said that the reason Black music is so strong in the whole picture of contemporary music is because no music of this century lacks a debt to Black music—excepting, perhaps, the Webern camp—that we have really given the world a universal approach to life.

Yet he said that we are brainwashed to believe with the masses that there's never any encouragement in Western society to become an individual. A social, political, and economic system that's built primarily on capitalism and technology excludes the individual. T. J. Anderson refers to this in *Black Music in Our Culture.* In our society, the minorities have suffered, and the individual has been forgotten. They dole out whatever benefits are deemed necessary for us, but they make sure that we know we are in the minority in every endeavor.

Tom got all this together when he said Black music is part of the general movement to reach back for feeling. It's the kind of thing Eldridge Cleaver discussed in *Soul on Ice,* when he was talking about primeval mitosis—the mind and body trying to get together. Mingus said that if Charlie Parker were alive today, he'd think he was in a house of mirrors because you can't turn on any show or play any record that doesn't show some obvious debt to the innovations of Charlie Parker, because Parker was the giant that preceeded John Coltrane. But what Tom said is repeated by almost every Black composer I've met, that there is this general feeling of trying to salvage something out of all this cold, dehumanizing atmosphere in which we exist. When you live in the United States, where money makes technology the *raison d'être,* you find us more concerned with the manifestations of that technology than in the effects they will have on people. In the midst of this antithesis of humanity, you naturally find Black music as a humanizing influence, and that's why Black elements are running all through non-Black music, even with Tom Jones—although that kind of syndrome ain't really got too much to do with it—and I'm not just talking about that music for popping your fingers or shaking your butt, either. That's fine, but those are just obvious manifestations. What we are talking about is a deeper thing, a kind of spirituality that transcends the car radio and tape player. And I don't give a damn whether you dig jazz or not, because I ain't nobody that has to be convinced but, if you dig it, do something about it.

The whole thing is that I see Black music as a humanizing force, even when it is used for propagandistic reasons, as it very often is— but that happens with dudes like Beethoven and Smetana too.

QUESTION: We don't all know about the AACM. Mr. Abrams, would you be kind enough to tell us about your goals and plans?

ABRAMS: We formed the AACM to have a power base from which we could play our music, but we also took on other vibrations, some of which we hadn't anticipated when we got started. You'll find the list of our purposes in *Black Music in Our Culture,* on pages 14 and 15. These goals had a good feeling about them, a good social feeling. When we set out to accomplish them, some of them took on changes. Let me give you an example. The seventh item is "to increase mutual respect between creative artists and musical tradesmen, booking agents, managers, promoters and instrument manufacturers." In that department, we found that the only way to create mutual respect between artists and musical tradesmen was for *us* to become *both* the artists and the tradesmen.

QUESTION: I'd appreciate a little amplification on the idea of Black music as a humanistic expression.

ABRAMS: Let us go back to the blues and before the blues, before that word existed, back to the cotton fields. Survival was laid out right there. Check the means of survival the slave used: sending messages through songs, tapping his foot, putting his head in the laughing barrel when the massah stumbled on the sidewalk and almost broke his neck. That's how he survived: being himself. The way to survive is to stop trying to be like other people and just follow the thought of who you are. You receive the things you need through the process of thought. These experiences and ideas come from inside and that's why they are humanizing.

QUESTION: But you don't mean you have to go back to the roots, back to something related to slavery times, to survive?

ABRAMS: No. Taking over our own destiny and entertaining thoughts of self-realization is an advanced idea of the laughing barrel. That's what I was saying. You have to take care of yourself. And if you get money from what you do and feel you should go and pray then, go do it. Do all of it. Do everything that has to do with keeping you within who you are.

BAKER: I can see where you're going: The whole notion like if you start dealing with capitalistic endeavors and distribution and stuff, how do you avoid becoming corrupted? A cat has to remember where he came from. You've got to keep those roots. And you cannot abrogate your responsibility because you all of a sudden have machinery to move with. I know a lot of dudes who are very honest and together while they're scuffling but, the minute they make it, it's like hanging up. The best example of people working collectively in Black music, and making it really work without all those hassles of exploitation, is the AACM.

ELLISON: With Coltrane, we had a man with all the intellectual and technical tools to go from now on, a man who extended the tenor saxophone range, a man who made several innovations in sound, a man who definitely made spiritual perception available and visible to all of us. A man with all of this going for him does not feel like a machine. When we try to stay on top, to exist politically or economically, we cannot surrender that basic African human element which is our heritage.

BAKER: I don't intend to let the world change me into something else. It doesn't matter how much I acquire in material wealth, how much I get going intellectually, how well established I get institutionally, those things will never be my master. Things like this we must use in a manner that increases our humanism, in a manner to benefit other people, because nobody can get nowhere by himself. If you get a little help from your friends, don't blow it on an ego trip, because your friends can put you right back where you started. I think we've got to keep on keeping on. I don't think you can go back home. But we can't move at the expense of that thing that keeps us human beings.

QUESTION: Mr. Abrams, how would you make a difference between jazz and Black music? Might it be that Black music must involve Blacks in its creativity, whereas jazz might not involve Black persons?

ABRAMS: This is what I mean, yes. There are many jazz stars, many very good ones, both White and Black. That's what this country is: synthetics.

QUESTION: Yet isn't the word *jazz* helpful? If there is to be a concert by Dave Baker, for example, and you say it is going to be a jazz concert specifically, won't that get a crowd? Sorry, I know that Dave gets his own crowd. What I mean is that doesn't *jazz concert* mean something more than just concert?

ABRAMS: It's true that we are manipulated in various ways, including economically, by this word. Some time back, someone asked, "Is jazz dead?" Right then, that question was destroying incomes, mostly of Black people. The same thing has happened to rhythm and blues but, if you tell your agent you've got a good rock group (not a rhythm-and-blues group), you're in. It's not just words I'm talking about. What do I care about a word? You can say jazz all day; it's all right with me. But it's not all right with me in *my* projection. All of us in Black music realize that the purpose of this whole revolution is to bring everything together, and the implications of the word *jazz* won't do that.

BAKER: If a dude comes up to me and says his name is spelled like I spell David, but he pronounces it like William, that's up to him. The people who make the music have the right to name it, and it don't matter how you spell it if you know what it means. In the group we talk about nigger and it ain't no scuffle, but if somebody else names us that, then problems start to exist. When Lou Alcindor changed his name, he said he knew tickets were being sold on the strength of the name he had, so he said that name could be used for a while. There's an analogous situation here too, so you can call it jazz until the transition is made.

QUESTION: You know, we can't assume that jazz is strictly African in its influences. The Black musician, perhaps like any other, will embrace inspiration from any source if it can be used in a creative manner for his own purposes.

QUESTION: To me, Black music means music of the Black people and it therefore has sociological implications, but this doesn't apply only to jazz. The non-jazz composer comes from pretty much the same sociology at heart, if not in fact.

ELLISON: To call it Black music or jazz doesn't mean anything excepting in implication. Because of that, I think labels can be important. They help a man to organize himself, and they also communicate things to others. If you tell someone you're going to Third Street, he knows what you mean. We've got to know that labels come from human reasons. Even though they might be bad at times, improperly applied and wrongly interpreted, they provide man with indentification and direction. After that, when you go down to the joint and listen to the musicians, you get all the possible truths of whatever is happening, and then you don't need the label any more.

TAYLOR: If we think of the Black experience, in music or art, there is a matter of the oral tradition which is passed from one generation to another. In this sense, *experience* suggests a linking of forces which can only be understood fully if that experience is part of one's total life style. On the other hand, we have the discipline within the traditional system, represented by the printed word or note. These two—the oral and the written—never merge fully. The aspect of improvisation in jazz or church music is not something which comes out of the hymn book or the charts; it comes from your experience. We've heard musicians say you have to be a part of it to understand it, meaning that a dictionary definition can't get to all of the implications and meanings. This is a matter of reacting to an experience, rather than being declared a musically literate or illiterate person. You have to have been there at one time or another.

QUESTION: We can discuss Bach on the basis of the printed page, but not in terms of Bach's own performance and improvisations. A musician who improvises cannot be discussed that way, as if his music were on the page. I think we have been faulting music history all along if we think the label and the printed page reveals all we need to know.

QUESTION: I'd like to know more about the origin of the word *jazz*. I read that when Black musicians syncopated the spirituals, they called it *jebbing*. I have also been led to believe that the French changed jebbing to jazz.

ABRAMS: Strip yourself of the label and you won't have to worry. They'll give you all the names you want, and they will change like the music does. And, with what their words suggest, they will show you what Black music means.

● "Strip yourself of the label and you won't have to worry?" How lost becomes the non-performer when he is robbed of his labels! Pierre Boulez once made reference to those "imbeciles" who insist on calling Debussy an Impressionist, and Malcolm cautioned us that labels kill. But if you listen to that music, certainly starting with *A Love Supreme*, you begin to understand this is not jazz. This is not the same kind of music we heard from Benny Goodman. There is something new, something very much different. We don't even need to worry about the possibility that the label was attached by Whites, but we do come to know this is Black music—and it is more than just music. It is far removed from those terrible shorts we saw in the movies, where directors got perfectly decent musicians to simulate jam sessions in the spirit of latter-day minstrels. That music from the past twenty years, which may be still termed jazz two decades from now, is a social expression through music of the Afro-American and, as with so many other idioms of Black music, it is more than music.

Of course, it is also political. Art is always political to the extent it has relevance to the society for which it was created. Those who want to appreciate it should be sensitive to the materials of the art and to the most subtle manners by which these might be used, but this is of no value in the end if the art work is not seen in its social context. That context within jazz is political. That context need not be Marxist, as Frank Kofsky advances in *Black Nationalism and the Revolution in Music* (New York: Pathfinder, 1970), but it is difficult to imagine expressions which would relate in a *positive* manner coming from Black Americans in support of recent Republican political thought. That antithesis gives more fuel to the belief that Black culture is subversive while, in truth, the United States has been hard at work from pre-Federalist days to define all non-Anglo manifestations as subversive. In his last visit to the Center as advisory chairman, TJ told a group of students that nothing associated with Black music will have full support until Blacks can assume their proper and distinctive role in American society. Those same forces which see ghetto language and life patterns as alien are the ones that wish us to continue thinking of jazz as the music of cheap dance halls, whore houses, and night clubs, that cannot see this music as a very honest and often idealistic expression of a genuine culture.

Very many of these ideas are qualified in the Summer 1972 issue of *The Black Scholar,* particularly in the exceptionally provocative article by Donald Byrd, "The Meaning of Black Music" and that by Max Roach, "What 'Jazz' Means to Me."

8. Jazz in the Curriculum

Cannonball Adderley, Dorothy Ashby,

and Robert H. Klotman

● Within the past fifteen years, the name of Cannonball Adderley has been ubiquitous at concerts, and with increasing frequency, his music and voice have been heard on many university campuses. His personality is filled with wisdom and good humor, and those ideas he verbally expresses are no less important than those coming from his saxophone.

Dorothy Ashby, respected throughout the harp world, has demonstrated the adaptability of that instrument for jazz expressions as documented on such recordings as Cadet S-690 (*Dorothy Ashby*), Cadet S-809 (*Afro-harping*), Prestige S-7638 (*The Best of Dorothy Ashby*), Cadet S-825 (*Dorothy's Harp*), Atlantic S-1447 (*The Fantastic Harp of Dorothy Ashby*), Prestige S-7639 (*Dorothy Ashby Plays for the Beautiful People*), and Cadet S-841 (*Rubaiyat*). The moderator for this session, Robert Klotman, established his friendship with this distinguished young lady while he served as supervisor for music in the Detroit public schools, a post he held prior to joining the Indiana University music faculty.

ASHBY: My experience in jazz and in jazz education has been diverse. For five years, my husband and I had a four-hour radio show in Detroit, twice a week. We talked about the new jazz releases, about the problems of jazz, and about the performers. I also spent some time as a record reviewer for the *Detroit Free Press* and, like Cannonball, I have spent much of my time playing in clubs and concerts— not with his financial success, but we're working on that. When Dr. Klotman was with the Detroit school system, we toured the elementary and junior high schools to perform and to talk with the kids about the life of the professional jazzman.

I speak often of the decade of 1950–1960 as being the best for the Black jazzman. The economy of the country was in pretty fair shape. What we missed out on in the way of post-war adjustments, we "made up for" with the Korean venture. The United States was becoming aware of jazz's role in international goodwill. The jazz festivals were born, giving jazz some of its greatest and most diverse audiences. Jazz was used in the films, like *Odds Against Tomorrow, No Sun in Venice,* and Miles' *The Elevator to the Hangman.*

That period passed, and now we're in a slump. Some articles claimed that jazz was dying in the mid-1960s, but we knew that wasn't true. Jazz has a long way to go in the academic community because some of those who teach have not experienced being with jazz people or jazz music, either from circumstance or choice, and continued to think of it as the music of disreputable people, to be performed in disreputable places.

As early as 1947, North Texas State University had a jazz program being supported by Wilfred C. Bain, who is now the music dean here at Indiana University. Before that, some of the Eastern schools had jazz courses. Many of the colleges in the country now have jazz in their curricula. The reason we are here today is to try to instigate more, to propagandize even more for our first love: jazz.

I mentioned a degree of distrust for jazz on the campus in some areas. There are those who fight it because of their own personal fears or shortcomings, perhaps anticipating the resentment they would feel if Blacks were engaged to teach (that is, those Blacks who were qualified, whether or not they have the letters behind their names). Most of us like the well-trodden paths and dislike having to discover or create new techniques, and we would have to in order to teach jazz. The old techniques won't suffice. The traditional academician would be uncomfortable discarding the safety of old labels and analysis forumlae. Instructors would be called on to distinguish styles and idioms which would be new. This requires a keen ear, one that really has heard all kinds of jazz for years. It requires a sharp mind, one that has learned jazz outside of the formal educational system. Of course, we learned the basics of music techniques at school, but we did not study the art of improvisation. Jazz, being the product of the moment, must have spontaneous creation. This is something we learned in those places where people were doing that kind of thing, not in college. So the teacher would have to differentiate among two hip beat, Latin, Afro-Cuban, gospel type, a slick rock beat and a funky rock beat, etc. These terminologies were created by jazzmen to describe their own particular colorings and shadings, and they are often terribly subtle. The answer might rest in the intensity of the beat, the complexity of the beat, or in that minute metronomical difference which could distinguish heavy funk from light rock funk. Those who have had experience in playing and writing jazz, who knew the recordings and the players, would be in a position to develop definitions for communication in teaching.

Many jazzmen who excel as players, writers and arrangers could very capably teach others certain musical principles: How to create endlessly varying melodies and rhythms in a particular idiom, using a given set of chords; how to fashion continuous harmonic variations for a given melodic line in one or a multitude of forms; and how to design combinations of melodic, harmonic, and rhythmic variations for this spontaneous improvisational form we call jazz. This is evidently a comtemporary counterpart of that instruction to which Baroque organists were exposed for their treatment of the chorale preludes, and relationships to the passacaglia and chaconne are not at all remote.

One summer, my husband and I taught some young people without any prior musical training. In just a few weeks, they could recognize the colors between major and minor chords, they knew what augmented chords sounded like, and they could play basic triads and had begun to learn inprovisation.

How jazz can be taught in concrete terms and not in poetic terms depends, of course, on the skills of the instructor and the grade level of the teaching. A particular set of methods will work for the young student new to performance. The form and analysis of jazz could be taught on the college level with applicable transfers of information from harmony and theory, with in depth stylistic studies of particular performers. Because of the manner in which the jazzman acquires his skills, he is probably the best qualified person to teach this essentially aural tradition.

Being able to teach jazz effectively also requires of the teacher an awareness of the jargon and, indeed, an awareness of the total life style of the jazzmen. The reason for some of our prowess in improvisation, for example, might stem from the fact that we've always had to improvise. We learned how to make do with the food left over from the plantation house—to make chitterlings, maws, and brains. When the season demanded it, we put cardboard in our shoes. We wore long hair before the style was called Afro, because we couldn't afford haircuts, and then that became the style of the jazz musician. In *Black Music in Our Culture,* you've read how Wes Montgomery improvised his own instruction and invented his own techniques. I guess, to an extent, I had to do the same thing—for want of money, and because I didn't have a harp until I was out of college. I began harp in high school. The school had only five harps, but there were thirty students. Scheduling problems forced me to design a fast learning plan so I could get as much accomplished as possible during the school year. Naturally, I developed some unorthodox techniques. Wes Montgomery developed skills other guitarists would have thought impossible, and he developed them out of his own necessity, lacking a teacher or a guide.

We also need to teach areas in jazz that are neglected too much: to tell those interested in jazz as a profession about the snares of booking agents and managers, about the creation of publishing outlets so you get the percentages and don't get exploited, about television residuals, and about record distribution. A jazz curriculum should cover things like this also, things essential for our lives in the business itself.

One final word on terminology: Don't get caught up in the desire to have labels. The person who wants to learn jazz, wants to know *how* it is done and not what you call it. If you've heard that wonderful old Black jazzman, Eubie Blake, you don't need to know his piano style is called "stride." You need to know how he swings his left hand, following tenths or octaves with chords to accompany what he's doing melodically with his right hand.

What is important is that the jazz student understand the amount of time a performer has to create and execute a musically logical idea, one which is aurally pleasing and rhythmically "on time," one which is suitable for the harmonic color and the expressive style of the piece. And a really good jazzman can consistently create valid ideas (and even different ones with each new performance of the same work) which will have still more than these qualities.

ADDERLEY: I wish I could say who I am. I've been trying to find out for some time. I imagine most of us have. We are victimized by things like identity, which means we have a niche, a category, something to do, a place, and an expected behavior follow-through situation. Actually, that's one of my big problems. It's very difficult for me to accept what has been done to this music. We have allowed it become categorized and placed in niches, numbered, detailed, and put into little things. We've come up with a departmentalized Black-oriented music. I imagine that the only reason there should be any emphasis on *Black* music is because there has been a concerted effort to be sure there hasn't been any information regarding the music that is of, from, by, and—largely—oriented *to* Black people. Consequently, some of us have taken an interest in trying to cancel those lines of demarcation that say this is jazz, this is bop, this is funky jazz, this is modern jazz, this is avant garde, this is gospel, this is spiritual, this is blues—well, blues may be another thing altogether—but I resent saying this is soul or rock and roll, or whatever you want to call it. From a pragmatic viewpoint, these are the realities we have to deal with in this society. Since I'm going to be a jazz chauvinist, I'll have to go along with these terms to an extent.

The things from early jazz (erroneously called Dixieland), from that music practiced by the New Orleans people, is all very beautiful. But it's very odd that Louis Armstrong became known as the first principal jazz instrumentalist, when Duke Ellington was doing his music in Washington at the same time. There has been no explanation in our research why we have said Louis' music belongs in the start of jazz history, while his contemporary is overlooked.

I am not a person who feels this music has to be developed and taught by a Black man. It must be taught by someone who knows it, loves it, and is competent. Although it is true that Blacks have a stronger emotional identification and can develop this enlargement of traditional European music which has become peculiar unto itself, I feel that anybody with the skills and love can develop it. I had a piano player for ten years who was an extraordinary example of this, a European: Joe Zawinul. He played jazz as authentically as any one. And on records, because you can't see the performer, it's difficult to identify someone ethnically or racially—even those as ego prone as I am. I once said I could tell the race of a player from the recording, but that is no longer true.

I'm one of those people who has concentrated on Black music and thereby created those little monsters who proclaim that traditional European music is of no value to them, because they are Black, because it cannot help them make a living, and blah, blah, blah, blah! Well, I don't think we should necessarily try to create performing musicians by our playing jazz. We should create people who *love* it and can get some insight into what music *really* means.

The worse thing in the world is the half-time football show. There is so much tradition around it that there is no room for imagination: all those people make letters and figures on the field, play popular tunes and the *Stars and Stripes Forever* . . . that's the dullest music in the world today, and it seems as if nothing has been done about it for generations. It's the same as it was years ago in New York and Boston. How can we make music a part of *living* within our society with this kind of activity in the school? I'm talking about the logistics of absolute scheduling. I'm talking about the introduction of music— that is of Americans, of our people—into student life the same way we deal with geography or arithmetic. I'm talking about studying the music they hear every day, so the pupils will have some frame of reference for change and improvement without having to resort to information from an expert about what is excellent and what is not. This means that I'm not thinking so much about the academic curriculum approach, but that I am concerned with the *humanistic* approach. That may be an innovation for people who are professionally identified with music, either as teachers or performers. It is unfortunate if we are exclusively musicians.

We are not comprehensive enough in our schools. Everything is so cut and dried, and people no longer have any real interest in anything except academic games. Except for the college level and a few other places, there is no consideration of jazz. A few high schools have stage bands, which may or may not rehearse during school time. But I don't think people have to be musicians to be taught about this music.

How can we make this music available in the general curriculum— not as a frill or elective for those who have no real interest. There must be some way to introduce music into the general school program to people in the chorus or in folk singing or whatever, and not from a racial point of view. With that, we start off with one shoe in the gutter and the other in a bear trap. When we identify music as Black in this racist society, we automatically create a limbo with that ninety percent of our students who don't happen to be Black.

There is a source of pride for our Black students who know they have something, but then we have so many Black students who don't have any interest in jazz per se. You say Black music, and they think only of James Brown, Brother Joe May, or Aretha Franklin. You say Duke Ellington, and they smile like that was something lofty that had to do with our past. It's like telling some kids who have been reading the latest poets about Langston Hughes or Paul Laurence Dunbar. They say they can't identify with that; they can only identify with what is here and now, what is current.

KLOTMAN: All of my early training was in the Western tradition, and I'm very much of a Johnny-come-lately to this scene, and it came about because of my urban experiences. I say this, then, with an apology, but I was concerned with those seventy percent of the Detroit students who were Black, and that isn't a minority group. I thought it was ridiculous that we were completely ignoring this majority and the cultural heritage of these students. When I started teaching in the 1940s and wanted an example of theme and variation form, I used Art Tatum's *Dark Eyes* as well as Haydn's *Emperor Quartet,* and that would be an example of music integration.

HARRIS: How much Western or European music should be included in the curricula you are considering?

ADDERLEY: The curriculum should be comprehensive. There is no other way to study music. In jazz, for example, we play European instruments and we use European notation. The music itself is an Afro-American style of European music. That's why it started off with songs already in existence, played by the Black marching and funeral bands.

ASHBY: I agree, yet we must know that there are special factors at times which require a different approach. Just a few days ago, I was here in Bloomington for the International Harp Conference. A fellow harpist asked if I were a Grandjany or Salzedo disciple. I had to say I was an Ashby disciple because, after all, I had to create my own technique to get what I wanted from the instrument. My elbows aren't always high, nor are my thumbs.

ADDERLEY: I'm not in conflict with that. What I'm wondering is how you teach somebody past telling them to do their own thing. You can teach them something that's proper and functional in terms of a technique but, when it comes to the *essence* of music, jazz is more complicated than simple phrases.

ASHBY: As an example, we can use the symbols of figured bass with the pop musician.

ADDERLEY: We use symbols in scores to get things done. There is no reason why we could not employ a notation previously not used in music, not even by the avant gardists, if this would communicate something to the jazz musician. Communication, however, is essential for formal, written music. Real improvisation is something else. I've seen major players with great reputations who can only improvise with the people they rehearse with all the time.

KLOTMAN: Oscar Peterson, who was on a panel with me in Seattle recently, told a student he should get as much *formal* training as possible, that it would not harm him and that it would provide him with background and knowledge he might not otherwise acquire. At a Chicago meeting of the Music Educators National Conference, a group of string players performed some music by Dave Baker as a demonstration. The first violinist, evidently well schooled, was not at all inhibited by the jazz style of this suite.

TIPTON: We know there is an abundance of music teachers, seemingly in every area but jazz. At Hampton, we are interested in starting a jazz degree program, but many of the practicing jazz musicians with whom I've spoken are reluctant to leave performance to the degree a teaching schedule would require. Is there any information source which will assist in locating such a faculty?

ADDERLEY: As we travel to various campuses, we have found some Black music or jazz teachers who are profoundly incompetent, who get a job teaching because of a local contact or regional reputation. I've seen this in major state universities—even in ones with fine music departments—and jazz falls down to its lowest possible level, diminishing its relevance and importance to the students and the faculty because of this incompetent teacher. We might be a little less concerned about finding jobs for people and more concerned with the rectification of some wrongs and with the quality training of promising teachers. I know that such organizations as the Black Music Center, the Afro-American Music Opportunities Association, and the Institute of Black-American Music will work in unison toward this goal, because I wouldn't like to seen anything that seems to be at cross purposes when our aim is to spread the gospel of what this beautiful music is all about.

ASHBY: I hope we will also find ways to keep alive the music and the tradition of those good jazzmen who are no longer with us, like Billy Strayhorn, Charlie Parker, and John Coltrane. It is particularly important that libraries stock their collections with recordings of these men before the records are out of print, and that they acquire whatever published music is available.

ROBINSON: We must not think that music is only one language; there are many languages in music. I am concerned that the language of jazz is not always taught to young people.

ASHBY: I agree with you, and I'm sure my fellow Detroiter Beverly

Williams feels the same way. We've got to be concerned with the development of young audiences, and it is not true that children hear jazz at home, on the television or radio, or from recordings.

ADDERLEY: I've done a lot of what you might call filibustering on this, particularly on the campuses. When people tell me they like jazz but they don't understand it, I ask them to tell me what music they *do* understand, what they understand about it, and why they think that music is easily understood. We come up with things like the Beatle's *Hard Day's Night,* so I play recordings of Ella Fitzgerald or Count Basie doing that, and when they do it, it's jazz. Don't worry about the sources for these things. The composer isn't important in a jazz performance, not *that* important. Jerome Kern and Cole Porter have written things which jazz musicians have used for development. So I take these things and show them how much they do understand about jazz. It just depends on whether or not they've decided that they understand. And I tell them I don't think it's necessary for them to understand any art, any art at all. All you have to do is come up with your own conclusions and what's there, enjoy it or not, get into it or dismiss it.

I've had the experience of being a teacher, and I understand the difficulties. One must develop teaching skills the same way he develops other skills. Even if you have a lot of information, it is not always easy to impart this to other people. I have mentioned before how I felt about degrees. I don't mean they are unimportant because we operate in a society that counts degrees. Ornette doesn't have a college degree, but Cecil Taylor and Archie Shepp do. Ironically, these two have college positions. I know Ornette very well, and I certainly respect him, but he is not a teacher. More than that, his music is not easy to read. I've commissioned pieces from him, and he writes music just the way he wants: no time signature, irregular bar lines . . . even the note heads don't have stems some times. We can't play his music until he plays first, and then we have to imitate what he does. So you see, a person who is gifted is not necessarily a good person for communication in other areas. And, on degrees, Ken McIntyre turned down his doctorate because like he felt it was insulting for that faculty to offer him a degree in Black music.

ABRAMS: You know, degrees are handed out by schools which set up their own criteria. If you talk about their thing and give it back to them when they ask, you've got the degree, but they're not talking about *jazz*. And the present system was not set up for the needs of Black people.

ADDERLEY: I'm glad you're here Brother Abrams, I'm glad to see you again. What you are saying is very important to our topic. Let us not misunderstand where we have been leading ourselves: We have been talking about jazz in the curriculum of *existing* schools. The whole school system needs to be revolutionized so we won't be hung up on these old-time traditions about teaching but, if we're talking about doing it in the schools, it's got to be introduced in the schools the way that the schools operate. Once the music is in the system, and once *we* are in the system, we will have to manage methods whereby the beauty of this music can be utilized aesthetically and intellectually.

MAULTSBY: How do you feel about the rejection of such musical terms as *melody, phrase,* and *ostinato*—words which have been associated with European music? I'm thinking about a White jazz musician, teaching in a university, who advocates doing away with these words.

ADDERLEY: Well, I think the man has to do what he thinks should be done. I don't agree with him, though. In order to get a wider number of people on the same consciousness level, we have to have a system that is not quite so personal. I don't know what this teacher is trying to accomplish *other* than teaching Black music, but if he feels he should reject these terms because they relate to music he is trying to get away from, then I have to accept it because I'm not doing his job.

QUESTION: I would be happy to hear what you might have to say about the blues.

ADDERLEY: I've always felt that the blues idiom is a feeling. Duke Ellington has said that some people like to travel and that a traveling man who has to leave his wife at home sometimes has need for another woman. If he has left his woman too long, she may find she needs the attention of another man. Duke has said that these feelings and reasons give rise to situations which lay the foundation for a blues expression. He said that sometimes the man is happy his woman found another man, because he didn't want her. Under these circumstances you can have happy blues, rather than sad blues. You know Count Basie's *I Know My Baby Gonna Jump and Shout?* That's the blues. But I don't know what the blues is, I just know how it feels to me. Definitions and rhetoric can't say in finite terms what the blues is all about. People just know.

QUESTION: On the matter of education and jazz, I wonder if we should start from the top and come down. In the hierarchy of education, what do you have to say about Black studies programs?

KLOTMAN: I'd like to have that question directed to Vice-Chancellor Herman C. Hudson, who is in charge of Afro-American Affairs at Indiana University.

HUDSON: The most essential element in Black studies programs is that there must be Black control. At Indiana University we are well aware of the fact that we're in a White institution and we know that White people may work for the program, but the control of the program, the directions and ideas that permeate its development have to be in the hands of Black people.

I am very much opposed to interdepartmental arrangements, institutes, programs, or appendages of any sort which many institutions have established to meet the exigencies of the time, because these will be abolished as soon as the pressure is over. The program must be integrated into the basic structural arrangement of the university, on the departmental level. Persons working in that department should have the same rights and privileges of all faculty members, including tenure and promotions. Their academic home is within the department, and its future must not rest in the hands of outsiders who make external judgments about their capabilities.

I also agree that degrees are not necessarily a presumption of competence. The reverse is also true: One cannot presume competence because he grew up in the ghetto. We are part of an educational institution with a lot of traditions, many of which are bad and most of which are not going to change overnight. Having academic degrees is part of the university life. It is not, however, an essential criterion in our Afro-American Studies Program. We are hiring at the professorial rank (not as only an artist-in-residence, which is a very temporary thing), engaging people who might lack degrees but who happen to be extremely competent for the job.

QUESTION: On a lower level, are we using a back-door policy by having subject material segregated in courses like Black music, or Black history?

HUDSON: The people who teach American history or music history have systematically excluded mention of the Black contribution for generations. I'm not ready to turn that over to people who have perpetrated this serious omission. For a period of time it is going to be necessary for us to develop materials on our own history and then later to get this into the overall educational picture. And I don't say that only Black students should study Black music. White students have been victims of educational policies in the past also.

ADDERLEY: The ex-coach and star of the Boston Celtics, Bill Russell, is a dear friend of mine. We were talking with Joe Garagiola of the *Today* show, and Joe took issue with the fact that there was a new magazine called *Black Sports*. He said he would be insulted if a magazine came out which was called *White Sports*. Bill and I simultaneously agreed that magazines would not be named *White Sports;* They just were. And history has been White history, and music has been White music.

Within the framework of American institutions of higher learning, we have excluded Black contributions to music and have influenced the emasculation to the extent that it has carried over into predominately Black schools, making those administrators effete who for many years have looked down on the music of the street, of the farm, of the road, and called it inferior. We've created this attitude with our own children. I deplore the fact that it has been necessary to establish these so-called divergent points of view because this should have been part of the whole thing all the time. As Chancellor Hudson has said, everybody has been deprived of knowing the truth by these guardians of the White ethnic image, by the status quo "policy makers." You'll almost never have Black history taught within a general history course unless a Black administrator is in the head chair.

ASHBY: By the same token, I think Black students should also have more than just Black studies, and I'd like to see the student of baroque music study jazz.

ADDERLEY: Along the line of Black studies, I was informed by the people on one major campus that over sixty percent of the Black students at that school are not involved in any way with the Black studies program. That's tragic. I don't think Blacks should identify only with Blacks, but it would be nice to know what it's all about.

● There are two articles which extend some of the implications brought up in this discussion, which I recommend. Neither of them deals specifically with jazz or music, but they tie in beautifully with thoughts offered by Dorothy, Cannonball, and Chancellor Hudson, and they both appear in the thirteenth issue (January 1971) of *Cultural Affairs on Education,* a journal issued by the Associated Councils of the Arts (1564 Broadway, New York 10036). The first of these is by Joseph Featherstone: "The Arts and the Good School." Second is W. H. Ferry's "Universities: Looking Black." I appreciate having these articles brought to my attention by our good friend, Madeleine Gutman. Mr. Featherstone amplifies manners whereby art education (including music) can provide students with knowledge and experience of value, and Mr. Ferry attacks problems and prejudices in Black studies in a most perceptive manner.

As for the particular points this duo raised, it is quite possible that Cannonball's "little monsters" will be shaken. Within the context of his statements, however, surely it can be understood that his interests are allied with those expressed by many at our seminars. If Dave can say that Whites don't own Beethoven, Cannonball can say that jazz belongs to those who love it. But he is also advancing the cause of a rehumanized education and of comprehensive musical studies.

Both Cannonball and Dorothy have expressed their thoughts quite clearly, but I was particularly delighted to find Dorothy had already thought of an idea which was taking shape in my mind: the relationship of jazz performance to baroque performance. At this point, I should have liked very much to include a translation of an article on exactly that point, written by Hans-Peter Schmitz, which was published in *Die Stimme* in 1949, and which was called to my attention by Dr. Erwin Jacobi of Zürich. Unfortunately it is not possible to make arrangements for this in time to include it, but I hope this article can be published in translation in the near future.

9. The Conflict Between Foreign and Traditional Culture in Nigeria

● The problems of cultural identity for a proud Nigerian provide a counterpart to those faced by his American cousin. The situation is not identical, as this article indicates. The Nigerian is aware of those elements from colonial days which have contributed to his culture—often as an imposition, but most seriously as a distiller of native values and techniques—and there appears to be no interest in negating the significance of European music. But the invasion is not only European: It is also Black American.

The author, a Senior Fellow in Musicology at Nigeria's University of Ife, has explored this delimma of acculturation shock in a newspaper article with the same title which appeared in the *Daily Times* (Lagos, October 1, 1970, pp. iv–v). When he was kind enough to send me a copy, I asked that he permit us to reprint it because the problems may be of special assistance in providing additional perspectives within the United States.

I also corresponded with the Music Director of the American Wind Symphony Orchestra, Robert Austin Boudreau, whose commission stimulated the article. He replied that "during the fall of 1962, I was invited to Nigeria as a guest of the Nigeria Arts Council, where I met several Nigerian composers. In the summer of 1963, as a result of this visit, we had the first Nigerian Festival in Pittsburgh. We commissioned three Nigerian composers to write special works for this occasion; one was Samuel Akpabot, another was Ayo Bankole, and the third was Akin Euba." The works resulting from this commission were *Overture and Variations* by Bankole, *Dance to the Rising Sun* by Euba, and *Cynthia's Lament* by Akpabot. The latter work was premiered in August of 1965. Mr. Akpabot had already composed *Ofala Festival* on a commission of the American Wind Symphony Orchestra for a July 1963 performance.

Regarding the composition of the 1965 work, the composer writes, "Cynthia Avery was the 16-year-old daughter of the White American Vice-Chairman of the American Wind Symphony Orchestra of Pittsburgh with whom I stayed during a visit in 1963 for the première of *Ofala festival*. After the performance, we went to the Conrad Hilton to have coffee with Mr. Boudreau. The rather silly waitress deliberately avoided serving Miss Avery and myself (we were seated together, a short distance from the girl's parents and Mr. Boudreau, who were served). This so distressed Miss Avery that she stormed out of the café into the foyer sobbing, 'I don't know what has become of my people!' I decided to write a short piece for her, and on my next commission two years later, I produced *Cynthia's Lament.*"

Along with two other Nigerian composers, I was commissioned in 1963 to write a work with a truly Nigerian flavor for the American Wind Symphony Orchestra of Pittsburgh. It was the first time that any of us had attempted this. We all had good grounding in Western classical compositional techniques, but how much did we know about African music? The results brought us to some moments of truth.

I remember vividly that halfway into a run-through of his work, one of my colleagues said, "Oh no, this is no good! This is not what I wanted!" Neither was I happy. I could not get away from the fact that my efforts were too strongly under European influences. Clearly then, our first attempts to write orchestral music with a genuine African flavor had failed to all intents and purposes. We had to try again.

This story could be duplicated by other Nigerian artists in creative fields I am sure, especially in music and the fine arts: we had made an honest attempt to create something really Nigerian, but we had to admit that the final results were not what we wanted.

In August of 1970, I went on a research and recording tour in southeastern Nigeria on behalf of the Institute of African Studies of the University of Ife. At Abak, not far from Ikot Ekpene, I came across a seven-man orchestra of two drummers, a wood block player, and a quartet of end-blown flutes known as uta, made from carved-out gourds and the horn of a deer. On examining one of the instruments, I discovered a length of tubing from an automobile wrapped around one end of the flute for protection, and I was curious about this because our forefathers had no access to motor car tubing. "Why do you use this?" I asked the leader of the group. With a wry smile, he told me our ancestors had used goat skin, but the tubing was "more respectable." So that was it: Goat skin was out, and automobile tubing was in as a symbol of respectability. I was then forced to ask myself how truly Nigerian was our culture.

If you travel to the ancient kingdom of Benin to purchase a carving, you will likely find modern works which have been polished with sandpaper.

As with many others deeply involved in traditional Nigerian culture, I prefer the unadulterated traditional style of music, of painting and of carving, handed down by our fathers through the ages, but then someone might stand up and ask what really *is* Nigerian culture.

We know that Händel, a German, wrote Italian operas, and that Lully, an Italian, composed French operas. How do we then define our own unique styles in Nigeria? Do they exist in the arts only because the creator is resident in our country? It is difficult to find an answer because there are many instances of works by Nigerians which have nothing to do with Nigeria excepting the name of the composer.

I would like to essay a definition by saying that a work under the umbrella of Nigerian culture must be by a Nigerian artist, in whatever creative art he is active. I would then go on by saying that, in order for it to exist alongside other Nigerian masterpieces, it must be steeped in and/or borrow lavishly from traditional patterns. Failure to fit into these categories completely disqualifies the validity of a Nigerian concept.

The Nigerian artist is doubly blessed. By virtue of his European training, he can compose a piece of music or create a piece of sculpture in the Western style which, if his efforts are good enough, may make an impact purely on its own excellent, and not for the sentimental value that the artist is Black. On the other hand, he can deliberately set out to use his father's idioms and traditions to create something really indigenous, which would communicate to his countrymen and, at the same time, evoke the approbation of foreigners.

This second route could be approached in one of two ways—either by making use only of traditional instruments and materials, or by fusing the two cultures, but in a manner which is heavily dependent on Nigerian traditions for its success.

This is what my colleagues and I set out to do in Pittsburgh in 1963. If we did not quite make it as we thought, it was because we were still heavily influenced by our European training. The results had moments of brillance, many patches of indecision, and sprinklings of confusion.

The traditional Nigerian composer or sculptor has a decided advantage over his European trained counterpart because his tools are less complicated and his ambitions rest within the confines of his limitations. The pitcher maker works in clay to produce some eye-catching pottery; the xylophonist draws warmth from his crude looking instrument with its pentatonic scale; the flutist, with only a few notes at his disposal, falls back on melodic rhythm; and the weaver is able to produce attractive handwoven Adire and Akwette cloths from his simple instruments.

I have seen the scores and listened to efforts of some of my contemporaries who wrote for traditional Nigerian instruments. This exercise, I sadly relate, has not been much of a success. Pleasant as the music might sound, it is not quite "with it." Ironically, the Nigerian composer who is steeped in the rhythms of Western music is strangely deficient in the traditional rhythms of his own country.

There is no doubt but that European influences have caused our artists to look down on our traditional culture. I was talking recently to a Nigerian painter and sculptor who had just returned from the United Kingdom. Among those works he was exhibiting in Lagos, I sought in vain to find a single work which I could identify as Nigerian. When I asked him about this, he was indignant. "Look," he said to me, "I am an artist. I make my sculptures as I like. I do not have to create something Nigerian to be accepted around the world." These words mean little to me.

The fact that my friend is trying to get away from his roots is perhaps the chief reason why his works will not win for him the acclaim he seeks. His view was that Nigerian art was, in the main, primitive, and he was trying to show the rest of the world that a Nigerian artist had brains. In his rather misguided mind, he saw Picasso as a stylistic improvement on traditional patterns.

Wrong. A thousand times wrong! In twenty years, when chances are that his works might be forgotten, pilgrims will still be coming to Nigeria to seek out and study the beautiful traditions of painting and carving of the "primitive" Nigerian artist. Sophistication is not a substitute for skill, and never has been.

The scene in Nigeria is a very interesting one today. When the country became independent in 1960, there was only one composer of significance, and perhaps only two others attempting to secure recognition. Today music and art are taught at Nssuka Univeristy, art at Ahmadu Bello. There is a resident composer at Lagos University, and the African Studies Program at the University of Ibadan is not far behind. The greatest experiment in the preservation and encouragement of Nigerian culture, I think, is now being carried out at the University of Ife, located as it is near the shrine of Yoruba culture. Nigerians knowing the Western tradition here are rediscovering themselves and are seeking out aspects of our culture which unfortunately were submerged in the colonial era.

I have mentioned the project at the Institute of African Studies of the University of Ife especially because this leads us to perhaps the most vital question in considering the future of Nigerian culture. How can we retain the roots of our cultural heritage amidst the strong challenge of foreign influences?

The first step is for those connected with the preservation and advancement of our culture to reasses their sense of values. From being outward looking, they must turn inward. The age of the White tie and tails is over and done in Africa; the promises of *agbaba* is very much with us for a long time to come. We can no longer look on the player of the bata, the goje or the uta as a *curis*. It is true that the goje is a one-stringed viol, but that does not make its music less passionate or effective. Does a xylophone mounted on banana stems produce inferior tones to one with a Bond Street finish?

Nigerian power must replace European power in the creative arts. Artists are traditionally poor people; it is this poverty which causes adulturation. The artist in Benin who sandpapers his carving—and even paints it with varnish—is doing so to attract foreign customers; the state and his fellow countrymen do nothing to encourage him. To most of them, he is an illiterate without the West African School Certifcate, a man who does not belong, a man alone, battling hard to preserve the arts and crafts of his forefathers. The colonial mentality, which saw only those with secondary or university education as worthy of recognition, must go. One might say there are more graduates with illiterate ideas than illiterates with a correct sense of values.

The state must first encourage the traditional artists by raising their standard of living with loans and by giving them workshops with conditions ideal for creativity. Secondly, the teaching and practice of traditional music must be made compulsory in primary and secondary schools. (I was introduced to music as a chorister for seven years in the Lagos Cathedral, and then as a student at King's College in Lagos. How much richer would my experience have been had traditional musical techniques been taught side by side with Byrd, Beethoven, and Brahms!) Thirdly, the radio stations must come to our aid. There is an amusing episode regarding one of my colleagues who was asked by the Nigerian Broadcasting Corporation in Lagos to compose some music for a choir. Before the end of the discussion, the official took my friend aside and said, "For God's sake, do not include any traditional drum in your work!" The deal fell through; Mozart, Mendelssohn, and Mahler were in, and Ikoro and bata drums were out—yet another case of the wrong sense of values. Lastly, the Nigerian Arts Council, as custodians of our cultural heritage, must join the universities and radio stations in helping to preserve and advance Nigerian culture. This body should be freed from the disciples of pre-independence Nigeria, reflect the twelve states of our country, and bring into the fold tried and tested men of music and the arts.

To preserve our culture, we must instill pride in our youth while they are yet young. There is nothing wrong with the current craze for "soul" sessions, but everything is wrong in a society whose youths think more of the passing fancy of American dance than in the beautiful and lasting traditional dances of their own country. James Brown, the high priest of "soul," sings and shouts, "Say it loud, I'm Black and proud!" and, in so doing, reflects the singing traditions and political sentiments of the American Negro. When our youths sing the same words, who are they telling? Of course, we are Black and proud. Nigerians in their music, dancing, painting and carving have been Black and proud for centuries! The indigenous musicians have been saying it loud for a long time. Alas, the sound of 100-decibel twanging guitars, the roar of electric organs, and the fanfare of blazing trumpets have turned the loud pleadings of traditional music and musicians into a whisper.

Thank God it is 1971! The Nigerians must now return to their tents!

● On we go, both suffering and benefiting from acculturation, that inevitable phenomenon which has destroyed and created more than one culture. It is particularly unfortunate that in Africa, where tradition has been a way of life, new ideas are imposing themselves and are changing, undoubtedly, more than just music. Mr. Akpabot is lamenting more the loss of the *quality* of a craft, however, than the *spirit* of it, and the quality is more basic to the art work. He is also complaining that indigenous aesthetics have been questioned by fellow countrymen who have been led to think European concepts have more validity. I remember Gunther Schuller was concerned about this at our 1969 sessions, as they applied to Japanese music.

On a recent visit to the Center, Hugh Tracey expressed his concern over the growing influence of Black-American music in Africa, which is hitting social factors within the lives of the Black African, and I have heard similar comments from others from Africa.

No matter how inevitable acculturation may be (and, it must be admitted, African influences sure messed up the Arne-type traditions the British brought to the colonies), it would be very sad if cultures in Africa would be eradicated prior to documentation, although it is very shallow to suggest that any culture should exist basically for anthropological research, and I don't mean that (I am reminded of a statement made by an American Indian who said that the typical Indian family consisted of a mother, a father, two children, and an anthropologist). What the world lost with the Aswan Dam may find a parallel in music, and Mr. Akpabot is anticipating this.

10. Journalism, Black Music and Black Dance

Earl Calloway and Carole Y. Johnson

● The profession of music criticism is far from overpopulated by Blacks and, no doubt, there are special reasons for this. As the distinction between African performers and audiences is blurred, so also is that of the listeners and the critics. Music and dance, in such instances, serve the corporate goals of society. Outside of that environment and regardless of the retention of African aesthetics, American music has other considerations, and the importance of individual opinion and leadership takes on special characteristics. The complex aspects of this question are presented in Addison Gayle's provocative anthology, *The Black Aesthetic* (Garden City: Doubleday & Co., 1971, xxiv, 432pp). Yet another obligation of the Black critic is the communication of ideas and events, and outlets for this service have not been open to Black writers to the extent that the American art scene requires. Chicago's distinguished journalist, Earl Calloway, describes his thoughts and experiences in this field.

The only journal known to us which gives special consideration to Black dance is *Feet Maganews,* issued by the Modern Organization for Dance Evolvement (MODE). This society, which has been partially funded by the New York State Council on the Arts, developed under the leadership of Carole Y. Johnson, a totally charming young lady with an international reputation as a dancer and scholar. MODE (whose mailing address is G.P.O. Box 2848, New York 10003) includes on its board of directors and advisory council such persons as Madeleine Gutman, Bess Pruitt, Alvin Ailey, Katherine Dunham, and Pearl Primus. Its work in dance is analogous to that of the Black Music Center in music.

CALLOWAY: A decade and a half ago, a little lady in Montgomery refused to get up out of her seat on the bus and move for the convenience of another individual. There were three reasons. For one, she was tired. Secondly, she was a lady. As a third reason, she felt she was equal. You know what happened. The whole nation became involved. From that small beginning, the people of Montgomery spoke through the voice of Martin Luther King, and an international movement for equality of *all* people really got started.

The Afro-American arts came together, and man saw he did have a heritage. Leontyne Price followed Marian Anderson at the Metropolitan Opera; the jazz performer stepped to the forefront of American culture with a new concept of himself; Arthur Mitchell, Rod Rodgers, and Alvin Ailey joined other dancers to demonstrate our great contribution to this art; we found outstanding conductors in Isiah Jackson, Henry Lewis, James De Priest, and Paul Freeman.

It was about that time that I graduated from the Chicago Musical College, ready for a career as a lyric tenor, but during an illness in 1960, when I started writing until I regained my health, I found that there was a need for someone to communicate ideas on the arts to the people, and I remained with the *Chicago Courier* for several years. I wrote for the Associated Negro Press and had a national column. Then, by 1965, I moved to the *Chicago Daily Defender* and my work broadened. I started writing for the Negro Press International and soon for the national edition of the *Courier* as well.

People refer to me as a music critic. I'd prefer to be known as a fine arts editor because my work encompasses more than critiques, more than music. I am involved with television, movies, drama, dance, music, and other aspects of the arts, and I am concerned with the whole question of aesthetics.

I go to a performance to enjoy it, not to be critical of it, but there are six criteria I have First is talent: the innate ability of a performer to dance, sing, speak, or play. I know that talent might be acquired, but the innate talent that has been disciplined is usually the one that makes the stronger contribution. Second in importance is creativity: the performer's ability to create or re-create an idea in a manner which can be understood by the audience. Third is musicianship. In addition to talent and creativity, the musician must have a distinct sensitivity to the materials of his art. Fourth is technique: the competence to enhance, to vary, to color, to make dynamic, to realize the concepts of one's musical imagination. In fifth place are all of those physical factors involved in the performance, having a stage personality which is harmonious with the music and the audience. Although last in my list, communication is not the least important. By this I mean the *ultimate* effect all of these elements in performance on the listener so that, in the end, the audience is different. I offer these points for your consideration if you are engaged in formal criticism or not.

As a writer, I am concerned with the dissemination of information and ideas on the arts to the community, Black and White. I want to get other people interested in art, to help preserve or elevate performance standards, to bring the artist and his audience together.

To get specifically to matters on Black music, I should first say that I use the term *Black* to refer to *all* Black people—in Africa, in the United States, in South America, in the Caribbean . . . wherever. *Afro-American* to me means Blacks in this country. Now even though our paper is Black-oriented, I think music is music, and theater is theater. There are standards no matter if the performers are White or Black, no matter if they are students or professionals. On certain levels, being Black or White is of no major consequence. When I hear a singer, I think how well he carries across his poetic thought, how he structures a phrase, how he colors his sound, and how he builds his dynamics. I'm also concerned about his enunciation, whether the text is in a foreign language or English. I'd want to see how he and his pianist cooperate and create one, unified performance. In these aspects, you see, there are basic standards which Black and White musicians share.

I jot down ideas at the recitals and work them into real reviews later. At this seminar, we have heard Natalie Hinderas perform. I noted her firm attacks, her sharp and vital rhythms, the vocal quality of her phrasing, the crispness of her technique, and her ability to see humor in the music. Of course, these ideas would have to be amplified. On Dave Baker's *Black America,* I merely wrote down that it was "vibrant with all the musical rhetoric of the Black experience and artistically profound." That is only a start.

Program building is part of the question of criticism. I've noticed that we usually place spirituals at the end of the concert, and it dawned on me that many of these spirituals might have roots which are contemporary with Bach or Mozart. Why couldn't we sing these early spirituals right alongside a Mozart aria, for example? Miss Hinderas didn't exclude Haydn or Chopin in her program, and she didn't put them at the end of it, either.

I was born in Alabama and spent a good deal of time in New Orleans. When I was little and my mother was working, we had a lady in the house that we called Big Mama. She was something like eighty at the time. She had lived in slavery, and the descendants of those people would still come by to see her once in a while and bring her food and money. When Big Mama was working in the kitchen or doing the washing, I heard her singing the old slave songs, and I learned a lot from her. This is a part of me, and it's probably a part of many of you. I just don't think you need to put those songs at the end of a recital.

I also heard music at the vaudevilles, at the circus, at Birmingham's Frolic Theater. I remember the street singers who played on tambourines and all manner of things, like bones. There were blind men who would stroke their guitars, carrying their songs with them from one place to another. There weren't too many places we could go in those days in the South, but we went on Sunday evenings to church, to be with the sanctified people, to listen to them and dance with them. These are the kinds of memories I have of the music of my people, and all of this is part of my background as a journalist.

I'd like to make a plea now that you cherish your newspapers. We may complain that we don't get anywhere, that no one recognizes a certain individual, but has this information been sent to the paper? If you spend your life doing something in the arts, others must know about it. I want to encourage you to communicate with me. If you are a composer, let me know what you have written and something about yourself. You should take advantage of letting other people know about your work, those outside your own community. This is particularly true with those in classical music.

We have a broad coverage; our chain of papers is not small. The *Chicago Daily Defender* was organized in 1905, and it has been at the very forefront of the Black experience—not only in the arts, but in civil rights. When no one else would speak out against lynchings, we did. I remember selling copies as a boy in the sandy hills of Mississippi and Alabama. I learned a lot from reading it, and most of the jazz and rock artists came up by way of Chicago, so our files have a rich documentation in Black music history.

We don't want to wait until someone is famous before we give note of him. You may all now know the name of Primous Fountain. Several years ago I heard about his talent, and I searched for him and did an interview. I told him I wanted to hear some of his music. At that time, I was conducting the Philharmonic Youth Choir, so I gave him $25 to have some music copied which we could perform at a banquet. We did it, and it was a beautiful experience. From this came a full page on him, and I encouraged radio station WLS to give a public performance of his music. They gave two, and then musicians from the Chicago Symphony got interested in his music. Later, he got a commission from them and a grant to go to Tanglewood. He has been offered a scholarship to the New England Conservatory by Gunther Schuller. Five performances of a work have been scheduled in Oakland, and a commission has come from the Pittsburgh Wind Symphony. All of this from an interview, but of course he is a very talented person. I was also able to help a comic pretty much the same way, who has since been with the Playboy Club in Atlanta and Toronto, in California, in Japan, Las Vegas, and so on. We have a circulation of almost a million, with special editions for certain states. Let us play a part in letting the rest of the country know about you. You see, then, my work is not just in music.

JOHNSON: As a representative of MODE, I want to tell you about our journal, *Feet,* which is the only publication that specializes in the dance as created and experienced by Black people. Before I go into that, I'd like to discuss some of the questions which have been posed to me by several of you about the music used by Black choreographers.

During the past four or five years, there has been a noticeable upsurge of activity in the dance that is created and performed in concert by Black people. In addition there has been a strong desire to share this dance with people in the Black communities who normally do not see their professional dance artists, even though many young people participate in numerous dance classes through the various recreational programs, Model Cities and Poverty Programs, as well as through the neighborhood Black-owned dance schools. Because of the various government programs that have been a part of the 1960s, more artists have been able to return to the Black communities today than were able to in the previous twenty years. The last time there was any such mass effort of art in the community, at least of dance, seems to have been during Roosevelt's WPA days of the 1930s. It must therefore be noted that this new creative period has a history of contemporary development that in many ways dates back to WPA days.

It is no wonder that you ask about the music that Black choreographers use because the history of Black people and their dance (both the concert and recreational forms) is more obscure than that of Black music. In fact, it's so obscure that the average Black student today is only slightly more aware of what is happening with Black artists than I was when I was a student growing up in the 1950s. Even though Katherine Dunham had a national press at that time, I'm not really sure if I had heard of her even though I had unknowingly been exposed to her technique in the few Afro-Cuban classes I took at the Sydney School of Dance, a local Black dance school in Philadelphia. Janet Collins, who gave a concert in Philadelphia, is the only Black dancer I am sure I knew about. I saw Carmen De Lavallade on television several times, but it was many years later before I realized who she was.

Even though much more is happening in Black dance today, I can be almost sure that the average dance students in, say, Minneapolis or Baton Rouge do not know about Alvin Ailey or Arthur Mitchell, despite the amount of national publicity they get. Many who have heard of them are not certain if they are Black or not.

Not until I was working on a research paper for the New York State Council on the Arts in 1967 did I learn how much was being done by Black people in the 1950s. I learned about Katherine Dunham and Pearl Primus who reached their peaks in the 1940s and have continued working to this day. I read about all the things that Talley Beatty, Donny McKayle, Louis Johnson, and Alvin Ailey were doing, as well as about the work of less well-known figures.

The music used by the Black choreographer is whatever he wants, and I'm not trying to be facetious—whatever music they feel will express the idea they want to communicate, whatever music inspires them. Sometimes an idea sparks one to search out suitable music and other times the music inspires the idea and movements. Their choices of music therefore run the gamut of the American musical experience: historical European music such as that by Bach, or contemporary music by Samuel Barber, Béla Bartók, John Coltrane, Duke Ellington, Alan Hovhaness, Heitor Villa-Lobos, Charles Mingus, or traditional Black music of the blues, spirituals, prison and work songs, gospel music, and material from Black folklore.

The choreographic works that were most successful, or at least the ones that moved me the most, were those that used music out of Black-American life, and the 1950s was the period when dance artists really got down to the nitty-gritty exploration of aspects of Afro-American life. They approached the subject differently than had Katherine Dunham and Pearl Primus in the preceeding decade. Talley Beatty's best known works are *Road of the Phoebe Snow, Congo Tango Palace,* and *Toccata,* which came from *Come and Get the Beauty of It Hot,* which used music by Duke Ellington, Billy Strayhorn, Dizzy Gillespie, Miles Davis, and other contemporaries. Donny McKayle used the driving rhythms, emotional harmony, and content of prison and work songs in *Rainbow Round My Shoulder*, the only dance work which has moved me so much that I left the theater crying when I first saw it. In *Games*, McKayle used street games and songs which grew out of children's play songs and games. Alvin

Ailey's *Revelations* is considered the classic statement in the use of traditional spirituals and of gospel. His *Blues Suite* used different kinds of blues, from the light and humorous to the sad and poignant, sometimes driving and sometimes slightly bitter.

I have recently been working with a young choreographer, Eleo Pomare. In his *Las Desenamoradas* (based on Garcia Lorca's *House of Bernada Alba*), he uses John Coltrane's *Olé*. His *Blues for the Jungle* has become a classic in its own way. I think of it as an accumulation of the explorations of Alvin, Donny, and Talley during the decade before, and it is a statement in tune with the attitudes of revolt that characterized the 1960s. In this work employs music by Charles Mingus and Oscar Brown, Jr., as well as electronic arrangements of traditional African music played by Olatunji and his group, and traditional Black-American music, His *Missa Luba* was inspired by that Congolese mass, and he has also created a dance for me based on three songs of Bessie Smith.

Rod Rodgers is a choreographer who came into prominence in the middle sixties. He has used music by Yusef Lateef and, I think, Freddie Hubbard, as well as Bernice Reagon, and poetry by such Black writers as Don L. Lee and Jackie Earley. Coleridge-Taylor Perkinson has written music for Rod Rodgers and for Arthur Mitchell, and he may be the first Black composer to have a commission from a Black dance company. This means that funds have been made available for Mr. Perkinson to create ballet music for Black companies, just as Whites have been doing in the past.

Howard Roberts did arrangements of traditional music for Alvin and Donny, and the first performance of *Revelations* was conducted by Howard Roberts, while the première of *Rainbow* was done by Robert de Cormier. Bob Cunningham, Clifford Jordan, Bill Brown, and Pat Patrick were among those musicians who led the Dancemobile companies, in accord with the original premise that Black musicians would be hired to write and play for the Dancemobile groups.

Many young choreographers are currently using blues, ballads, rock and roll, folk, and gospel music for their productions. Odetta, Leon Bibb and Aretha Franklin are a few of the favorites whose recordings can be heard in dance classes and productions which cannot afford live music.

There is a big influence now from the African dance companies that are touring the United States. These had started in the late 1950s with Les Ballets Africains, from Guinea. Companies from other countries participated in the New York World's Fair of 1963–

1964, and followed their New York season with nationwide tours. At the present time there is always at least one truly African dance company on tour each year in the United States. In addition, there is a growing number of Black-American companies developing traditional African dance in New York, Washington, Philadelphia, Chicago, and other large cities. These companies, which always use live musicians, have a wide variety of African percussion instruments in the orchestra.

Other Black choreographers who were producing in the 1950s and 1960s, whose names should be better known than they are, include Arleigh Peterson, Ronne Aul, George Mills, Stanze Peterson, John Coy, Ronnie Arnold, Raymond Sawyer, Bill Frank, and Gus Solomons, Jr. I should also mention a few of the choreographers who are developing now and who look as if they might become well known: George Faison, Glenn Brooks, Fred Benjamin, Chuck Davis, and Ron Pratt.

Please remember that I have been talking about only a few of the better known choreographers and the music they have selected from the wide range of American works. Perhaps at another time we can explore the use of music by composers of other ethnic backgrounds.

I have never forgotten a statement often repeated by Norman Lloyd, my music history teacher at Juilliard, who said that Martha Graham might never have been understood had it not been for the appreciation of John Martin, dance critic for the *New York Times*. He was able to educate people so that Martha Graham's new approach to the art could be understood and appreciated. This is something no Black choreographer has yet had, and it will take someone, as Earl has indicated, to bring the names of our artists and their ideas to public attention.

Dance Magazine and *Dance News* are the major dance publications in the United States. If you didn't know which dancers and choreographers were Black a few years ago—to an extent even now— you never would have known from these publications. I think many of our contributions get "whitewashed" in the major publications. When you read about a new personality in the magazines, you always assume the person is White (unless it is made known to the contrary) because the American attitude suggests that good things come from White sources. A few years ago there were almost no feature articles on the Black dancer, and not too many photographs, so many of the names would have gone by undistinguished by race.

MODE established *Feet* so that special attention could be given to these "faceless" people. The philosophy behind MODE is very much like that on which the Black Music Center was based. We wanted to reach to the public—especially the Black public—to let them know about the dancers and the exciting work they are doing. The reaction to *Feet* has been very positive, and that is wonderful. It is difficult to get artists to work together, but we have a common goal and, as a result, MODE has won a lot of support. *Feet* allows the choreographer a voice, and it is a workshop for writers and photographers interested in dance.

CALLOWAY: We ought to say that Carole Johnson is also a dancer, and has appeared with Rod Rodgers and Eleo Pomare. She has been a panelist at meetings of the Association of American Dance Companies, and the American Dance Guild, and was affiliated with the Dancemobile in New York.

JOHNSON: That was from 1967 through 1969. The first year I was able to raise funds from the city, state, and corporate sources and I went through the Harlem Cultural Council which sponsored the project, so that dance could get right to the people in the community.

CALLOWAY: Would you tell us how *Feet* got started?

JOHNSON: In April of 1970, I had a meeting with Katherine Dunham about the necessity of having a Black dance conference. Miss Dunham had previously talked about this with Ruth Beckford Smith, a dance person from the Bay area of California. I thought these talks were so important that I wanted to get the word as fast as possible to the dancers in New York and have some feed-back on the ideas. We had thought that we would have the beginnings of our planning session in the summer of 1970.

Leona Johnson (no relation), a dancer who had worked in California with Miss Beckford, was with us at MODE and felt that a newsletter would be better for information on Black dance than the word-of-mouth tradition. Primarily through Leona's efforts, we were able to issue a mimeographed version of *Feet*. We were curious to see the response from the dance community. Well, it was so great that we changed to the current format with the fourth issue that November, with aid from the New York State Council on the Arts. Now we want to develop a large circulation and get *Feet* to the libraries and public on a national basis.

QUESTION: On the matter of criticism, I think performers often come off pretty well, but I think the composers suffer a great deal because the critic does not understand new idioms, techniques, or experiences.

CALLOWAY: Quite true, but we must realize that all composers might have this problem. It's a problem for the critics too. I think of Steve Chambers' *Sound Gone,* which we have heard Miss Hinderas play. This was really new music for me. I liked it, and it made sense. The composer may have had something else in mind than what I was able to grasp, but I likened the pathos of the bass to suffering and the glissandos in the treble to suffering. This composer is gifted at any rate, and I think the public must know here is a man with a wealth of ideas.

QUESTION: I'd like to ask Carole if my observation is correct, that the high school dance teacher is less shackled in terms of the Black experience than the music teacher.

JOHNSON: I'd have to say you are right, but there is actually not much dance in the schools. Dance is mostly approached as an extracurricular activity, like a club or after-school event. Because there isn't a real curriculum and little tradition for teaching it, dance is often approached in a fresh manner. The classes, however, are always dependent on the experience and qualifications of the teacher.

DE LERMA: I suspect there are not too many music critics whose ideas are thought valuable by musicians, but I'd like to apologize in particular for an inane review which appeared locally of Natalie's recital. If you saw it, you noted that it had nothing of any substance on the music or her performance, but the most ridiculous thing of all is that the critic was impressed to see Indiana University's piano faculty at a concert given by a Black pianist. The audience then suggested a stamp of approval. I know we have a distinguished piano faculty, but Miss Hinderas is distinguished also. And I think it is offensive to have suggested that our professors might not have been interested in the recital which the Black Music Center sponsored. So my apologies to Miss Hinderas, to you, and to our faculty.

CALLOWAY: Duke Ellington toyed around with the idea of a ballet, *The River,* for something like ten years. He went to see Alvin Ailey about it, and they decided to get to work. Well, they are both traveling all the time, and Alvin Ailey told me, "Man, it's real crazy. Every so often I get bits of the score from Honolulu, from St. Louis, from Chicago, and such."

QUESTION: Isn't there an important problem here which the Black arts can solve? I am distressed by the interdisciplinary gaps that exist, which have made those in one art isolated from their counterparts in other media.

CALLOWAY: This certainly is a serious matter. I am working now on plans for a January showcase for all of the Black arts, which will be held at the Museum of Science and Industry in Chicago. This will be our second "edition" of this project.

● Mr. Calloway has said he does not regard himself as only a music critic. There are, in fact, few newspapers in the country which can afford to engage a writer only for music. But in Mr. Calloway's case, it is not so much a matter of economics as of reality. Despite the work of the Black Music Center and the Modern Organization for Dance Evolvement, Black society and its arts cannot be compartmentalized to the extent that European art has been curricularly compromised. When Carole Johnson replies that Black dance in the school is approached in a freer manner than music teaching, she states that this is true because dance is not weighted down with the burdens of tradition.

No matter what kind of dance is being considered, some interdisciplinary factors force themselves into the picture. When we deal with Black dance, it is all the more obvious that dance is tightly bound to a society, and one cannot speak of feet positions or costumes as ends in themselves. It is equally shortsighted to speak of orchestration or harmony as the final goal of music study, but traditions of education and of degree majors have encouraged this. In Black journalism, we can then be thankful that Mr. Calloway sees himself as a servant to more than music.

His definition of *Black* is exactly the one used by the Black Music Center, permitting the latitude of substantially broader coverage within an area that bears varying degrees of unity. He also has sufficient perspective to see that there may be universal standards of performance that can be applied without inhibiting the realities of a given culture or style, and he laments those programs that put Black music in the footnotes.

The matter of communication, to which he and Miss Johnson both address themselves, is critically important. We need to know who our Black artists are and to know that they are Black, and we need to provide support for the young artist whose talent and potentials merit recognition. On the basis of this information, we can seek performances of persons who might otherwise be required to divert too much of their creative energies in trying to locate a public.

I lament the ideas of a critic who suggested, in essence, "Natalie Hinderas *must* be good! George Bolet went to her recital!" We don't need this kind of criticism. The newspaper wanting that kind of review should send a society editor and a photographer, but we don't need that kind of approach at any more "cultural events" either. This is only one reason why we must have aestheticians sensitive to Black music, who need to read what Addison Gayle, Leroi Jones, and Earl Calloway have written, but we also need more Black critics who may react to, rather than reflect, the essentials of Black culture.

11. A Periodization of Black Music History

David N. Baker

● David Baker had already established himself as an outstanding trombonist before he joined the Indiana University faculty in 1966, on recordings, concerts, and tours. Following an injury, he gave exclusive attention as an instrumentalist to the cello and bass, but he used this interval also to synthesize his rich experiences in music to write several primary books on jazz performance and to explore new worlds in composition and arranging.

Within a matter of almost months, he had tackled the history of Black music as well and initiated four courses in Black music history. Despite his achievements in this area, he senses yet other potentials and has plans for the future in scholarship, education, and performance which cannot help but prove monumental contributions.

To understand Black music today, one must grasp certain ideas about the social, political, and economic milieu from which it comes. The racist attitude of White America forces a balancing set of attitudes from the Black artist. The Black man in this country has been exposed to two attitudes. One relates to the efforts to dehumanize us, the other relates to the efforts to deify Whites and Western culture.

In *Beyond the Melting Pot,* Nathan Glaser and Daniel Patrick Moynihan say that we differed from European immigrants in that we did not participate in the same kind of clannishness, that we did not identify ourselves as Carolinians in distinction from those who lived in Virginia, that our life in these regions was not different enough to stimulate local attachments. "Without special language and culture, and without historical experiences that create an élan and a morale, what is there to lead them to build their own life, to patronize their own?" A statement that is attributed to us is that "everyone else sticks together, but we knock each other down; there is no trust among us." I'm going to try to disprove this.

The dehumanization process has taken many forms, sometimes subtle ones. The Jim Crow process of the last century pictured us a subhuman, morally degenerate, and incapable of being educated. We were depicted in the movies, novels, and radio in that light in this century. Think of the Africans in the Tarzan movies, about Stepin Fetchit and Willie Best. Think about *The Birth of a Nation*. But the idea of a barbaric Negro is a European invention. There has been a continuing attempt to make us amnesia victims. Moynihan has said in effect that Black Americans were created *ex nihilo*. True, it is difficult for those who prefer to ignore Black history because we are labeled a "non-literate" people and because sources in formats of European traditions are not available. This notwithstanding, Black culture and history are as old as man himself, as we have already stated in *Black Music in Our Culture*. To be non-White does not mean to be uncultured or uncivilized. Let's stop implying that the Egyptians were European.

History can be written to support any assortment of facts. History is only a point of view. In London, they teach that John Hancock was a Boston smuggler, and in this country that he was a great patriot. I'm reminded of the child who came home from school and asked his father, "If it is as you told me that the lion is the king of the beasts, why do we read that White hunters win all the battles?" His wise father said, "Lions do not write history books."

Whites have a pathological unwillingness to accept evidence about African history and, when parts of it are accepted, it is as a footnote to British economic history. It was colonial policy to impose anonymity on Africans. They gave us our names, defined us, and selected our heroes. They have given us a cultural psychological problem which has been a continuous burden, but now we're taking that off. The White man invented racism to ease his own anxieties and guilts. Black life has become a set of reactions to pressures exerted by the dominant White culture, forcing us too often into a negative stance and dissipating our precious energy and creative spirit. The politics of capitalism have always been a matter of human oppression and exploitation. All facets of Western life have conspired to create Black self-hatred, self-denial, and slavery.

The other side of this two-headed monster is the attempt to deify White man and his culture. I have called this Anglo-Saxon ethnocentricity. This is a view which assumes a superiority of Western values and mores, of perpetuating English institutions, language, and cultural patterns. This view assumes that Blacks become "proper" Americans by adopting the prevailing Anglo-American forms and standards of life, and all aspects of that life are aimed at the perpetuation and reaffirmation of this concept.

The entire curriculum of educational institutions, their administrative framework and goals, is a reflection of a middle-class society and is therefore hostile to Blacks. The conveyors of Western thought and tradition has been guilty of unmitigated arrogance in their complete disregard of other cultures. Almost any music course will totally ignore the contributions of Indians, Orientals, and Africans. This attitude may be difficult to take in the White majority, but its effect on the subjugated people is devastating.

Blacks have studied long in an effort to approximate White cultural habits and behavior patterns. We have been respected in our community only after the White world has made us legitimate. The White press has been the Black man's Bible, and the President his God. In order for any Black man to succeed and be accepted in music, or any other field, it is mandatory that he accept White values and try to imitate these. That process, by the way, is a denial of his unique heritage.

As many Blacks believe that Black people can help to save the world, many composers feel that in Black music lies the seed for the salvation of American music. Even the most casual observer can see that Western music is not the predominant musical concern of young people any longer. White Americans need to come to terms with the awakening consciousness of Black Americans as a people and to recognize that a symbolic and ideological awakening brings symptoms of the need for fundamental and political change. Social reality for Blacks in the United States is not what it is assumed to be by the country at large.

These ideas are offered as the foundation for those implications of my discussion of Black music history.

The first music that Blacks made in this country was African. One is then obligated to understand those traditions within the context of slavery, but the essence of African musical culture is a prerequisite. Music is the center of African culture, in all of its manifestations. Three basic divisions of African music might be made. Secular music is the common property of all the people, regardless of cult or affiliation. When a new "composition" is created, the elders judge its acceptability. Second is ceremonial music, employed for festivals and ceremonies. The third category is esoteric music, which comprises the bulk of African music and usually belongs to a particular cult. Only members of that cult use this music. It is true that master drummers might change from one cult to another, but they do not divulge the secrets of any cult.

Music is a functioning part of all aspects of the culture, and this is a factor we will find retained throughout Black music history. It will appear for political, social, economic, religious, and historical purposes. In a political framework, music serves most obviously in songs of praise for a leader. You will find instances of drums regarded as symbols of political power, owned by the royal family. And you will find music playing an important part in the settling of legal disputes. Music is used for social reasons (such as births, rites of passage, marriage, and death), and, as Hugh Tracey has indicated, these social reasons might relate to protest. Such music can express criticism of the pompous, the cruel, and over-bearing, those who perpetuate social injustice. The misdeeds of a wrongdoer might be expressed by "thirty or forty strapping young men before all the people of the village" or the pride of a petty official might be subjected to criticism as the young men jeer at his pretentiousness. "What better sanction could be brought to bear upon those who outrage the ethics of the community than to know the poets will have you pilloried in their next composition," Dr. Tracey notes. Yet another instance of the social function is that of passing news or gossip, or even as a medium for blackmail.

In economics, music serves principally as an aid to cooperative labor. When a rhythmic pattern of the work song is established, the work is easier. The combined strength of many men, using rhythmic coordination, is far more effective than it would be if they were acting as individuals.

The role of music in religion is varied. Music is so important in the ceremonies and rites that the event will be postponed if the right music is not available. This is not just a matter of the sounds. The instruments themselves can become objects of worship, or they may serve other important functions within the religious context. The elaborate symbolism for certain instruments we will find carried over into rural Black-American music.

Music functions within history through those songs which relate important events in the history of a tribe or lineage: battle songs, epics, stories of family history. The singer thus becomes a keeper of records, one who memorizes the history and has immediate access to that information, who relates it to others by song.

Musical instruments facilitate communication. The talking drum is the most obvious example. Drum signaling is widespread in the

Congo and in West Africa, and exists to a greater extent in East Africa than we had once thought. The basis of this drumming is linguistic and has to do with the concept of phonemic tones. It reduces the language to two tones. The types of instruments may vary, but their sounds carry some distance and they are usually capable of two different pitches. What is particularly important here is that these instruments (drums, whistles, flutes, trumpets) are used for *verbal* communication, that music actually becomes a *genuine* language.

Proverbs are important sources in many parts of Africa for song texts and provide yet another link between music and oral tradition. These texts might allow the expression of thoughts which might otherwise be repressed. I think of a song from the Congo, in which, verse by verse, plantation workers notified their employer of their greviances, ending with the threat that they would seek work elsewhere if the recently instituted salt and oil rations were not discontinued. Without the song, this discontent might not have been expressed. We're going to find some analagous situations when we get to signifying songs and the like in Black-American music.

A problem arises in describing the basic characteristics of African music because we often have to borrow terminology from European musical analysis. This is not a necessarily valid procedure—particularly when we bring European implications of the term with that transfer—but Western terminology is what we have to work with. In my comments on African music, you will note that I am speaking particularly of West African music, because the majority of slaves were drawn from there. And this cursory consideration is by no means an effort to eliminate reference to the important scholarly studies of African music by anthropologists and ethnomusicologists.

Contrary to common belief, every group of musical instruments is found in African culture: idiophones, membranophones, chordophones, and areophones. You'll find xylophones and xylophone types (certainly including the *mbira* or *calimba,* or thumb piano), drums and rattles, natural horns made of ivory (whose pitches follow the same harmonic series as those in Europe), the single-string musical bow, prototypes of the zither, the harp, and the violin. Through Alan Merriam's extensive experiences in studying African music, we have arrived at two basic generalizations about African musical instruments: Both instrumental soloists and groups are found in Africa; and accompanied songs are perhaps more important than solo instrumental performance. The implications of the latter statement include the fact that, when an instrument plays a song, the words are conceptualized although not verbalized. A relationship to the words of a song is retained, not only in melodic form and rhythmic stress, but in sonority. You can compare Louis Armstrong's trumpet sounds with his singing voice, if you want an extension of this idea.

African melody appears to have a wide range of contours. It has been noted that it is often more diatonic than Oriental or American-Indian music, thus being more like Western folk music. Depending on what authority you consult and what music he has examined, the music either uses a small range or a very large one. A study of African melody will certainly have to take into consideration the capabilities of the instruments, both in terms of range and of tone color.

Antiphonal singing is a primary factor in African music. This alternation between a solo singer and the chorus we all know as call and response. The lines of the chorus remain basically unchanged, leaving the leader free to improvise—and improvisation is an essential element in most Black music. Solo songs will also be found, as well as song cycles (sometimes specific songs to designate the start and the end of the cycle). Hugh Tracey has found something like a symphony: a lengthy work including both vocal and instrumental music, as well as dance and poetry.

A form which has been very important in recent Western music, as seen in Stravinsky, Lukas Foss, Gunther Schuller, and others, is the additive form. Sections of the music are added, one after another, without any necessary regard for development or the relationship of these sections. This is a contrast to the litany form, in which one or two melodic phrases are repeated for a long time, and that idea is also very widespread in Africa.

The matter of form reminds me of a movie I saw on George Gershwin: The idea was that he had arrived when he wrote a piece that lasted twenty minutes. There is no pre-determined length in African music. It the ceremony takes seventeen hours, that's how long the music lasts. One of the things Webern was reacting against was the idea that long music is good music. No such kind of value judgment exists in African music.

There is probably no concept of a scale which is peculiarly African, and in fact, the idea of a scale is usually alien to African musical thought. We can speak of A as having 440 vibrations per second, but that pitch will vary in Africa according to the singer's expressive interests. We are going to see obvious manifestations of this in the music of Ornette Coleman, for example, who says without hedging that he resents someone's complaint that he is "out of tune" because he selects different pitches for the same note at different times. The fixed tuning of the piano has no doubt brainwashed us into thinking pitch freedom is a bad thing. At any rate, the African *practices* broader ranges in pitch than is common with the contemporary academically trained musician.

A.M. Jones has said that during the twenty years he has lived in Central Africa, he has never heard the third or seventh degree of the major scale sung "in tune." What he has been hearing, as he states, is of course the blues scale. This scale is certainly very important to Black music, but varieties of pentatonic scales also exist.

African harmony has been described as a sort of organum, or as polyphony resulting from the overlap of call and response, but it has generally been thought harmony is either without significance or is completely non-existent. Richard Waterman contends that harmony exists in traditional African music and that, in fact, this accounts for the harmonic precedence in slave music. He is not speaking of harmony as it has been codified and used in Western music, he is acknowledging the existence of a broad intrusive belt of Arabic influence which isolated and hid the harmonized music for some time, and he also feels that harmony was not presented in evident enough a manner for the ethnomusicologists to note it in their transcriptions if, in fact, they actually heard it. Several things might have encouraged faulty conclusions: (1) the early recordings were poor in quality, (2) the analyst was not often in contact with the performer, and (3) the non-harmonic music from Africa which was examined was assumed to be representative.

The open sound of the African voice is produced by a full utilization of the head cavities. The result is open and resonant, very much like the sound produced by the European folk singer. But the African adds something else, and with this you get into the intrusion of color and personalization by way of vibrato and inflection.

The level at which African music seems to be most highly developed is that of listener and performer perception and participation. It is generally agreed that rhythm is the single most outstanding factor in African music, that this element differentiates it from the music of all other cultures. It is not uncommon for observers from any period to devote large portions of their discussions to drums and drumming. For one thing, this is common to the West and to Africa; for another, Westerners have a romantic fascination for the talking drums; thirdly, the highly developed skill and artistry of the drummers is truly impressive. Now, what we must emphasize is that rhythm has a different place in the heirarchy of Black music. In the West, the primary elements are melody and harmony. The Western listener in Africa is not psychologically prepared for fourteen layers of intricate rhythms going on simultaneously. It just doesn't register. To the extent that it does, he can't translate it. By the same token, I can understand an African who, on hearing Brahms for the first time, might see the music as primitive because Brahms, for all of his marvelous rhythmic subtleties, cannot begin to match the complexities of African rhythm. So the dude tells his brothers, "Boy, they don't have it together at all!" We have to understand that African music is complex and that —no matter how advanced rhythm gets with Elvin Jones or Tony Williams—jazz is naive when you put it beside *bona fide* African music. African rhythm is based on a constant conflict of rhythm, with rhythm being born simultaneously with the other components of the music. It is not added later, and it is not something so mild as syncopation.

When we speak about African music in the earlier days of this country, we find many of the same things. Music was still a part of the life of the people. That dude that was out picking cotton ain't talking about going to no concerts that night. If he wanted music, he made it himself. They let him sing, because that was supposed to keep people happy, but they took away his instruments.

Ante-bellum music consisted of spirituals, shouts, gospel tunes, hollers, and work songs. You find three categories of spirituals. The first is syncretic: the adaptation of African ritual to Christian liturgy, the attempt to find similarities between the two. It was not difficult for the guy one generation from Africa to see a relationship between baptism and his river gods, between spirit possessions and the holy Ghost, or between West African gods and the Trinity. Secondly was that spititual spontaneously created by the preacher and his congregation, with its interlocutions and exclamations. You can hear this at any Black church now, with the preacher doing his thing on Sunday morning. The third variety consisted of variations on White tunes. The first thing the Black man had to do was take care of the rhythm, so he introduced syncopation to the tune. Then he had to change the words, so that massah he's talking about was the one up there in the front house. And then he brought in the blue notes to personalize the music, giving the melodies flat three and fives and sevens, or making the tunes pentatonic.

If you listen to a group of singers still relatively close to their African background, you'll see the tenor usually marks the beat, the alto and soprano fill in the spaces, and the bass complements the other voices with little rhythmic runs and other fillers. This idea can be discerned in modern rhythm-and-blues groups, and White groups have copied it too.

The work song was a type which was closest to the African tradition. The call-and-response pattern is here too, along with the vocal inflections and intonation colorings (slides, dips, screams, and slurs). It was unaccompanied because you can't play the banjo while you're picking cotton, no matter what the movies said. The type of work also influenced the form and style of the music, as well as the text. The holler was a thin vocal cry, usually of short phrases and very highly personalized, and was used for communication. You could tell when so and so was coming across the field by his holler. We have this surviving in the street cries. It's fun to listen to Miles Davis playing *Porgy and Bess*. The crab man and the strawberry woman. Listen to them sell their wares! I can remember like in Indianapolis when I was little, hearing a dude come through with a little high whistle and cry about selling hot skins. Now they call it pork rinds. You could hear dudes hawking watermelons or cantalopes, and each one took pride in developing something that was uniquely his.

The musical and cultural contacts between the slave and his master were also important. The Protestant music of the Danes, Dutch, and British stimulated one thing, while the Catholic music of the French, Spanish, and Portuguese was different. It's hard to imagine a spiritual coming from a Catholic province, for example, because this was Protestant-type music. These geographical settings brought about a different set of musical, moral, ethical, and social relationships. Some dudes would have trouble swallowing this, but slaves changed the whole mythology of the South. Brer Rabbit modeled childhood for generations of upper-class Southerners. Black church ceremonies took Whites on the path from Wesley to Whitfield's 1728 mission, to the Red River camp meeting of 1799, to the African Methodist Episcopal Church in 1816 and the Holy Rollers and Holiness faith healers. And through all of this runs the cultural thread of African origins and influences, changing the behavior patterns of the entire Protestant South. We've got to give the plantation system a plus: It helped preserve African culture. Like Russian serfdom, it helped in the retention of the artistic tradition.

Let's see briefly what these were. We lost the African songs and dances when they served no function, but we kept those which could be adapted or fitted to the new economic patterns: work songs, love songs, lullabies, play songs, song games, wedding and funeral songs,

and some magic songs. We lost the epic songs and battle songs about
our African heroes. Whereas Western languages take pride on being
exact and to the point (technology and clocks have a lot to do with
this), Africans enjoy indirect statements and find direct expressions
unimaginative, if not crude. Even though we find contemporary ghetto
language being appropriated by our presidents, it is still ours. You
talk about a pair of shoes being your pair of kicks, about your girl
being your rib. That's colorful. Our educational systems don't like
this kind of talk because it ain't good English, you dig? But it is
important in Black music that it can translate itself from one period
to another, still veiled in ever-changing paraphrase. The minute
Whites cop one part of the language, it changes. We change it. It's
gone before you can even get hold of it. Unless you're right there
in the middle of it, you're going to be a year or two behind the times.
I'm talking about music and language both, you know!

The roots of the whole American pop music scene rest in the
minstrels. If pop music were divested of those things which came
about because of Black people, it would cease to exist. Minstrelsy
was originally social, born in the slave quarters of the South. In an
environment in which the slave was viewed as subhuman, music had
to fulfill an outlet. Music in Africa had been propelled by social
motivations. It had been conceived as a participative music which
was meaningful to the *entire* community. When we talk to the Black
composers today, you will find many of them still think in these
terms. No popular music has escaped the Black influence. Those
people who say jazz is influenced by rock and roll (White rhythm-and-
blues) are just naive, or misinformed. The flow continues to be as it
always was: from Black to White, as in the route from minstrelsy to
the Broadway musical, from rhythm and blues to rock, from jazz to
pop.

Various social factors provided the cultural climate needed for
the birth of jazz in New Orleans. This city was the largest in the
South at the time, and it was relatively "liberal." The French and
Spanish residents winked at what their WASP neighbors would have
found immoral. In this easy-going city, the Black man had more
freedom than anywhere else in the South, at least by 1900, and the
higher wages attracted many Southern Negroes. An additional stimulus
was the fact that New Orleans used music for practically all occasions,
and that fitted right in with the African thing.

The instruments the early players got were generally second-hand,
from a Confederate band. In addition to these conventional instru-

ments, you had a body of *ad hoc* instruments like fly swatters, jugs, washboards, combs, buckets, plungers—any thing that could make sound (and we've always been a resourceful people; TJ called it "inspired intensity"). Any book on jazz will describe the marching bands of 1870 and 1890 which played for parades and funerals. Fraternal and labor organizations had their own bands, just as they do today in Indianapolis. You go in now to the YMCA band and find usually older dudes with awful instruments, but these cats still want to play and do their thing. Most of the Indianapolis musicians who made names for themselves came through something like this, like the Prince Hall Elks Band, where J.J. Johnson got his start. He still gives credit to a little old man with one leg too short who started him off. Freddie Hubbard came through one of those bands. I came through more than one because I didn't play so well and I had to do a lot of traveling.

The dance music used before hot bands got going was sweet stuff, using strings and piano. Salon music. The hot brass band, from around 1890, marked a revolution in popular music. Ensemble playing was heterophonic, rather than polyphonic, and blues was the common denominator. Instrumental jazz developed from the mergings of the New Orleans band tradition and urban blues. The art of group improvisation, like the blues, was associated with the uptown section of New Orleans. As in folk music, two creative forces were involved: the group and a gifted individual. The tension between the collective harmonic rhythm and individual rhythms is what later came to be described as swing.

Despite the brass and marching band precedents, jazz was different from march music. The early jazzmen depended on their imagination and preferred (in many instances from necessity) to improvise, rather than read music. It was not all improvisation, of course. From the very beginning, jazz musicians used what we call band "arrangements," but they weren't written down. They simply came to be because they were played that way several times and got crystallized.

The music came from a millon sources. Many of the pieces were stolen from old marches. Band leaders stole tunes and, because they couldn't read, played the tune with many variations. After the leader showed the trumpet player the way he thought the tune went, the trumpeter would play it for the band and then the players made their arrangement. It was every man for himself, with the trumpter taking the lead. True to the oral tradition and that of personalizing the music, the early jazzmen infused their music with speech and vocal qualities: growls, pitch variations, slurs, smears, and the cadence of conversation. The idea of ensemble playing was on the surface an imitation of brass bands, but it was more than that when one considers the music from social and psychological viewpoints.

The classic form of the New Orleans band crystallized with Joe "King" Oliver, the first master of referential improvisation (i.e., using a melody for the point of departure). We're going to see some dichotomies set up here in a minute, but his whole philosophy was based on the perfect rendition of a completely predictable result. Ensemble music, Black or White, jazz or not, always has this goal. The music produced excitement from its effective realization. The excitement of the performance came from the perfected rendition of certain traditional devices and patterns, the unanimity of conception. The greatness was within prescribed limits. Gunther Schuller, in *Early Jazz,* calls this "a circus psychology where each succeeding performance had to top the original." We know that's a dead-end street. The only tolerated surprises were the breaks (and these, by the way, were direct links to spirituals, work songs, blues, and—when they were expanded—they became the first solos in jazz).

Once a single player could hold the listener's attention, the collective ensemble was no longer as important, and that brings us to Louis Armstrong. When the soloist begins to predominate, we have one-voice music over a two-beat metrical bass. The next stage would be four-beat harmonic bass for collective improvisation, as we had with King Oliver. The third stage, which is the gateway to today, is the emergence of a soloist coming from the ensemble's homophony. Satchmo was able to break free because he had a technical prowess unmatched by any other player of his time, and he had a fertile imagination, an unbridled sense of solo construction and influences from King Oliver and Bunk Johnson. His innovations were in rhythmic treatment primarily. He relaxed the time and effected the departure from what has been described as a ricky-tick rhythm section. He introduced rhythm to the straight tone (what Gunther Schuller calls "terminal vibrato"), and you could recognize this in his playing all of his life: that vibrato that widens and almost breaks at the end of a tone. He was one of the first to play outside of the triad and who tried not to be limited to the overtone series (what I call the *Waldhorn* syndrome).

Ragtime (1895–1920) was essentially a White music, despite the fact that it was pioneered by Black players, while jazz was essentially Black. Ragtime was composed, and jazz was improvised. A ragtime piece stood alone as a complete entity, but jazz was *based* on an entity. Ragtime was played pretty much the same way each time, whereas jazz almost lost itself once it got written down. The limitations of ragtime rested in these restrictions, while jazz remained flexible. Ragtime also demanded a high level of discipline. It was formally structured with something like four clearly distinct themes set in orthodox harmonic frameworks, like much White music of the time. The rondo-like form of ragtime differs from the ternary pattern of jazz *tunes*.

Soon after the First World War, Chicago had clearly become the center for jazz development. Blacks were recording in the South Side, Louis Armstrong and King Oliver were important, Jelly Roll Morton was active as perhaps the first jazz composer, and the band became less a predominately percussion ensemble. But the East Coast was important also, with Fletcher Henderson and Duke Ellington, both from the growing Negro middle-class (unlike Armstrong and his New Orleans confreres.). They both were pianists with no small degree of sophistication. They borrowed from the relative primitivism of New Orleans, but they polished it up so it would be palatable for the uptown Black and White folks whose physical and mental make-ups were not geared to such intense energy, and this was also in keeping with the orientation of the eastern Negroes (who were more often academically trained).

Economics provided larger bands, and no matter what their musicianship or talent, they were not expected to improvise. By the end of the decade, even Oliver's and Armstrong's groups were playing written arrangements. Henderson's prime influence on jazz was shaped by the arrangements he and Don Redmon made, and their approach is still the predominant one with large bands today. Duke Ellington completely changed the aesthetic, and he is in my mind (and in the thinking of many people) one of the greatest of all American composers.

The seeds for jazz were firmly planted by 1931. Great strides had been made in instrumental technique, giving the soloist an equal footing with the ensemble. The harmonic framework had been enriched and expanded. Vertical and horizontal structure was evidenced and the emotional latitude went from hot to cool. There developed two camps: those musicians who wanted as few restrictions on their music as possible and those who wanted to absorb various European ideas.

The big bands reflected the hope of recovery from the Depression, but the big-band concept had other social implications. Factory production lines suggested a certain kind of efficiency, perhaps akin to the written arrangement that predestined some musical effects with a degree of security. The liberalism of the Roosevelt administration was mirrored in the increasing number of bands with players from both races. They had existed in the 1920s, but for recordings not for public appearances. Concert music was looked up to by many jazzmen, many of whom accepted some values as their own. Leroi Jones called swing and ragtime "the debris of vanished emotional references," meaning they were White realizations of a music that began as emotional music.

The wind players of the time were fleet fingered. The performances tended toward eight- and sixteen-note patterns in place of ternary beat subdivisions. Phrases were larger and harmony became more important than melody (one of the first really beautiful examples of was Coleman Hawkins' *Body and soul*).

During this time there was a lot of activity by the non-jazz Black composer: Edmund Jenkins, William Grant Still, William Dawson, and Florence Price. Concert works of this time were in the "Negro idiom"; but for the thematic references, the music was largely White. Margaret Just Butcher said of Florence Price's piano concerto that it "vindicates the Negro's right of choice to pursue the broad road of classicism, rather than the narrow, more hazadous, but often more rewarding path of racialism." I'll have to think about that statement from the standpoint of value judgments. These composers were frequently inclined to ignore their folk music because of the insistent claim that this was their one musical province, and the sensitive, ambitious, and well-trained artist saw this (with some warrant) as a threat which would lock him in a musical ghetto. In his most violent reaction, he would have nothing to do with this rich heritage.

For a long time, those who defended the folk forms were in the minority, but they were virile voices. J. Rosamond Johnson and Will Marion Cook projected a Negro conservatory of music, and along with Harry Burleigh, they popularized spirituals (yet there remained many older singers and young choruses which refused to sing them). Clarence Cameron White, Nathaniel Dett, and John Work all championed the cause of the folk music.

The early development of bop is not documented on recordings because of the musicians' union ban on recording from 1942 to 1944. Bird and Diz, to some people, popped out of a shell like Venus because of this ban. We miss things like the experimentation which took place in Earl Hines' band, and it looks as if a new music appeared all of a sudden in 1945 or 1946 which had no roots or past at all. People like Louis were really up in arms. Boppers were guys who flatten their fifths, and one cat said, "I don't flatten my fifths, I drink them." With bop, harmony gained equal footing with melody and rhythm. The players needed a good technique, finely developed ears, and the ability to construct music at a fast tempo. It was multi-metered, rich in syncopation. The wind players imitated the pianists. Phrase lines were asymmetrical, and the soloists had a wide choice of notes from what I call the chord and melodic referentials. Drummers let the bassists keep time and became freer in their own expressions.

Rootlessness was a way of life for many people at this time, just after the war. The past was gone, and society was in an upheaval. The first boppers were young Blacks, sensitive to the fact that Black music had been exploited by the Whites and that it had been debased as a result. Some sought to make their styles too difficult to imitate. They thought of themselves as artists, not as entertainers. The days of second-class citizenship for music were over, and there was a significant departure from the aesthetic of New Orleans. Increased consideration was given music's artistic quality, its form, and its harmonic and thematic development. Though most of the young musicians were not from large metropolitan areas, they were nevertheless big city men and their speech, dress, and mannerisms were urbane, sometimes even flamboyant. But they were pure musicians for the most part, unwilling to compromise their art to the expediencies of commerce. They would not hesitate to offend bourgeois tastes.

The new jazz retained the collectivism of the old, but now the collective improvisation was exclusively between soloists and the rhythm section. Ensemble work was usually unison, and intensity was at an explosive level.

Despite the aura of revolution, and notwithstanding the high artistry of some of its practitioners (Charlie Parker, for example, was to prove as influential as Armstrong had been a decade or two earlier), bop was a more restrictive music than jazz had been in its earlier days. Playing within the demanding harmonic framework called more for clever minds and nimble fingers than for true creativity. From the sociological viewpoint, by its emphasis on harmony and instrumental facility and the use of European concepts, bop was considerably more White than Black, despite the social stance of the beboppers, and yet the effect of bop on jazz was great. It led to a significant rise in basic musicianship (according to the best of European standards), it increased the number of rhythmic and metric choices open for expressive reasons, its best players served as reference points for more than a generation, and the seeds for further evolution of jazz as an artistic expression were planted.

The big bands generally served more as synthesizers, rather than innovators. As is true with Western music, innovations took place in the chamber-like ensembles ten or twenty years before these ideas really reached the bigger groups.

Jazz music of the 1960s was perhaps more diverse than anything which came before it. First of all, there is the "mainstream" which was partly a synthesis of that which came before, and almost all of the major players today come from the bop tradition. Soul music is something we will consider elsewhere in more detail. A third idiom is that which is ethnic-influenced, generally Caribbean and Afro-American. In fourth place is the avant guard. Most of these players are Black, more socially aware than were earlier jazz figures, often rather far left in their political philosophies, and very concerned with the world as a unit. They don't claim to be in jazz, but in Black music. Even this might be divided into two camps: the intuitive and the cerebral, with someone like Ornette Coleman illustrating the former, and George Russell the latter. One more idiom is that of the third-stream, a term coined by Guther Schuller, in which John Lewis is one of those Black musicians active.

Not necessarily distinguished by style, but by function, is liturgical jazz—which sounds like a contradiction in terms—with Duke Ellington and Mary Lou Williams being important figures. There is also jazz music of a sort in radio, television, and the films, with such significant musicians represented here as Quincy Jones, Oliver Nelson, Benny Golson, and Tom McIntosh. Quincy and Tom have both told me that, when the film producer sees he has a Black composer, he says, "Now wait a minute. I don't want any jazz." The assumption is that this is all we write!

If the picture isn't right yet for Black composers, it must be nearly hopeless for Black conductors, even if there are a few (and very few) who are being engaged on a regular basis. There remains the myth that Blacks are not adroit in cognative skills. When we watch pro football, we see the brothers can take care of that business out on the field, but how many Black quarterbacks are there? We can run fast, you see, but we can't think. The same is true in the attitude toward the conductor. It's one thing to be playing *in* the orchestra, but something else to be *leading* it! And many orchestral instrumentalists can't get jobs at the local colleges unless they are in the orchestra, and there's not a whole lot of us making that scene, either.

Black music must have an articulation and description of its needs from the Black perspective. This is axiomatic. In the past, all aspects of our existence have been defined by the White man and that situation has produced the intolerable syndrome of Blacks having to adjust to White standards, White sanctions, White rewards. However well meaning some Whites may have been, they cannot evaluate the Black experience.

We cannot abdicate from our culture and give it to those who exist outside of it. If we are seriously interested in our present and future needs, we must examine social institutions with respect to the Black community. Foremost is the educational institution, and this is where we must introduce, develop, and perpetuate a complete Black aesthetic. This can only be done by a total restructuring of the conventional academic procedure. The curriculum, administrative framework, and educational goals in these places reflect White middle-class society, and this is anathema to Black people. The function of a university has been to maintain and promote the political, social, and economic foundations of that institution, and this means a perpetuation of Anglo-Saxon ethnocentricity.

The study of Black music, as with Black studies in general, must have the following basic ideas:

1. Psychological and emotional liberation for Black people, a movement away from inappropriate White standards.

2. Establishment of a proper perspective of the Black man in the world and in world history.

3. Discovery of non-White experiences as values in their own right.

4. The development of Black power in skills and intellectual strength.

The university must be an innovator, but it must also be a custodian, and it is possible and necessary for it to serve both roles. It must not try to communicate with us about Black culture with the use of White terms which don't fit. It must be willing to change its curricula and its methodology. It must employ Black teachers to teach Black culture whenever possible so that the information can come from the Black perspective. It must support research in Black culture so that such references don't end up as a footnote in someone's dissertation.

⬤ How ardently and with what articulation does Dave plead for the proper recognition of Black music! But it is not mere rhetoric; he has the facts and he sees the history as one which can teach the techniques of musicology to a student as readily as traditional paths of study but—more than that—he is alert to the implications of the information. What he has compressed here is a taste of the facts and ideas he offers to students in his lectures at Indiana University.

12. Art Music of the Blacks in the Nineteenth Century

Geneva Handy Southall

● Dr. Southall is a dynamic and dedicated scholar. Her formal training was secured at Dillard University, the American Conservatory of Music, and the University of Iowa (which awarded her the Ph.D. degree in 1966), with additional work at Aspen. As pianist and musicologist, she has served on the faculties of Paul Quinn College, Knoxville College, South Carolina State College, and Grambling College. In 1970 she moved to her new post as associate professor in the Afro-American Studies Department of the University of Minnesota.

As concert pianist, she has toured extensively in the United States and has given a series of concerts in Germany under the sponsorship of the United States Information Services. She has shared the findings of her research, particularly in Afro-American music, on many college campuses and at meetings of the American Musicological Society.

Both charming and straight shooting, she comes from a musical family from New Orleans. Her sister, D. Antoinette Handy, is a professional flutist and is on the faculty of the Virginia State College. As. Dr. Southall indicates, her daughter is carrying on the family tradition of activity in the arts, and the challenge for her young grandson is already posed.

The present concept that Black is beautiful and a thing to be proud of is not new. It was in 1853 that the famous Black Harvard-trained ethnologist and well-known abolitionist—probably our first recognized Black nationalist—Martin R. Dulaney said "I thank God each day for making me a Black man."

It must be remembered that an important part of the Black man's culture lies in his music. At the same time, we must be aware that no serious or sincere investigation of Afro-American music is possible without some understanding of the social and cultural history of Blacks before they arrived on this continent. We must know the conditions of slavery, and the social and economic pressures they encountered subsequently as "free" men. Any close examination of their creative efforts will show how these are interrelated with their entire society.

In a recent article,[1] William Grant Still stated that no participants in the history of music may have been so greatly influenced by social, environmental, and economic factors as the Black man in America. These influences reach the type of music he has created, as well as all aspects of his professional activities.

Despite the significant role the Black man has played in world civilization since the beginning of time, his contributions have been omitted or distorted in our history books. Since it has become fashionable now on many campuses (and, I assure you, very necessary on some campuses) to correct this blurred image, a little effort has been made by television stations, publishers, and other communication media to set the record straight.

Margaret Butcher in *The Negro in American Culture*[2] says that the right and most effective way to look at the Negro's relationship to American culture is to consider it not as an isolated race matter and minority group concern, but in the context of the whole of American culture.

Afro-American music consists of three main types: folk music (which may be sacred or secular), "academic" or "art" music, and popular music. Each type has its own technique, its own idiom, and its own sociology and must therefore be judged by different critieria; each type has its own individual function. Zelma George made the first comprehensive critical analysis of Afro-American music in her bibliographic index to Negro music,[3] which included 9,592 titles for the Moreland Collection of the Howard University Library. She distinguishes these three main currents saying that folk music, the bulk of which includes spirituals, shows the expressive melodic and racial feeling, character, and expression of the people, and that it is generally anonymous in origin and is orally transmitted. In contrast to this, Zelma George finds "art" music with a technical tradition which is in the possession of a small group of highly trained specialists involved both in its creation and performance, while popular music (blues, ragtime, jazz, and soul, as examples) involves both the folk and

---

1 "The Negro Musician in America" in *Music Educators Journal* [Washington] 56 (January 1970): 100–101, 167–171.
2 New York: Alfred A. Knopf, 1956.
3 *A Guide to Negro Music; An Annotated Bibliography of Negro Folk Music, and Art Music by Negro Composers or Based on Negro Thematic Material* (Ed.D. Dissertation), New York University, 1953; Ann Arbor: University Microfilms, 1954), 302 pp.

academic traditions; it is more faddish, more concerned with contemporary life; novelty is a key ingredient, and although some of the music is written, the art of improvisation is a necessary performance tool. We must be aware that these types result from reciprocal cultural interchange and that the degree of their mutual independence is determined by the amount and type of musical exposures in which one has participated.

While it is generally conceded that Black Americans have given this country its own true American music in their spirituals, blues, and jazz, there is a serious lack of information to show that the Black man's contributions in the academic areas are likewise noteworthy. The myths perpetuated by Uncle Remus stories, by Black-faced minstrels, and by stereotyped clowns have portrayed him as an undesirable, lazy, shiftless lover of chickens, as a socially inferior person incapable of reaching artistic heights. The constant pointing to the Black man's vocal ability as a natural talent has further deprived him of working at other crafts, tending to relegate him to singing or performing only certain types of music. Too many Americans, Black and White, educated and illiterate, are unaware that the Black man was active in the creative and performing arts prior to the Civil War in both the North and South.

In *Music and Some Highly Musical People,*[4] published only thirteen years after the Emancipation, James Monroe Trotter includes biographical sketches of Black musicians who were active between 1820 and 1870 and also presents actual music written by them. Had this book been in our libraries, Black youth would have been inspired toward greater pride for our musical achievements, and their own confidence in their resources would have been raised. It might also have prevented some of the bigotry had White youths known of the artistic achievements of this minority element in our society. It is unfortunate that four scholars of American music (Louis C. Ellison, John Tasker Howard, Gilbert Chase, and H. Wiley Hitchcock) do not refer to Trotter's book and do not include information on the Black man's academic musical pursuits of the Nineteenth century. Although the most recent edition of Howard's *Our American Music*[5] sees fit to include Trotter's book in the bibliography (showing an awareness of its existence), it makes no effort to include the material

---

[4] New York: Johnson Reprint Corporation, 1969, 1881, 353, 152pp. Basic Afro-American Reprint Library.

[5] For a brief resumé of the extent to which Black music is included in selected textbooks, see Appendix 3.

in the body of the book, despite the fact that many of the musicians were acclaimed by the press and reputable people in the music world, both at home and abroad. It is unfortunate that encyclopedias still tend to restrict Negro music to that produced in this country, and even there the documentation is very incomplete, failing to mention contributions before 1900. Information has already been provided by ethnomusicologists, anthropologists, and historians showing that African slaves were influencial in Arabian music as far back as the seventh century. Musicians of color have been sufficiently important to have had their names recorded for many centuries. Maude Cuney Hare devoted several pages to the African slave influence in Arabian music in *Negro Musicians and Their Music*.[6] She had the nerve to write about a Black man doing something in music, and doing it well. It is unfortunate that she died broken hearted, that she had such trouble getting her book published—a book which, within twenty years, was to prove one of the most sought after and authoritative in its field.

Let us now look at some of the earlier Black figures in music. In the eighteenth century there was Ignatius Sancho, the Chevalier de Saint-Georges, and George Bridgetower, all offsprings of African slave parents.

Ignatius Sancho was born on a slave ship in 1729, en route from Vienna to the Spanish West Indies. His mother died in childbirth, and he was taken to Greenwich in England and given to three maiden ladies. A frequent guest at their home was the Duke of Montague, who noted the boy's unusual aptitude for music. The Duke frequently took the little Black boy home with him and taguht him how to read, to write, and to play musical instruments. His mistresses resented the child's eagerness for learning and threatened to sell him, but Sancho continued to develop his literary and musical interests, in secret. He wrote many books, pamphlets, and essays on the evils of slavery, and became a noted music critic of the day whose writings were also respected on the Continent. In addition to his creative talents, he published a theory book which was highly respected. His high esteem in England is witnessed by the fact that Gainesborough painted his portrait and that he was buried in Westminster Abbey, although Thomas Jefferson ridiculed him in America.

The Chevalier de Saint-Georges was born in 1739 of an African slave

---

[6] Washington: Associated Publishers, 1936, 430pp. Of peripheral interest in this respect might be Ernest Borneman's "Jazz and the Creole tradition" in *Jazzforschung* [Graz] 1 (1969): 99–112.

and a French father. He became celebrated as a composer and a soldier. His father, who held a high position in the French government, took the boy to Paris and saw that he received major educational advantages, including music, fencing, and horsemanship. Saint-Georges studied with Jean-Marie Leclair and Gossec, and became a noted writer of string quartets, operas, violin concertos, and orchestral music. He was assistant director of the Opéra and director of the Concert des Amateurs. Lionel de la Laurencie[7] shows that the publication of Saint-Georges' six string quartets in 1773 places him with Gossec as the first French composer for that ensemble. As violinist, he was considered one of France's most brilliant virtuosos.

Bridgetower,[8] also a major violinist, was of Polish and African descent. Although a composer of some worth, he is best remembered as the mulatto who first performed Beethoven's *Kreutzer Sonata* in 1805, five years before he was awarded the Bachelor of Music degree from Cambridge. Also to his credit is an important treatise on piano study.[9]

Three major Black musicians from Latin America should be mentioned: Claudio de Celebrantes (a noted violinist-composer, active as director of several musical and dramatic societies in Havana before 1844), Joseph White [10] (winner of the 1856 virtuoso prize of the Paris Conservatory, which engaged him for its faculty in 1864), and Antonio Gomez (Brazil's chief musician of the nineteenth century, composer of *Il Guarany* which was performed at La Scala in 1870).

Dena Epstein, in "Slave Music in the U.S. before 1860," [11] shows that fifteenth-century explorers, travelers, and slave traders were impressed by the musical ability of the Blacks and made such references

---

[7] A translation of the writings of La Laurencie on Saint-Georges is projected by the editor to assist non-French readers in their studies.

[8] Prior to the publication of *Black Music; a Preliminary Register of the Composers and Their Works,* interested persons might consult de Lerma, "Bridgetower: Beethoven's Black violinist," in *Your Musical Cue* [Bloomington] 5 (December 1968/January 1969): 7–9.

[9] *Diatonica armonica for the piano-forte* (London: R. Birchall, 1812). A reprinting of this by the Black Music Center is anticipated.

[10] Various works by this Afro-Cuban composer have been acquired for Brooklyn College by Professor Paul Glass, a member of the Black Music Center's Honorary Advisory Committee. Among these works is White's violin concerto, scheduled for its American première by Indiana University Professor Ruggiero Ricci.

[11] In *Music Library Association Notes* [Washington] 20 (Spring 1963): 195–212; 20 (Summer 1963): 377–390.

in their accounts.[12] While there are only incidental descriptions of the instruments and the music in these sources, we may readily assume the full story was not recorded.

In his notes on Virginia, Thomas Jefferson grants Black musical superiority when he writes, "In music they are generally more gifted than Whites, with accurate ears for tune and time, and they have been found capable of imagining a small catch." Even in slavery, Negroes had cultivated their precious musical gifts with enough skill to impress Thomas Jefferson.

Too little was written, unfortunately, about any aspect of the slave's musical life other than his singing these religious or sorrow songs on the plantation. An examination of many advertisements for runaway slaves nonetheless discloses descriptions of several as being instrumentalists. Unlike slave dealers' ads, which were filled with salesmanship to sell their wares (that was us), those for a runaway had to be honest and give precise information about physical traits and special accomplishments, making it easier to identify and recover the property.

Despite the fact that the treatment of slaves was supposedly milder in New England than elsewhere in colonial America (particularly due to Puritan and Quaker influences), the slaves still preferred freedom, and many ran away to secure it. From an investigation of sixty-two advertisements for runaways, taken from eleven eighteenth-century newspapers in the various New England colonies, Lorenzo Green found at least six which mentioned unusual musical ability. Five played the violin, and one advertisement said the slave not only played the violin well, but he had taken his master's instrument with him, so we can imagine that man really searched!

While there was seemingly a preference among Blacks for string instruments (and it really makes you sick to know that the orchestras are just now looking for string musicians, because this was our thing),[13] there is ample evidence to show the slaves also performed on other

---

[12] Several sources to which Dr. Southall refers have since been reprinted by Eileen Southern in *Readings in Black-American Music* (New York: W. W. Norton, 1972), 302pp.

[13] During his intermission from the trombone, David Baker proved his talents on the cello and double bass. This experience stimulated "The String Approach in Jazz" in *Orchestra News* [Cleveland] 9 (March 1970): 5–6; 9 (September 1970): 10–11; and "The String Player in Jazz" in *Down beat* [Chicago] 37 (5 March 1970): 37–38; 37 (30 April 1970): 37–39; 37 (28 May 1970): 34–35. The extensive activity of Blacks as violinists and string composers, documented in Eileen Southern's *The Music of Black Americans; A History* (New York: W. W. Norton, 1970), provides additional support to Dr. Southall's statement that "this was our thing."

instruments. One runaway was advertised as playing the fife well in the July 10, 1719, issue of the *Norfolk Chronicle*. In the *Virginia Gazette* of 1753, one owner offered to sell a slave who played the French horn extremely well. John Murant, a free Black born in New York City in 1755, who moved to Charleston, tells of his musical experiences as a professional violinist and French hornist during his days in South Carolina in his autobiography, *A Narrative of the Lord's Dealings with John Murant,* in 1783. The chapter in question is "The Conversion of a Young Musician," and it tells something about his musical activities, but it also throws light on non-plantation music in Charleston, about the church service, and about music—about life itself.

In some cases household servants were encouraged to develop musical skills so they could contribute to the pleasure or social prestige of the masters. Cy Gilead, a body servant to Lord Bielcorf, was official fiddler at the state balls in Williamsburg. Leonard Briggs became his assistant when the Virginia capital was moved to Richmond, and Briggs was reputed to be equally skillful on the flute and clarinet. Who said we didn't play woodwinds? [14]

Newport Gardener, a slave in Newport, Rhode Island, became so proficient from his lessons that he excelled his teacher, and when he won his freedom in a lottery game in 1791, he opened his own music school, teaching both Whites and Blacks (including his former mistress). Since it was he who became schoolmaster when the state's Blacks sought to have their children educated in the early nineteenth century, one can assume he was knowledgeable in non-music areas as well. I should add that this information came from three different books, published no more than three months apart.

Long before the Civil War the first professional entertainers were among us. These were sometimes slaves, managed by their masters (who also collected the fee). Two slave brokers, Toller and Cook, advertised the celebrated George Walker in the Richmond *Daily Inquirer* (1853) as being "for hire, either for the remainder of the year, or by the month, week, or job" stating that Walker was "admitted by common consent to be the best leader of bands in all eastern and middle Virginia."

---

[14] It should be noted that the clarinet and horn were not generally popular instruments at this time, except in England and France, as indicated in my dissertation, *Wolfgang Amadeus Mozart: The Works and Influences of His First Ten Years* (Indiana University, 1958; Ann Arbor: University Microfilms, 1958), p. 119. Evidence of their use by Blacks in Colonial America may therefore be of particular note.

There were many travel accounts of soldiers, foreigners, and visitors from Northern cities, and the diaries of Southerners, which refer to the musicianship of the slaves, the economic use of their talents by the Whites, and discussions of the social and civic community life—particularly the personnel of the bands and orchestras needed for balls and other festive occasions. Proof of the economic worth of such Black musicians can be seen by a bill filed in October 1844 in Louisville. The plaintiff asked for money to recover his damages because there had been unauthorized transportation of three slaves on a steamboat to Cincinnati, from which point the slaves escaped to Canada. They were described as "scientific" musicians who had played for some years on various instruments at balls and parties, who were each worth $1,500. The plaintiff further asked for money to cover the musical instruments, clothes, and books which they had taken (I like the fact that they took the books, too). The three slaves were obviously skilled because, prior to their escape, they had been permitted to live with a free Black in Louisville, where they studied music and were allowed to perform in nearby towns. For this reason, the defendant said the judge should consider the quality of these musician-slaves when the damages were being assessed, that their habits of independence given by their master had generated restlessness and a desire to be free, so he really was to blame for their getting away.

Solomon Northrup, the well-known Black who was kidnapped in Washington in 1841 and illegally sold to a Louisiana slave-holder for twelve years of bondage, wrote an autobiography, *Twelve Years as a Slave; A Narrative of Solomon, A Citizen of New York.*[15] He throws a great deal of light on the musical activities of the plantation. Northrup was a scholar, and he was smart enough not to let the White folks there know he could read and write. He had skills as a violinist, and he used them. They thought they knew him, so they let him get out—and that reminds you of what they said when the civil rights started: "We thought we knew you!" They gave him an opportunity to get off the plantation to play at these fashionable parties, and when he got out there, having opportunity, he made contact with his New York friends and he escaped! Because of this, we have a beautiful autobiography of a dozen years of slavery about slave life from a scholar and a musician.

Irving Wiley, who made a study of Southern Negroes during the Civil War, discusses the musical role of Black musicians in the Union

---

15 Buffalo: Derby, Orton & Mulligan, 1853, p. 336.

army, noting that a few were sometimes called on to act as musicians for the units. The 1862 Congress, in its first session states that the Black musicians were to be paid the same as the enlisted Whites.[16]

The most famous of all slave musicians was a Georgia-born prodigy, Thomas Bethune, known as "Blind Tom." I hope to publish an article on him before long, because I'd like to prove he was not the "idiot" claimed by some sources. Tom's remarkable musical talent was demonstrated before his second birthday, when he unexpectedly joined in the singing of the Bethune girls on the veranda. They were both trained in music, and they were astonished to hear him singing a second part. A more shocking exhibition took place when he was four. The boy slipped out of his mother's cabin, went into the parlor and played on the piano the music he had heard that day. From then on, he had access to the piano, and the family gave him lessons. He absorbed his teaching so fast that, by the time of his fifth birthday, he was famous in the community as a performer, and also as a composer of music which imitated nature. Before long, he was a sensation in southwest Georgia. Crowds poured into the Bethune home to see and hear the blind boy, and to marvel at his musical genius and his ability to imitate anything he heard. Colonel Bethune rented a piano from an old German music teacher in Columbus who had a music store, and held public exhibitions. When he requested the German musician to give Tom lessons, the old man said, "I can't teach him anything; he knows more about music now than we can learn. All you can do is let him hear it, and he will soon work it out by himself."

Accepting this advice, the Colonel saw to it that every amateur or professional musician who played in or near Columbus was heard by Tom. The boy gave his first concert when he was eight, after which he performed in most of the major American cities, naturally becoming the subject of widespread discussion. Many articles were written about his unbelievable skill—a skill which would have been remarkable even for a sighted person from a middle-class background. He was tested by scientists and sceptics whose findings were reported in such journals as the *Atlantic Monthly* and Dwight's *Journal of Music*. Throughout the war he performed in both the Confederacy and the North, and was then taken on a European tour where he was similarly tested. After a concert in Glasgow, one critic compared him to Mozart, feeling Tom's talent was superior in the power of retention and tone production.

---

[16] Quoted in Wiley, Bell Irvin. *Southern Negroes, 1861–1865*. New Haven: Yale University Press, 1938, p. 366.

A picture of him, when he was about nine, apppears in a 1940 issue of *Etude,* with an article by Eugenia Abbott.[17] Standing there, he is as cute to me as the little, precious, golden-haired Mozart. Yet the picture most often used of him shows him as an old man, sitting like an ape in vaudeville. The *Etude* portrait shows you how he looked when he was going around Europe.

He appeared before royalty and was heard by the leading European performers. When he returned to the United States, he gave a command performance at the White House, and his Philadelphia concert brought a testimonial from seventeen music teachers which was published in *Harper's Weekly.* According to one review, he displayed an accuracy of fingering even when he turned his back to the keyboard. Other musical feats included the ability to play a different piece with each hand, yet his mature grasp of the elements of music made him different from those who played only by ear, yet, in truth, Blind Tom also played by ear. He could also recite the speech of a public orator, word for word, in the speaker's voice.

It is said that he had a repertoire of over 7,000 compositions, including works by Bach, Beethoven, Mendelssohn, Chopin, Thalberg, and others. He wrote more than one hundred compositions: songs, waltzes, marches, and—especially—descriptive pieces. One of the songs he wrote was only an accompaniment to a melody he heard his mother sing, about freedom. Even though she was what they called a "house nigger," she knew what she wanted, but never really got. And Tom also wrote his own poetry.

Colonel Bethune shrewdly claimed that Tom was an idiot, that his genius was due to occult practices. After the Emanicipation, he persuaded Tom's mother to have him appointed Tom's guardian so he could continue to profit from the boy's talent. Charity Wiggins was her name,[18] and she lived to be one hundred. Like many fromer slaves, she learned to read and write, and she tells in an article how she came to deplore her separation from her son who was, in truth, stolen from her.

When Colonel Bethune's son died, his widow remarried, and she waged a court battle to secure custody of Tom, and she won. She took Tom to Hoboken where he spent the last fifteen years of his life in a few concert appearances and—as you might imagine—in vaudeville, because this was what we were expected to do. Tom was exploited until his death in 1908. Despite the break of the Bethune family over

---

[17] "The Miraculous Case of Blind Tom; The Enigma of the Famous Musical Genius Who Astonished the World," p. 517.
[18] In the last years of his life, Blind Tom wished to be known as Thomas Wiggins.

this suit, there was a kind of affection for him and Colonel Bethune's youngest daughter secured permission for Tom's remains to be returned to the family plot, twenty years after his death.

Among the free Blacks, there were many highly trained performers and composers who enjoyed the friendship and encouragement of the best people in their community and often acclaim from the press at home and abroad. One such person was Elizabeth Taylor Greenfield, known as the "Black Swan." This is one thing you find all through the nineteenth century: Everybody who is going to be considered great will be a Black "somebody" who is White. I don't care how good they were, there was still a comparison to a White person. Because of Jenny Lind, Elizabeth Greenfield had the secondary status of the "Black Swan." She had been born in Natchez in 1809 and was taken to Philadelphia by a Quaker who gave her freedom and a liberal education. When it was noted the young lady had the phenomenal range of three and a half octaves—something like the range from the bottom of a real contralto to the top of the coloratura range—her benefactress saw to it that she had proper training.

When her patroness died in 1844, the singer had no support. She decided to visit friends in western New York and, while crossing the lake, she sang for some passengers who arranged for her to sing in their city, and she was soon signed by some prominent gentlemen from Buffalo for a series of concerts. In January of 1852, she sang for the governor and other state officials in Albany. After concerts in New York, Boston, Toronto, and other Northern cities, a Buffalo benefit concert (attended by 4,000 persons) made it possible for her to go to Paris to study under Manuel Garcia, where she remained for a year. She then toured England and, on May 10, 1853, gave a command performance for Queen Victoria with Sir George Smart serving as her accompanist. On her return to the States, the *New York Herald* reported that "the Swan now sings in a true, artistic style. The wonderful power of her voice has been developed by good training." She returned to Philadelphia, where she opened a vocal studio and continued to concertize until her death in 1876.

Despite these artistic successes, she never forgot she was a Black woman, and she made constant appearances at anti-slavery meetings (which is more than I can say for some twentieth-century follks). She was also an accomplished pianist, guitarist, and harpist. Further evidence of her esteem is her portrait, hanging in the Louvre.

The existence of Miss Greenfield should have removed doubts concerning the ability of Blacks to sing opera and Lieder, yet the notion persisted that we could only sing in minstrel shows. It must be remembered that plantation sorrow songs had not yet come to the public's attention because so many of the spirituals were still being sung on the plantations and farms.

Minstrelsy, as portrayed by Whites, was very popular during this period, and many free talented Blacks felt compelled to negate this parody of their culture. Thomas Bowers, a Philadelphia tenor, was one of these. He was called the "American Mario." Bowers stated that he resented minstrelsy, that what induced him to go to the public was his interest in belying Negro minstrelsy. His repertoire, presented before eastern and midwestern audiences, consisted of arias from opera and oratorio.

He refused to perform at a Hamilton (Ontario) concert when he learned from a Dr. Brown (who had bought the tickets) that six Blacks were not going to be granted their first-class seats. Back then, he used his artistic worth to protest discrimination. Until I came across this in my research, I had thought Roland Hayes was the first who refused to perform before segregated audiences. By the way, Bowers was a student of Elizabeth Greenfield, and he also appeared at anti-slavery programs.

It seems that Philadelphia (perhaps because of the Quaker influence?) had many talented free Blacks. There were many instrumentalists and composers in that city, where the Black man received support from the state, charitable organizations, and the more affluent Black citizens. Here was the first of many literary and scientific societies, of library clubs and lyceum series, established by Blacks who wished to further their own cultural growth. The October 1936 issue of the *Journal of Negro Education* carries a lovely article about American literary societies by Dorothy Porter, the curator of the Moreland Collection at Howard University.

There was Frank Johnson, who concertized with his orchestra in the United States and Europe and who, in 1843, was given a silver trumpet by the Queen of England as a sign of her esteem. His successor was Joseph D. Anderson, who had skills on many instruments. William Appa was an accomplished pianist who taught for twenty years in Philadelphia and New York, equally in demand as a French tutor, numbering among his pupils wealthy Whites in the community. J. Andrew Connor had literary interests, contributing to literary magazines of the day, and was a leading piano teacher and a published composer. We could go on with James Hemingway, W. H. Davis, Isaac Hazard, Andrew Burroughs, and other composers. I didn't say they were writing the greatest music in the world (neither were the White Americans), but they were composing, and they are a part of American music history.

Many of them were skilled violinists. There was Peter O'Fake, who was the leader of the Newark Theater Orchestra, and William Jackson, who was compared with Paganini. One name we should not forget is John T. Douglas, trained in Europe and New York, who toured extensively as a performer and was active as a composer of music for piano and for orchestra. It should also be said here that he was the first violin teacher of David Mannes, who paid tribute to him, but you won't find that mentioned in too many encyclopedias or histories.

There were many musicians active in Boston, where the conservatories and schools were open to all who could afford instruction. In addition to such men as Henry Williams and Fred N. Lewis, we find Justin Holland. He was born in Norfolk, to free parents who were farmers, and moved to Boston at the age of 14, where he began study of the piano, flute, and guitar. Recognizing the limitations of his general education and aware of the liberal attitude at Oberlin, he moved to Ohio for additional education at the age of 22. He was one of the authors of a publication concerned with moral reform and settled soon afterwards in Cleveland, where he established himself as a leading teacher of piano and guitar. Among his students were the wealthiest Cleveland families, as well as the daughter of the governor of Massachusetts and her husband. The major technical books on guitar playing at this time were in foreign languages and, in order to understand them, Holland learned French, Italian, and Spanish. When his comprehensive guitar method was published in 1874, it was a musical landmark. A critic in the *United States Musical Review* for that year wrote, "I must confess that in its present state, this is the best book in this country— the most thorough, explicit, progressive and satisfactory work ever written in this country or Europe. The method is elaborate, and contains many points not heretofore touched on in works of this kind." [19] He further added that Holland's ability as a composer and skill as a performer qualified him to write this book. I examined a few of Holland's publications at the Louisiana State University Library (he spent his later years in New Orleans), and I was amazed at his compositional virtuosic-demanding skill.

There were many singing family troops traveling throughout the North before the war. You may have heard of the Hutchinson family,

---

[19] Quoted in Hare, Maud Cuney. *Negro Musicians and Their Music.* Washington: Associated Publishers, 1936, p. 206.

a White group. Well, their friends, the Luca family from Kentucky, didn't make it into some of the books, but they were very important. The family consisted of three sons (two violinists and one cellist) and their parents. One of the boys also played piano, and he was only ten. The youngest son, Sam Luca, finally went to Liberia and composed their national anthem. The family appeared at many concerts, including the May 1853 event for the Anti-Slavery Society anniversary in New York, attended by 5,000 persons. The newspapers report that the audiences were wildly enthusiastic, that many persons were overcome and wept. They toured throughout New England and the Middle West and, in 1859, sang with the Hutchinson family in Ohio, bringing criticism from those who objected to Whites and Blacks performing together.

In St. Louis there was J. W. Posterwelt, an early composer, but I am reminded of John Cotter's thesis on *The Negro in Music in St. Louis.*[20] This man had made a study of just one city! The story of the Black musician and his contribution is numbered in these cities and these towns. That is where your history is. Each person is going to have to become isolated almost and develop a history of his own locale. Mr. Cotter's book is one bit of evidence of what happened in one city. Everyone keeps talking about New Orleans, but let's not sell St. Louis short.

There were outstanding composers in the ante-bellum South, especially in Charleston and New Orleans. We find that William Gibson from Kentucky had been one of the first to put instrumental music in the church, and he opened a singing school so they could sing anthems.

When you are doing your research, don't stop anywhere. For example, I belong to the Association for Negro Life and History and, as a result, I get their publication, the *Negro History Bulletin*. A while back I was reading an article on Sidney Hinton, the first Black legislator of Indiana. I jumped for joy when I found that his mother had been the leading piano teacher in Raleigh. The article was not about his mother, but it gave me reason to think Raleigh had some musical activity in the Black community back then.

New Orleans and Charleston were centers where the free Blacks acquired the most economic security, as indicated in E. Franklin Frazier's *The Negro Family in the United States*. The Blacks of Charleston were ranked early in the nineteenth century by some as being economically and intellectually superior to any other free Black

---

[20] Washington University, 1959.

Americans. As early as 1810, they organized the Minor Society to provide education for orphans, as an example of their interest in providing educational opportunities. Among those actively engaged in music was the famous Lord family.

It might be expected that it was in New Orleans the free Southern Blacks made the greatest contribution to music. They lived in an environment primarily dominated by French influences, and opera reigned supreme. Seating arrangements were made for free Blacks, and even for some slaves when they came to the opera with their masters. Many Blacks were of French extraction and were accordingly given musical training at home, or in Paris. Opportunities for professionally trained musicians were plentiful in New Orleans, and the immigrant French, German, and Italian musicians had no prejudice about teaching Black students who could pay, and in time, the more talented Blacks began teaching pupils of either race. Outstanding people were Lucille Beraise, Samuel Snare, Lucien Lambert, and Edmund Dédé (the great violinist who finally returned to Paris). There were enough trained Black musicians there to organize a Negro philharmonic society for the study and preservation of the classics in 1830. Many brass bands were established, and since they resented segregated seating, the Théâtre de la Renaissance opened for free Blacks in 1840, presenting comedies, dramas, vaudevilles, opéras comiques, and other musical presentations. The theater also contained a ballroom which no slave nor White could enter. Of course, we are going to find out that they lived in that third area of society—the middle stratum—until about the 1880s, and then "them folks" had to come on back the other way, and this is when they became members of the jazz group. They were the other kind before, but they found they were wading in the water by themselves.

Henry Kmen, who did a study of New Orleans music during the ante-bellum period,[21] said that one of the first orchestras at a New Orleans ball in 1802 was of six Negro violinists. A Black Creole in the early part of this century wrote a book in French about famous Black New Orleans Creoles,[22] and I have a translation of that book, made by Miss Julia Julianne who heard of my interests.

Please remember that the card catalogs of the Moreland Collection at Howard, the Schomberg Collection in New York, the James W. Johnson Collection at Yale, the Azalia Hackley Collection in Detroit, and the Library of Congress reveal holdings of a considerable number

---

[21] *Music in New Orleans; The Formative Years, 1791–1841.* Baton Rouge: Louisiana State University Press, 1966, p. 231.
[22] Desdunes, Rodolphe L. *Nos hommes et notre histoire.* Montréal: (n.p.?) 1911.

of compositions and writings about Black musicians from these early days and before. The present interest in Afro-American music must seek to include *all* of this music, not just the folk and popular music. And we must not forget the Booker T. Washington College at Tuskegee, where James Monroe Trotter worked as Recorder of the Deeds, to keep the history of the Black man going. I've mentioned Trotter's book already, but you should remember there is a lot of information in *Who's Who in Colored America,* a Tuskegee publication.

Well, that brings us up to the Civil War, and I want to mention just a few more major things in the nineteenth century.

The reason the Black man had to use vaudeville and the minstrel show was that this was the only way he could be professionally active in music many times. It was only at the end of the century that he had the audacity to stop making fun of himself and go into musical comedy, to portray himself as a human being again. This was also the time we find Afro-American folk music influencing what I called academic music. We begin to the see the "art" treatment and pride in the culture, brought about to a large extent because of the singing of the Fisk Jubilee Singers. The first publication of these slave spirituals came out in 1867, by three Northerners [23] who didn't understand all the words with their double meanings. Harriet Tubman wanted the other slaves on the Maryland plantation to know she was leaving, so she sang, "I'm sorry I gwine leave you. Farewell, farewell! But I'll meet you in the morning, 'cause I'm bound for that promise' land on the other side of Jordan," and she was on her way. When we say the spirituals were about a faith in Jesus, we've got to remember that we didn't know about Jesus when we came over here. The slaves were singing songs of anger often, and they had to camouflage their real intent. Whites only understood half of the words and made fun of the Negro dialect, not knowing that this dialect was telling about some stuff they would like to know. You've got to realize spirituals were not all "I'm happy, massa, and all I want is to meet Jesus by and by," because he wanted to meet Jesus on earth. Nobody likes to be held in bondage; everybody wants to be free. If you want to know how the slaves really felt, check their narratives, look in the early music periodicals and newspapers, go to folklore, read Lydia Parish's *Slave Songs of the Georgia Sea Islands,* and Dorothy Scarborough's *On the Trail of Negro Songs.* That's where

---

[23] *Slave Songs of the United States; The Complete Original Collection (136 Songs) Collected and Compiled by William Francis Allen, Charles Pickard Ware, and Lucy McKim Garrison in 1867* (reprinted New York: Dover Publications, 1970).

you'll learn about the ballads, dance songs, and lullabies. And if you really want to understand the lullabies, read the article on the role of the Black mammy in slavery which appears in the *Journal of Negro Education*. Remember to check the work songs, the animal nonsense songs (which were the ones they started with in minstrelsy), the railroad songs, chain gang songs, and the Creole songs and dances.

There was a very good article by George Washington Cable (a New Orleans journalist who got a little too pro-Negro and had to leave town) which appeared in *Century Magazine* and has now been reprinted in *The Social Implications of Early Negro Music in the United States* edited by Bernard Katz and published in 1969 by Arno Press. See what he says about the quadroon systems, love songs, voodoo (which is very important), wood and water songs, and the bamboola. Also read the work of Camille Nickerson, who was at Howard for years. She is from New Orleans and has devoted a great deal of time to the Creole folk song.

Your research will show you that minstrelsy began in England. Examine Hans Nathan's study [24] and look at the picture of Mr. Jim Crow as he was portrayed on stage, and of Brother Zip Coon with his "New York Dandy" self. He's still a man to be made fun of. The idea with both is they are trying to be smart. After the war, the Negro gets into minstrelsy. He blackened his face and whitened his lips because he felt he had to. Don't believe that every Black person—or White, for that matter—approved of this ridicule. There is evidence that Whites did not always appreciate these impersonations because they knew they did not represent the skill of the Blacks. See, for example, the criticism in Miles Fisher's *The Evolution of Negro Slave Songs in the United States*. In the October 27, 1848, issue of *North Star* which is quoted in Leon Litwich's book, *North of Slavery,* one can note the anger of free Blacks for the White minstrels. They called them the filthy scum. "They stole from us a complexion denied to them by nature." [25] When you examine minstrel history, you will see how the Black company, the Georgia Minstrels, moved on to musical comedy.

If you want to find out about how us educated folks felt about ragtime, read the autobiography of W. C. Handy. He throws light on the minstrel show, but he also tells of his experience as a young teacher

---

[24] *Dan Emmett and the Rise of Early Negro Minstrelsy* (Norman: University of Oklahoma Press, 1962). xiv, 496 pp.

[25] Quoted from *North star,* issue for October 27, 1848, in Litwick, Leon. *North of slavery; the Negro in the Free States, 1790–1860. Chicago:* University of Chicago Press, 1961, p. 99.

about 1900 at Alabama A. & M. American music was not allowed there. The president was so uptight, you couldn't play anything unless it was by a composer with a European name. So Handy fooled him and played some ragtime on a concert, saying it was by someone with a high fallutin' European name, and when the program was over, the president said it was the greatest thing he ever heard.

Every book you read will tell you Paul Laurence Dunbar wrote the libretto for Will Marion Cook's *Clorindy.* My daughter is in theater, and one day she read something about Cook (I've got the whole family in this; one of these days, my grandson's going to come to me with some information). "Mother, here's something about a man I've heard you talk about." There in a *Theatre Arts* anthology from 1945 was a statement by Cook that Dunbar had been asked to write the libretto, but that he didn't use it!

We had a discussion about rag tempos. The Marks Music Corporation has published many rags, and my daughter thought I was playing Joplin's *Maple Leaf Rag* too slow. Well, I got my hands on a recording of Joplin playing it himself, and his tempo was almost exactly the same as mine. It is true that he later went into faster tempos because of the pressure brought on him by younger virtuosos. If you want details on ragtime, get Rudi Blesh's book, *They All Played Ragtime.*

There are still other academic musicians I'd like to mention in greater detail had we the time, such as Ann Baltimore, the Hyer Sisters, Flora Bergen, and Madam Salenka Williams (they confused her with the "Black Patti" just because she was Black and she sang, but if you want to know about the real "Black Patti," read Willa Daughtry's highly-documented dissertation), but all this only proves that we have a lot of facts to correct, and a lot of careful research to do before we can compile a new and accurate history of our role in nineteenth-century music.

● Dr. Southall has spoken basically about those Blacks who contributed to the European musical tradition. I know she can speak with as much detail on the history of any other idiom in which Black talent has been invested. It should be evident to our readers that many of us enjoy chicken, but that splendid little fowl can be fried or served as *coq au vin* or in *paella.* For one, I categorically reject any dietetic laws not of my own making, and that decision defines me. It does not disenfranchise me. That argument could be carried on to retaliate against parochial interests advanced by a few well-meaning critics of

Black Music in Our Culture, with whom I long to have public discussion.

Dr. Southall has illustrated that Black talent manifested itself even in times of slavery within idioms not immediately related to African culture. Not "immediately" related? Well, if we knew more about Black-African influences on Arabian music, more about Moorish and Black influence on medieval and renaissance European music, and more about the African roots of Greek and Egyptian music, quite a few ideas about European music history might be changed.

The truth of the matter is that Black music can never be defined without consideration of Roberta Martin, Max Roach, George Russell, Joseph Jarman, Ulysses Kay, Blind Tom, Rev. James Cleveland, Olly Wilson, Saint-Georges, Dollar Brand, Eubie Blake, Carlos Gomez, Akin Euba, Bessie Smith, Joseph Hayes, Oscar Brown, Grace Bumbry, Paul Freeman, and all the Aunt Janes and other unknown bards—each of whom represents at least one contrasting aspect of the totality of Black music history. It is an incredibly large area, calling for an extraordinarily large number of diverse analytical and critical skills and aesthetic viewpoints. This is not to say that gospel music and jazz are of lesser importance, but the lack of information on "concert" music by Black composers should not be the basis for dismissing it or its performers from our considerations and remedial actions. I am reminded of a statement made to me by a leading Black musician with reference to another musician whose name I had mentioned. "Oh," he said, "she just discovered she's Black last season." Well, okay. I think that's fine. In truth, however, I suspect her previous bookings may bear evidence that others knew she was Black. Problems with the White liberal not withstanding, we should remember the comments of a major Black educator when, at a meeting, he heard a Brother rip into an important Black music history book, written by a member of that race: "We don't need Black folks to tear apart serious study of our art. White folks have better experience in this."

All of this sounds like an apology for aspects of that work undertaken by the Black Music Center or Dr. Southall's topic. I feel it is an idea that had to be expressed, and this was a good time to do it. No one needs to make an apology for Dr. Southall's scholarly talents, but notice must be given to a historical area of great importance which has largely remained untouched, and to those techniques and philosophies which are manifest in her research.

13. Soul Music

Phyl Garland

● One of the major books on the history of Black-American music is *The Sound of Soul* by Phyl Garland, published in 1969 by the Henry Regnery Company of Chicago. This handsome young woman is no novice to music or writing. She is associate editor of *Ebony* and the magazine's regular music critic. In addition to her studies on Ramsey Lewis, Aretha Franklin, Oliver Nelson, Duke Ellington, and other major musical figures, she has prepared the scripts for *Black Journal* telecasts and written about many subjects outside of music. Within a deeply eloquent style, she is able to capture the rhythms and sonorities of Black music, providing at the same time information and syntheses of great value.

It can be misleading to extract a melody from a musical work for identification purposes to one who is not familiar with the composition. Ms. Garland, in her talk, made brief references to sections within *The Sound of Soul*. I have elected not to include these in this transcript with the assumption that all of our readers already know this book, or that they will not hesitate to read it.

The matter of soul music is something which touches on all areas discussed at these seminars and, like the other subjects, has always been outside of the classroom. It is wonderful to know how active we have been in writing symphonies and concertos, and to know this has been going on for some time but, when you get down to the kind of music I'm talking about, we are at the concerts of the poolrooms, the bars, the street corners, and the storefront churches. The fact that the educational institutions have not been interested in these kinds of concerts is, to me, a tragic reflection on the institutions, not on the music of the people.

Many tend to think of soul music as something commercial, which has been packaged, marketed, put on the juke boxes, and had its sales charted in *Billboard*. Actually, it is the contemporary popular music of the Blacks and also of many Whites (particularly the younger generation). It is music drawn from the same old Black roots, in many instances a combination of blues, gospel, and jazz. It is often an interplay between White and Black music, between White and Black performers.

It is not easy to define soul music to the extent that you can say what is soul and what isn't soul. The heavy beat jazz we hear today, full of gospel influence—shouting and bluesy—is what we call soul. Some people have called rock music a sort of White soul music, but we can find the same Black elements here so that it is sometimes difficult to say where one stops and the other begins. We should consider it one great body of music, drawn from many basic roots in musical history, and deal with it that way.

A distinctive thing about soul music is its heavy gospel influence, which we find increasingly in jazz. And jazz, as the blues, has also influenced soul music. I discussed this with B. B. King, and we agreed the sound of soul is often the sound of gospel. B. B. is from Mississippi, a blues-rich part of the country where the style is passed on from one generation to the next by relatives or friends, at picnics and socials. He came from that tradition and moved to Memphis, and then further north, and he absorbed many jazz elements into his style. He said he didn't know how this music was defined in dictionaries and textbooks, but he saw the separation of religious music from the blues coming about when the Black man first came to this country. They sang religious music after they got here too, and they prayed to God, but they saw they were being kicked and beaten, so maybe the "man upstairs" wasn't listening. Then they started singing about whatever was on their mind, and that's where the blues came from.

The blues has always been an expression, a very honest expression, of what one was going through. This is something we all know. This is the outstanding characteristic of Black music. It reflects what is on your mind and what is happening. Go back to the chants, to the work songs, the classic blues, and the spirituals (even ones which have found acceptance in complex and elaborate arrangements) and you will find there is always a underlying message, a deeply personal feeling within the music. This is the essence of soul; this is what it is really about.

I've written about this in *The Sound of Soul,* not in a cold, academic style, but in terms of the impression it has made on me.

When we speak of soul, we're talking about people like Aretha Franklin and Otis Redding, the Supremes and James Brown, but we're also talking about all the other musical forces that helped to shape not only their music, but their lives and the texture of life today. The study of soul is as much a study of sociology as it is music. It has been the thesis of Leroi Jones that Black music secured its identity in this country because of certain African influences and the changes these underwent because of exposure to certain European influences, but also because of the position the Black had in this society.

Nina Simone is a Black girl who came out of a small Southern town. Her mother was a revivalist, and she accompanied her mother's singing from about the age of six. When she was exposed to blues, her mother wouldn't let her play it in the house. She could use the same chords and all, but not those words. She went north, to Philadelphia and then New York, where she studied music formally, and this is reflected in her style also. We were sitting and rapping a while back and she said "Music is one of the great forces in the world, and ever since I can remember, I've loved music, and I've been interested in *all* kinds, and I always will be."

I've had heated debates with friends who believe that the whole world began and ended with Ray Charles, Aretha Franklin, or James Brown, and I say it's cool to get into those things, but we can't ignore the musical beauty that man has produced, in *any* culture, from *any* time. It is important that we bring Black music into the total body of music, and not to isolate it. I mentioned to a friend that I was disturbed by an article in the *New York Times* about how few Blacks were in the major symphony orchestras. He said, "Well, I can't be bothered about that," which to me was very sad because we can't close out one thing in order to include another.

I think it was February 14, 1920, when the first blues recording was made. Because of this recording and those which came after it, it was possible to Blacks all over the country to hear major artists expressing ideas they all knew, even if they would not be able to hear the artist in person. Sterling Brown wrote a poem, *The Hand Is on the Gate,* which has been recorded on Folkways (S-9040). This poem will give you a good idea about what the blues are all about, and it will point up what B. B. King has said, that blues is soul.

I'll not attempt a résumé of the development of the blues or its effect on jazz in the 1930s and 1940s. Instead, I'll move on to more recent times. I remember, for example, when I was growing up in the 1950s there were many rhythm and blues groups, such as the Spaniels, the Platters, the Drifters, the Coasters, the Dominoes, and individual artists like Sam Cook and Dinah Washington. We all knew this music; it was a part of us.

The first White musician to make a really great impact with basically Black material was Elvis Presley, who grew up in Memphis, that hotbed of Black musical activity for many years. With clever promotion, Elvis was able to take Big Mama Willie Mae Thornton's *Hound Dog*

(I still prefer her singing it) and make the money. This was symptomatic of that idea that only Whites could make Black music acceptable to the majority, but that idea is changing.

Then from England came the Beatles, who had been listening to Elvis and to Chuck Berry and others, and this group re-did the R & B tunes. We all know what happened then: Black music came back to the United States, performed by British Whites. From this came the current rock movement, which is music performed primarily by and for Whites. The British were willing to state that their songs and musical ideas came from Blacks, unlike many American Whites.

There was one other important channel coming from the 1950s, and that was Ray Charles, originally a gospel artist, but he never forgot his gospel roots. Listen to *Drown in My Own Tears* on Atlantic 8039, and hear what he does with a chant. If you've ever set foot in a Baptist or Sanctified church, you'll know where that came from! Ray is preaching!

Now, if we're going to talk about soul, we've got to consider a few new approaches to the whole subject of music teaching. It is not a matter of throwing in a little Black music at the end of the semester for the sake of integration; I'm talking about dealing with it effectively and thoroughly.

I'm unhappy when I hear people talking about the universities dealing with something that's separate from what's out there in the world. Right now, that "out there" needs the universities. The schools must accept a responsibility to make an impact on society. When you read the final chapter of *The Sound of Soul,* you'll know that I think there are more important things than the number of records which get sold or who makes it to the top spot this month.

One of the reasons some schools have given attention to jazz is because it is sufficiently complex and intellectual to be regarded as somewhat respectable on the campuses, but we need to get more of it into the lower levels. Why should a student have to wait until college to learn anything about Black music?

Charles Bell is a friend of mine. He is a jazz musician who went into teaching, and he began experiments with elementary school children, although his primary post was in music education at Hunters College. In working with the kids, he decided he'd like to do a little opera for the students to perform. They asked for something on animals, and what came out was *The Zoo,* which was performed by fifth and sixth graders. The music was in a style they could relate to right away, and it took only about three weeks for them to learn it.

He went on to use music to help the students learn to read, approaching words as things made up of sound which, he said, is the thing musicians have been working with all along. He devised a method so he could raise the reading level of students who were behind. They learned their vowels by a song, and they'd swing it out! He had spectacular results with children who were as far as two or three grades behind, and he used this technique to help them with other reading problems they might have had.

I have recorded an interview with him, something we did in the middle of the night because of busy schedules, which I'd like to share with you.

GARLAND: Charles, you are identified as a jazz musician. In recent years you have become very active in music education, working with musical styles the children already had some familiarity with. Why did you do that?

BELL: First of all, I wanted to teach, and as a musician, it seemed the most logical thing I could do would be to have the music of the culture in the schools.

GARLAND: You went into the classroom and found out you had to go to where they were?

BELL: That's an interesting point, because teachers so often talk about where the children are. The question really is getting to that reality, whatever it is, which children belong to and which they are continuing.

GARLAND: That's not the way music education was approached in the past, was it?

BELL: No, that hasn't been the case, but that doesn't mean it shouldn't be. The children love music, and they love the world we live in. I suspect that anything anyone loves must be good. If people love it, it must have some validity. The music that dominates this century is the music most of the people in this country love, and the children love it, so it should be the music of the school. The majority always rules, doesn't it? As a Black man, I can *really* understand that principle. My first effort was a failure. I had taken one of the top ten tunes, arranged it for the group and . . . well, if I told you the kids were bored, I'd be complimenting myself. I had been involved in third-stream music, as you know, and I was just learning rock and roll chords and beats. What I did then was to tell the children to forget the clever lines I had written to the song. I told them I'd just play the chords and they could sing it anyway they wanted to. They gave me something that was out of sight.

Then we'd take a record and listen to it carefully. If we heard something played on the horn, I'd teach that part to a group. I'd do the same thing with the violins or the guitars, and then we'd put it all together. At a point, we had six parts being sung at the same time and nobody was looking at the music.

GARLAND: These were tunes they already knew?

BELL: Yes, but not only that. They were making things up for themselves, and they loved it. They were even invited to sing at a jazz festival, there in Pittsburgh.

GARLAND: Do you feel this was a better experience than if they had learned music in the traditional manner?

BELL: They'll remember what they were into much longer than if it had been Händel's *Hallelujah Chorus*. This was an experience which moved their bodies and minds. After I left that job, I kept getting letters from them. They tried to keep together by themselves. There was a feeling, and it was beautiful. They'll remember that experience all of their lives.

GARLAND: Those were junior high youngsters who might have had a certain degree of sophistication. Since then you've been involved with younger kids, and written *The Zoo*. Would you say something about that?

BELL: This is the most important thing I want to communicate to all of my Black brother musicians: Music has powers outside of those commonly accepted. It can communicate not only itself, but it has the ability to communicate anything. In working with *The Zoo* I found that little children can take on and deal with everything we so-called adults think life is about. Those sixth-grade kids understood concepts it took me thirty-seven years to get together. The work has a fabric of musical *and* intellectual counterpoint, but I think Jesus Christ made a very intelligent statement when he said that children can lead us.

The word *children* to me is as racist a word as *Nigger,* as *White,* as *woman* or *man.* What are you saying when you speak of children? You're saying you have preconceived ideas about the ability of a child to behave or learn.

GARLAND: Is this why you were able to get into some rather complex ideas about where they were leading you in *The Zoo?*

BELL: That's right. It was all just happening, just going on. Like I was no sophisticated, groovy, together musician condescending to play with these little children. It was just like these human beings together, making music in expression of living experiences. We all knew on which levels I was their teacher, and they were mine.

GARLAND: You've also been involved recently in teaching children how to read through music, a "frustration-free phonetic system." You were dealing with a fourth-grade class—the slowest class in the school.

BELL: I'm a descendant of a people who were so deep into their language that they could beat it on a drum. Right from that point, my experiment was not illogical. I think music can do just about anything, and I've speculated that information can be more thoroughly and quickly communicated through music. I worked on this experiment for four months with that class. Their reading levels ranged from first through third grades, even though they were fourth-graders. I've just finished video-taping twenty of these kids, and they were reading words college freshmen would mispronounce, or not be able to say at all. The results of my studies tell me that one year with the system will give the child—no matter his grade level—the ability to read every English word and that, in the following year, he'll be able to read all of the language without the system.

This system was primarily based on nine symbols for every individual sound of the language. The system always stays the same, and I even teach that in the music. The kids wants to sing a song over and over. Triangles and tambourines set up the rhythm. Then we go through the science of putting the language back together.

When I first became interested in the subject, I asked the teachers what was the process of the child as he learned to read. No one could answer that. If you were not taught phonetically, you were never *really taught*. Your memory just took over for you, and you learned sight recognition. A lot of the kids who were reading at first-grade level in my class knew the word "delicatessen" because they passed this word every day. That's how most of us "learned" to read. I was fortunate because I was a slow learner and I can remember the process, but not all of it.

When I bring music to the class, I have to be ready to change it. I could write one song, say, and then have the kids look at me like I'm a little silly (even though I was very impressed with the music before I got to class). I can't act like I'm at a session with this group of brothers and get them to do what I've done if they like it or not. I've got to keep flexible, run home and write another song, even if I think my first one might be worth a million dollars somewhere else. I've got to have songs to help my Puerto Rican students with "sh" and other sounds in English they aren't used to.

GARLAND: You have plans for another group of students now, right?

BELL: Yes. I'm going on with this reading thing. Once I get the schools going on it, I'm starting to think about the Chinese abacus in mathematics. I work with the abacus every day, trying to find some new methods here also.

GARLAND: How do you see yourself in the role of teacher?

BELL: If everyone gets down to where it's supposed to be, where man as a teacher can say that he teaches human beings, we will have gone a long way. I hope to leave my gifts before I go, and I suspect that the first people a Black teacher has to teach is his own people.

● Soul, as Phyl and Charles have suggested, is far more than a manner of singing. It is even more than a manner of living. It seems to be a manner of dealing with life, of coming to grips with it on humanistic terms. It is allied with that African concept of music, which makes the art an element within a social fabric and not an extraneous factor. It makes music relate to human conditions and needs—from blues to protest, from Coltrane and Sun Ra to Joseph Jarman. It is a spirit of love, such as is manifest in our legacy of Mahalia Jackson's voice and as can be seen in the Socratic teaching of John Lovell. It is an awareness of brotherhood—from Martin Luther King to Malcolm—which has the potential of including non-Blacks of fraternal inclinations. It is that quality which gave courage to the pioneers. It is the essence of mankind, not perverted by technology or capitalism. It is an expression which reaches out from the depths of one's free inner-self to touch and communicate to teach. It may be the heaviest of the Black man's burdens, but it is also the most natural of all.

If it is musically expressed within the modesty of Beverly Glenn or the great enthusiasm of Aretha Franklin, it is not any the less present, but it is not to be measured in terms of *fiorture*. It is a feeling of being home. To my brothers, it is the smell of garlic being browned in Spanish olive oil, the Phrygian cadences on a guitar, Rodolfo's sobs on Mimi's death, the combination of *cristianos y moros,* the sight of another Brown face. We all have a home. Samuel Akpabot called it a tent. It is the cradle of our cultural existence, but it is not our fortress. If we are secure in our concept of soul, we can receive appreciative guests and accept their invitations. We can play whatever jargonistic games our professions might impose on us, or we can share our at-homeness with business colleagues.

Phyl Garland has seen in the work of Charles Bell something which is an extension of the popular concept of soul. I think he is an outstanding example of one who takes home to school, who takes music to his people, who is committed to changing the world as best he can within his work. Perhaps nothing is more touching or impressive than his observation that those students fortunately entrusted to his care come from a culture which knew language so well that it could be expressed on a drum. Are these youngsters "culturally deprived?"

14. Gospel Music

Thomas A. Dorsey

● This venerable patriarch of gospel music must be one of the most influential figures in twentieth-century music. When one thinks of his activity in the early blues, the transfer he made into highly personalized religious music and the effect this has had on so much of the world's music, we cannot help but be in awe of Professor Dorsey's accomplishments. His warm and enthusiastic spirit makes his age irrelevant, but the richness of his life and experiences prove how meaningful those many years have been.

I begged him to remain in Bloomington for the concert which was scheduled for the evening of his talk, when Bernadine Oliphint and Carol Stone provided a superb song recital which was followed by a program offered by the chorus of Crispus Attucks High School in Indianapolis. The choral program was, by itself, a moving event; Anderson Dailey, the school's conductor, was leaving Crispus Attucks for another position. It was obvious that the students loved and respected him deeply, and that they had not minded the summer rehearsals for this concert, Anderson's farewell to this school. I had approached him beforehand to see if he would be willing to have the chorus end the concert with *Precious Lord*, in honor of the composer.

Professor Dorsey was seated right in front of me and, when Anderson announced this encore, it was evident this grand old man was touched, and the performance was excellent. Rather than merely acknowledge the enthusiastic applause from the packed house, Dorsey ran down the aisle, shook the hand of the conductor and the solo vocalists, sat on the edge of the stage, and—in the style of a real preacher—lined out the gospel hymn and lead the entire audience, all of whom remained standing in honor of this true gentleman.

As we left the hall that evening, everyone felt that special kind of warmth which we were later to feel at the première of Joplin's *Treemonisha*, after Hubert Walters' 1972 talk on the liturgy of the Black church, or Leila Blakey's song concert during that same seminar. We knew then that this is what music is all about, and the world owes Thomas Dorsey an enormous debt for having elevated us with his music.

My father was a country preacher in Georgia. You don't get much money for preaching, you know. Sometimes you didn't get any. I liked to follow my father around. I was between three and five at the time (it was about 1906 or 1907, maybe earlier). Maybe you didn't get any money, but the sisters fed well. They'd give you a chicken or something to carry home, and, while you were there, you got plenty to eat.

My family was mostly a musical family. My mother and father both could play. They didn't have the notes down so well for there were no teachers in those days, but there seemed to be some stream of music in my family. Lena McLin is my niece. Most of you know that, and I think she's great.

I got the chance in my early days to meet many of the stars of that time, like Bessie Smith. I knew her. Ma Rainey? I knew her. In fact, I traveled with her; I was her jazz band leader for three seasons on the old TOBA time—Theater Owner Booking Association. The man who booked you, owned you. There were no middlemen. If they wanted to fire you, they fired you, and nobody could do anything about it. I became Ma Rainey's jazz band leader and traveled on this circuit for three years. We played at theaters where I'd sold pop as a boy from eight to ten. We got all the pop we could drink, and we could see the show. I met the best performers who came along, and I got a pretty fair chance to learn music there. Eddie Hayward, Sr., was the pianist for the theater. He cued the pictures and played for all the performers, with Eddie, Jr. (just a little fellow then), around his father's knees.

At the National Baptist Convention there was an evangelistic singer named Professor Nicks. He was great! He was powerful! One Sunday morning he rose and sang a song, *I Do, Don't You?* Maybe some of you know it. He rocked that convention: shouts, moans, hollers, screaming. I said to myself, "That's what I want to do. That's good gospel, and I want to be a gospel singer!" That's where I first got the gospel word, and I was converted at that meeting. I was profoundly impressed with what he sang. I wrote a song then and there, that week, for *The Gospel Pearl*, a song book which may still be distributed by the National Sunday School Board of the National Baptist Convention. It's on page 119. I never got any royalties for it, I just let them have it.

I always had rhythm in my bones. I like the solid beat. I like the long, moaning, groaning tone. I like the rock. You know how they rock and shout in the church. I like it. It's a thing people look for now. Don't let your singing group die, don't let the movement go out of the music. Black music calls for movement! It calls for feeling. Don't let it get away.

This rhythm I had, I brought with me to gospel songs. I was a blues singer, and I carried that with me into the gospel songs. These songs were not just written. Something had to happen, something had to be done, there had to be feeling. They weren't just printed and distributed. Somebody had to feel something, someone had to hand down light for mankind's pathway, smooth the road and the rugged way, give him courage, bring the Black man peace, joy, and happiness. Gospel songs come from prayer, meditation, hard times, and pain. But they are written out of divine memories, out of the feelings in your soul.

That's where soul comes in: You bring peace and joy and understanding among men. I don't write songs for Black men, or White men, or Red men, or Yellow men, or Brown men. I write songs for people, and I want *all* men to sing these gospel songs if they can. I've been more than halfway around the world with songs like *Sometimes My Burden Is so Hard to Bear* and *Come unto Me All Ye That Labor and Are Heavy Laden and I'll Give You Rest*. I've introduced these gospel songs in nations where they've never been heard before.

One Sunday morning I was in Egypt and they had a Protestant meeting in the hotel where I was staying. They wanted to sing *Precious Lord, Take My Hand*. You know, there are many people in Egypt who know that song, including Arabs? That was good news to me. We had a great meeting there, and that brought *Precious Lord* up in my estimation. That song has been translated into about thirty-two languages and dialects, and has been sung around the world a million times. We used to send the music to soldiers during World War II when they had asked for it. Before the Communists took over China, we had a customer among the missionaries who ordered many copies over the years. They know it wherever I go, in Paris, in Africa.

QUESTION: Would you tell us something about your recent activities?

DORSEY: I have been an assistant pastor at the Pilgrim Baptist Church in Chicago for eight years. I'm also president of the National Convention of Gospel Choirs and Choruses, Inc. We've got a big meeting in Los Angeles in a few weeks at Trinity Baptist Church. If you're in that vicinity, don't fail to drop in. You'll see some rare acting. One of our accomplishments has been the construction of an eleven-story building at 4048 Lake Park Avenue in Chicago, where we had our school and home for singers for so long. The old building has been demolished, and we have a big, modern air-conditioned structure there now. I think that's quite an accomplishment.

QUESTION: Could you say when you first were converted to gospel music?

DORSEY: About 1921. I was converted in 1921 but you see, brother, we had to eat. I couldn't leave the blues right away. I couldn't leave the stage right away. I stayed on about a year and a half, but I was out of it about 1923.

QUESTION: How did you make the first money in gospel?

DORSEY: I opened my own publishing company, or the Lord opened it for me 'cause I didn't have a cent. I still retain that company, and I have a few other publishers here and in Europe. The first song I ever published was *Someday, Somewhere*. I'll tell you how it happened. I had just taken a new wife on my hands, and I got sick. I had about $13 in the bank, and I had to spend that. I got my song to the printer, in hymn book size. I got addresses of missions from a magazine of the National Baptist Convention. I borrowed $5 and got 250 two-cent stamps (you could mail a letter for that much then.) I put the songs in the mail and sent them off to the churches. What do you think happened? Nothing! Do you know it was a year and nine months before I got a reply? I got discouraged, and so did my wife. This was about 1925. Then I met Frye at the National Baptist Convention in 1930, and he came with me in 1931. Frye, Lucy Campbell, Ed Isaac—these were the people that put me over. I had met a lot of people at that meeting. Believe it or not, I sold $10 worth of music then. Sally Martin and I discovered each other in 1933. She had a lovely voice, but she needed a little of the roughness knocked off. I went to see her teacher, Mrs. Dennis Rogers, and she was a great singer. She could make those high notes go up into the sky, and Sally was so low! Her voice was heavier than mine. I told Sally to come over to my place, a place I called my studio, and she did. I trained her. She was working some place for the city, but she wasn't getting paid. I told her to come work for me, for $4 a week. And she did. She helped me make this publishing business. Sometimes I didn't have the $4 and I had to borrow it, but she stayed on. From then on, we've had an association. She's the national organizer for our convention now. She was my gospel singer. There have been others through the years, but she was the closest and the greatest.

QUESTION: Where in the Atlanta area did you secure any of your musical training?

DORSEY: Mrs. Graves was the only music teacher who taught the Black folk at that time. She gave me my first lessons. My grandfather was an alumnus of the Atlanta Baptist College, and I went there. I can't think of the name, but there was a fellow out there teaching music who helped me quite a bit. Then I told you about Eddie Hayward. If any of you go to Atlanta, visit my brother-in-law's church, Mount Calvary Baptist. B.J. Johnson is my brother-in-law.

QUESTION: Have you ever heard one of your own compositions and not recognized it, or been disappointed?

DORSEY: Oh yes, sister, I've heard them butchered, but I don't complain. I want somebody to sing the song. One fellow might not know how to do it, but I give him credit just the same. Then somebody comes along and does it right, the way that touches me, and I give him credit too.

QUESTION: Using your own music as a basis, how do you view what has happened to gospel music in the last twenty years?

DORSEY: I don't judge it. I can't do that. I'm glad if I've been an inspiration for them. Some of them are doing well now, monetarily, for which I'm grateful. I'm glad for them. There are many gospel songwriters now with a different beat. They have different movement in the melody and different progressions, but I never fight with any of them. I agree with them all; we're all going the same way. Now I'll tell you, this Hawkins boy—Edward Hawkins. I like his beat. He's got something new there. I like his style.

QUESTION: How many pieces have you published?

DORSEY: I don't know. I can't count them. Only one thing: I don't let the copyrights run out. I have a group in New York which watches out for that for me.

QUESTION: Have there been any major changes in gospel singing style in your lifetime?

DORSEY: Well, not exactly major, but there have been changes, and some to the good. Take *O Happy Day*. I've sung that song since I was a boy and nobody paid very much attention to it, but then Hawkins comes along. I guess he was inspired from on high, and he put beat into it. Not only beat, but the curves, the rhythmic curves, and the harmony. It creates a new style in gospel music, and I think he did a wonderful job. I'm for him, and I hope he gets rich on it. There are others singing gospel songs who have lost the melody. All they have is the beat. When there's no melody in gospel songs, you can't get much of a story, you don't get much of a message. They can put all the beat in it they want, but the melody is the foundation. You can take a melody and add all kind of harmony to it, but unless there's a melody—I don't know if that's satisfactory or not.

QUESTION: What advice would you give a young person who wants to get into gospel music?

DORSEY: First, he'd have to know music, of course. He'd also have to know some of the key people in the field. If you've got a good number and you've got some money, find a good singer and have that singer carry it out. Put it over like that. But there are a lot of gospel song writers now, and not all are successful. If you're going to be successful, you've got to work hard. Don't forget your song, no matter what happens. Nothing beats a failure but a trial.

QUESTION: Pearl Williams Jones, a fabulous pianist and singer, has a definitive article on gospel music which was included in the Howard University publication, *Development of Materials for a One Year Course in African Music* (1970), developed by Vada Butcher.

DORSEY: Say, we don't want to lose this heritage. I struggled so long before I could get any recognition! So many of my own folks fought me. Now don't you fight anybody. You can't make it like that. If another fellow's got a product, speak well of it. Don't try to raise your product by pushing his down.

There's just two more things I want to say. You may want to read this article about me that was published by the National Gospel Association. They said I was the beginning. I might not have been, but I'm the only one they know of. It's all there, a half-dozen pages: Sally Martin, Magnolia Lewis Butts, Lucy Campbell. I wish a Black company had put this out. Why couldn't we do this?

15. Information Sources

Dominique-René de Lerma, Frank Gillis, and Don Malin

● Frank Gillis is associate director of Indiana University's Archives of Traditional Music and a person with an abundance of qualifications for his work in Black music. He is a graduate of Wayne State University, Columbia University, and the University of Minnesota, and is well trained in jazz history, sociology, and library science. He began professional work as a jazz pianist in 1938 and recorded fourteen sides with his own group, The Dixie Five, in Detroit (1949–1951). He is an avid collector of recorded jazz and has an exceptionally large collection. For several years he served as editor of *Ethnomusicology*, a journal doubtless known to many persons engaged in Black music research.

Don Malin is certainly one of the best known personalities in the music publishing industry. Educated at Iowa State University, his present post as Educational Director of the Edward B. Marks Music Corporation has brought him in touch with most of the nation's music teachers, salesmen, composers, and performers. A member of ASCAP, he has been engaged as choral composer, arranger, editor, and translator of many publications, including *Renaissance Choral Music, Choral Perspective,* and *Rediscovered Madrigals.*

MALIN: The Edward B. Marks Music Corporation dates back to 1894 and is one of the two oldest music firms in this country to remain under the ownership of one family. Music of the people has always been particularly represented in our catalog, starting with those sorrowful songs from the so-called "Gay Nineties" such as *In the Baggage Coach Ahead* and *The Little Lost Child.* These were Broadway hits of the times, as were the Cole and Johnson shows whose tunes came into our catalog early in this century.

The policy was established quite early that we would issue music for the public and that we would also address the educational community. We didn't fit into the "long-hair" or "short-hair" camp to which most publishers of the times belonged; we were active in both fields. In our catalog today you will find contemporary composers such as Roger Sessions, Norman Dello Joio, Mario Davidovsky, and

Hale Smith. We had one of the first two Black music editors in James Rosamond Johnson (the other was Ricordi's Harry Burleigh). Hale Smith was with us as an editor for a period and is still under contract to us as a composer.

We published James Rosamond and James Weldon Johnson's *Lift Every Voice* in numerous versions, including the festival arrangement for orchestral accompaniment which Hale Smith has recently finished. We've published music by Hale Smith, Oliver Nelson, Oscar Brown, Jr., Billie Holiday, Eva Jessye, Paul Johnson, Rogie Clark, Lena McLin, Ollie McFarland, Clarence Jackson, Jester Hairston, Scott Joplin and James A. Bland.

Some publishers have shown varying degrees of interest in Black music, with the major activity coming from Black-owned firms, as would be expected. I think of Thomas Dorsey's company, of the Jobete Company in Detroit, and of course, of Handy Brothers.

Some representative works of earlier figures still are in print, people such as Harry Burleigh, William Dawson, R. Nathaniel Dett, William Grant Still, Clarence Cameron White, John W. Work, Edward Boatner, and mention may be made of younger composers who are published, such as T.J. Anderson, Ulysses Kay, Rogie Clark, Margaret Bonds, and others whose names are known to you. However, if you look at the listing of the present holdings of the Black Music Center, which may be representative of the available literature, you will find substantially more publications *about* Black music than publications *of* Black music. This means that more people read words than read music. We still have gaps in the area of published music.

While looking through the Center's collection in the Music Library yesterday I was amused to find collections of spirituals and folk tunes which had been published in France and Germany, with French or German texts. There was a certain delight in finding *Die Gospel-Eisenbaum kommt* ("The Gospel Train's A-coming") and in seeing translations of *When the Saints Go Marching In*, but there are two lessons to be learned from this. For one thing, we've known all along that European support of Black music has been strong, but we also see that Black music needs the consideration of Black people, just as any ethnic study may benefit most from the work of those who best know that culture.

Publishers today are looking for Black music, produced by Black people. Right now we need a song collection for Black school children which can be used in the middle grades. All music publishers are aware that there is little material for the earlier grades, and there is a special problem here related to reading skills. Too many children go through school and never learn to read music, and that inhibits the music publishing market. The economic problems which have been on the rise lately also have hurt the business, particularly when school systems drop their music programs.

Music publishing is not a highly profitable business. The total volume of sales in all music areas (not including records) came to almost a billion dollars in 1969. The sale of printed music was only nine percent of that total, and that figure was based on retail prices. The actual volume of business by publishers would be around $45,000,000—just about five percent of the total music volume. I happen to be a Director of the Music Publishers Association of the United States. This group now has only 47 members. In the past fifteen years, the number has dropped because of mergers, but also because at least fourteen companies have gone out of business.

I've mentioned the need for materials on the elementary level, but there are a few which are available that should be cited as having particular value. *Wake Up and Sing*, a Marks publication, is a collection of songs, adapted for young children, compiled by Beatrice Landeck and Elizabeth Crook. There are songs here by Huddie Ledbetter, Massie Patterson, and Eubie Blake, as well as Woody Guthrie, designed for children from Kindergarten into second grade. Miss Landeck has also published *Echoes of Africa* (David McKay, 1969), a book for older students which is based on her own research in Africa and which shows the spread of the African musical influence into both North and South America. She has also compiled *Git on Board* which has a good sampling of Black music (J. Rosamond Johnson arrangements are used) for unison or part singing, issued by Marks. John Work's *Jubilee* (New York: Rinehart & Winston, 1962) is another classic in the field which may stimulate educators or potential compilers. We should certainly also mention the Dett collections, published in the 1930s by Schmitt, Hall and McCreary, and Clarence Cameron White's *Traditional Negro Spirituals* (New York: Carl Fischer, 1949) and John Work's *American Negro Songs* (New York: Crown Publishers, 1940). There are also Frederick Hall's three collections of spirituals, published here in Indiana by Rodeheaver, Hall & Mack, and Edward H. Boatner's *Thirty Afro-American Choral Spirituals* (New York: Hammond Music Co., 1964), which provides a Biblical reference for each spiritual in question. William Henry Smith has a good anthology, issued by Kjos in Chicago, and Viking has recently produced a paperback edition of James Weldon and James

Rosamond Johnson's *Books of American Negro Spirituals.* For the solo voice, there is Rogie Clark's *Copper Sun,* a Presser publication. Clark has recently published two sets of Afro-American spirituals for SATB, and one for Christmas and one for Easter. Both of these are in the Piedmont catalog, handled by Marks.

With regard to Mary Allen Grissom's *The Negro Sings a New Heaven,* we have an example which I hope will be continued. This source book of spirituals was originally published by the University of North Carolina Press in 1930. It is now available in a reprint from Dover, issued in 1969.

As for piano music, we know that a great many Black children are interested in the piano, but we need more teaching pieces in this area. Marks publishes Oliver Nelson's *Blues and the Abstract Truth,* and Hale Smith's *Faces of Jazz,* and there is an excellent little book by David Kraehenbuehl, *Jazz and Blues,* published by Summy-Birchard, but I don't see much easy piano material based on spirituals or non-jazz sources. Those who teach and play piano might be encouraged to write for it. Of course, there is *Twenty-four Traditional Melodies* by Coleridge-Taylor, published in 1905 by Ditson. If this is still available, it could be secured from Theodore Presser, who bought the Ditson company some years back. It's interesting to note that then, at the start of the century, Coleridge-Taylor was using materials he got from Africa. These pieces are written with bravura. They take big hands and some degree of skill. What we need is more material, from the same sources, designed for young people.

In the field of instrumental school music, there is still a lot of room for development. William Grant Still has been active in this area, for band and orchestra. Hale Smith has written several works for band, and T.J. Anderson has at least one. But most of these are for relatively skilled groups. We need something for the middle school, for junior high. A successful example is the Marks publication of *God Bless' the Child,* arranged by Ed McLin for band and two-part chorus. There is a need for more Black instrumental music at this level.

Let me urge those of you interested in preparing music for publication not to overlook the folk element. While it is absolutely true that we need works such as Hale Smith's *Three Brevities for Flute* (published by Marks) and T. J. Anderson's *Tolson Variations* (Composers Facsimile Edition), we also need compositions such as Undine Moore's *Afro-American Suite* (in manuscript) and John Carter's *Cantata* (Southern Music Publishing Co.), both of which are highly original compositions, based on traditional tunes. Don't forget the folk elements found in the music of Bach, Beethoven, Bartók, Vaughan Williams, William Grant Still, Rimsky-Korsakov, Stravinsky, Delius, and others. Look up Michael Tippet's *A Child of Our Time*, and see how he uses spirituals.

Finally, I'd like to impress upon you my belief that the most important thing in the school curriculum is, in a sense, music. It can bear on everything you teach: language studies and reading, mathematics, physical training, and social studies. When you invest in school music, you are investing in the *whole* school, not just the music class. Politicians are finally admitting the economics of the country is not in a good state. Many of you have known that for quite a while. When that happens, the arts get a back seat, and that is unfortunate. The arts are essential to the curriculum.

GILLIS: Ethnomusicology is a broad and relatively new field developing out of musicology and anthropology. It studies the music of all cultures in the world, concentrating on folk, popular, and other musics which are carried in the aural rather than the written tradition. The primary source document for such music is not the notated score but the phonorecording, which captures and preserves for us an objective and accurate record of the original performance. The phonorecording thus provides us with data which can be used time after time for transcription and analysis and for gaining new insights into cultural change and diffusion.

Archives collecting and preserving ethnomusicological phonorecordings first came into being in Berlin and Vienna at the turn of the century. A number of such archives were established in the ensuing years in many countries. In the United States, the Archive of Folk Song was founded as a part of the Library of Congress by John A. Lomax in 1928. Other archives were developed after this date: the Rodgers & Hammerstein collection at the Lincoln Center Branch of the New York Public Library; the library of the Institute of Ethnomusicology, University of California—Los Angeles; the Rutgers Institute for Jazz Studies, originally the archives and library of the late Marshall Stearns; the New Orleans Jazz Archives at Tulane University; the Audio Center, which is part of the Popular Culture Collection at Bowling Green State University (Ohio); and the Archives of Traditional Music at Indiana University.

The Indiana University Archives of Traditional Music is based on phonorecordings collected by George Herzog at Columbia University beginning in 1936. His collection was brought to Indiana University in 1948 and officially became a part of the resource collections here in 1954. Since that time the Archives' collections have served many scholars in music, anthropology, folklore, linguistics and other fields. The holdings of the Archives include over 100,000 separate items—songs, stories, interviews, and the like—with representations from the greater part of the world's cultural regions.

A large body of phonorecorded data documenting the Black musical heritage is preserved in a number of archives throughout the world. Field recordings of African music and oral data, dating back to about 1902, are located in the Berlin Phonogrammarchiv, the Phonothèque Nationale, in Paris, and in the archives in the United States mentioned above. Commerical recordings date from the 1920s.

The earliest field recordings of Afro-American music—blues, worksongs, spirituals, and so forth—were collected from the mid-1920s on. Commercial recordings date back to the early jazz-oriented popular music of James Europe and W. C. Handy orchestras, from 1913 on, the piano music and musical shows of Eubie Blake, the vocal blues of Mamie Smith, Ma Rainey, and Bessie Smith, and the New Orleans jazz groups of Joseph King Oliver, Louis Armstrong, and Ferdinand Jelly Roll Morton, among many others.

The Indiana University Archives of Traditional Music is particularly rich in both field and commercial recordings of Black music. Of special significance are recordings collected by Frederick Starr, from the Congo in 1906, and those of Dr. and Mrs. Melville J. Herskovits, from West Africa, Surinam, Brazil, and Trinidad, in 1928–1942. There are many others collected chiefly by noted anthropologists in Africa and the New World.

There are several problems one might encounter using phonorecordings of Black music for research: first, determining who had recorded what musical material; second, locating a copy of the recording itself; and third, obtaining a use copy of the recording. Thanks to the work of many dedicated and industrious individuals interested in the history of phonorecordings, we have a number of discographies which provide us with valuable data. The jazz-blues discographies by Brian Rust—*Jazz Records, 1897–1942*—and J. Godrich and R. M. W. Dixon—*Blues and Gospel Records, 1902–1942*—are arranged alphabetically by performer and give titles recorded, date and place of recording, and record company label name and number. Using these reference sources it would be relatively easy to find titles recorded by certain performers. Finding materials within a particular genre—spirituals, worksongs, rhythm-and-blues, and so forth—or of specific song titles is more difficult, and only the catalogs of, or correspondence with, individual archives may help in providing such data.

In-print commercial recordings are generally available through the local record shop. Locating out-of-print commercial items and original field recordings for study or teaching purposes is difficult. Published guides to institutional and individual collections may be useful. Two such guides are: *A Preliminary Directory of Sound Recordings Collections in the United States and Canada* (New York Public Library, 1967) prepared by the Association for Recorded Sound Collections; and *Director of Ethnomusicological Sound Recording Collections in the U.S. and Canada*, prepared by the Archives Committee of the Society for Ethnomusicology (Room 513, 201 South Main St., Ann Arbor, Michigan 48108). Both of these compilations give the locations of major collections, alphabetically by state or province, and the major areas of concentration within each collection.

The major obstacle one encounters in working with phonorecordings is in requesting a copy from the original, which is to be used for educational purposes. Since one who copies commercial recordings for public distribution is open to civil suit, curators of archival collections and many individual collectors will generally refuse to make copies. The researcher will thus have to travel to various archives to listen to material he wishes to study and can only study within the confines of a particular archives. It is possible that the present copyright law of 1909—which does not apply to phonorecordings—will be revised so that single copies, especially of out-of-print recordings to be used for educational purposes, may be permitted.

Archives collecting phonorecordings share many problems, chiefly centering on the lack of funds for personnel, acquisitions, and the cataloging, classifying, and indexing of collections. As a result, archives cannot provide adequate service, they may lack important recordings, special files, and indexes, and they are unable to publish catalogs of their holdings. It is unfortunate that this situation exists at a time when there is a growing interest in the study of jazz and world folk and popular musics at academic institutions.

It is hoped that in the future funds will be made available for the collection, preservation, and servicing of these valuable aural data. We would also hope that provisions may be made to permit the copying of those phonorecordings which are generally unavailable and which are to be used for serious study and for general educational purposes.

DE LERMA: Most of you attending our seminars are aware of the kind of work the Black Music Center is engaged in during the year, and you have had an opportunity to make full use of our research and our printed and recorded collections. It ties in a bit with what Frank said when I mention that, as Director of the Center and as Music Librarian for Indiana University, I am unequivocally against regulations, laws, policies, and attitudes which are primarily designed to keep important information secret or away from those who need it. I have great sympathy for those individuals who have one, two, or more items of rarity, who do not know the informational value of these materials or who are unaware of methods to protect and preserve the items and, *at the same time,* share these with all interested persons. Librarians, curators, collectors, and "researchers" may establish whatever policies they wish, but the only requests the Black Music Center has gently turned down are those related to extensive material we plan to publish in the near future (so that, for one thing, we might develop a more secure financial base from royalties) or those which —if freely given—might diminish the income of a creator.

Moving on to other matters, and without tracing again the history of the Center, I'd like to share with you a story that suggests what might be done with your research. Fairly soon after I came back from an extensive research trip throughout western Europe in 1970 (not, alas, on the subject of Black music), I received a letter from Dr. Ruth Blume, editor of *Die Musik in Geschichte und Gegenwart*—the most important encyclopedia on music today—who wanted to know if I would be willing to write the article on Robert Nathaniel Dett for *MGG*'s supplementary series. My first reaction was concern for the fact that someone as important as Dr. Dett would be placed in the *Anhang,* but I remembered that John Cage and William Boyce missed out on the initial volumes of this multi-volume encyclopedia. I was impressed by the fact that Dr. Blume knew of my research on Black music at a time when there had been little local notice, but I was also concerned because the article really should have been written by Dr. McBrier, whose excellent dissertation on Dett was barely a few years old. The article was due by the end of the year in Germany, however, and I knew Dr. McBrier was on sabbaticial and that this was a chance to check our research. I reached behind me and pulled out the notebook with Dett entries and found one hundred titles with publishers. I knew how helpful it would be, right there and then, when we were ready to publish this research.

As soon as that year's seminar was over, I flew to the Library of Congress to see if they had more information than we had gathered.

I spoke with William Lichtenwanger, Carroll Wade, and Elmer Booze, all of whom were characteristically helpful. After that, I went down to the Hampton Institute to examine the library holdings there and to speak with people who had known Dr. Dett. My entré was Professor Maurice McCall, who had already been at our initial seminar and was someone I quickly came to know as a friend and a gifted composer. Substantial additional help was provided by Kenneth Billups, who later became a member of the Center's Honorary Advisory Committee, and I was assisted by friends with the libraries at Eastman and Oberlin. After corresponding with Dr. William Grant Still, I found that our research had not been complete, but that it was in the main quite accurate.

This work also put me in touch with Dett's publishers. He had several, but the major one was Summy-Birchard. They became alert to the fact that such a monument as *In the Bottoms* was no longer in print, as well as a number of other works by Dr. Dett. I had been impressed by his style when writing for the piano (the *MGG* article will state that *The Ordering of Moses* "ist ein Werk von sehr unausgeglichen Qualitäten"), and I felt some distress that so much of his keyboard music in particular was no longer available to piano students and concert artists. Through this contact, I began corresponding with Roberta Savler, the Administrative Editor at Summy-Birchard. In my letters I suggested that we had *Gesamtausgaben* on Mozart, on Bach, on Schubert—even on Schönberg. Why not one on a Black composer? This was before Vera Lawrence's two-volume set on Scott Joplin. Why could a library not be supplied with the complete works of Dett, of Clarence Cameron White, or of William Grant Still? I was not concerned with the financial problems which might occasion such a project because I think one should consider them after the concept of a project is thought valuable. It was a delight when Roberta wrote me later to say that Summy-Birchard was picking up the idea and planned to issue an anthology of various major piano works by Dr. Dett.[1]

QUESTION: Are record companies willing to open their vaults for special purposes?

---

[1] The applause which greeted this announcement bore witness to the frustrations evidently already plaguing many at the seminar. At last report, the anthology may be on the market quite soon. With respect to my MGG article on Dr. Dett, incidentally, I am honored that Dr. Blume has also requested one on Ulysses Kay. I'm sorry that our communications did not start until after work had been done on that area which would have included Anderson and Baker, for example.

GILLIS: Some will cooperate. Columbia has been very generous in this regard, and Victor has been helpful in several instances. Decca closed its doors long ago—not only the vaults, but the files. But I don't think any of the companies will make copies of items within the vaults. If enough people pressure a company for certain reissues, they might market them. John Hammond at Columbia has been particularly sympathetic in this regard. The reissues are not always commercial successes, but they eventually pay for themselves and help those of us with desiderata to fill in certain gaps in our collections.

DE LERMA: Incidentally, when John was with us in 1969, he emphasized the Black American debt to England as the preserver of this culture at a time when the U. S. market was failing. We have with us, among our several overseas guests, David Horn from the American Documentation Centre at the University of Exeter. Perhaps he would share with us his reason for honoring us with his presence.

HORN: The situation in England is rather interesting. Our concern for Black music, which Mr. Hammond mentioned, is still with us. Unfortunately, there is no good library collection of these materials, even though we have many private collectors with splendid libraries. Of course there are many fine music libraries, but none has made a special collection of Afro-Americana. Some places now, such as the University of York, include some study of Afro-American music in their curriculum.

DE LERMA: Wouldn't that seem strange, to find there are schools in England offering course work in American music, in music which not all schools in this country consider?

QUESTION: If you will glance through the bibliography being developed by the Black Music Center, you will find books on Black music in at least ten foreign languages. That will give you an idea of the interest in our music which is shown from almost all European countries.

DE LERMA: That is quite true. There are important books in German, of course, and French and Italian. Swedish is certainly not far behind, but you can find material in Dutch, Portugese, Spanish, and Czech. I've seen Marian Anderson's autobiography, *My Lord What a Morning,* in a Tamil translation as *The Cooing Cuckoo.* All of this reminds me that a very high recommendation should be made for *Jazzforschung,* a serious annual issued by Universal Edition and the Hochschule für

Musik und Darstellende Kunst in Graz, Austria. Not all of the articles are in German, but I can foresee language requirements getting built into jazz history curricula when this subject is finally regarded as "legitimate." I do hope we will all support the various journals for Black music, not just *Down Beat* (that grand old patriarch), so they will not fall by the wayside.

UNDINE MOORE: Many of you know that Altona Johns, author of *Songs of the Deep South* and one of the early researchers in our music, is with me at Virginia State College. Our Black music project there, funded by the National Endowment for the Humanities, includes videotaping the many concerts we have sponsored—jazz, gospel, spirituals, so-called "serious" music—and we have permission to make these tapes available to interested persons without charge. These tapes are not professionally prepared and some might need editing, but I personally think there is a charm in them because they are not so slick.

MALIN: I'm aware of the interest many of you have shown in Scott Joplin. Marks has published an anthology of rags, *Giants of Ragtime,* edited by Max Morath, will includes some works of Joplin not previously available.[2]

DE LERMA: The reconstruction of Joplin's *Treemonisha* by T.J. Anderson should be commercially available before long also. Am I right, TJ?

ANDERSON: Yes. I think it will be issued through Composers Facsimile Edition.

DE LERMA: . . . Which has issued all of your works thus far.

ANDERSON: But Vera Lawrence is publishing the complete works of Joplin, excepting three works which were withheld by the copyright owner.

DE LERMA: Yes, I think all of us interested in Black music are looking forward to that publication. It is being issued through the New York Public Library, by the way.

QUESTION: Could we have the address for the Society of Black Composers?

DE LERMA: It is 148 Columbus Avenue, New York 10023.

---

[2] This collection was issued in 1971.

16. Field Work in African Music

John Blacking

● The news that Professor Blacking would be in the United
States came from Charles Adams, who dropped by to see me
after two years of research in Lesotho. I brought this to the
attention of Dr. Alan Merriam, Chairman of the Department of
Anthropology at Indiana University, who expressed the wish
that we might be able to bring Professor Blacking to Bloomington
from Western Michigan University, where the British ethnomusicologist was serving for the year. With the cooperation
of Indiana University's African Studies Program, the campus
benefitted from a short visit by this young, vital, and distinguished scholar.

His initial comments convinced me that Professor Blacking
had a profound grasp of the meaning of music, both on its own
terms and with respect to the society which produced it, regardless
of the culture or the traditions involved. We were all so stimulated by his warm insight that it became mandatory to impose
on him once more, so that he could share his ideas with the
seminar registrants only weeks before returning to his continuous
post as Head of the Department of Social Anthropology at Queen's
University in Belfast.

He is one of the world's leading ethnomusicologists and
specialists in African music. Originally trained in traditional
Western music, a repertoire he has not surrendered, he has
dedicated his life in search of the real meaning of music to
people. Until being "awarded" an exit visa from the Union of
South Africa, his time was spent in extensive research into the
music of the Black Africans, particularly that of the Venda.
His published research has provided essential factual and
philosophic material for all persons interested in this literature.

The Black Music Center is proud to have Professor Blacking
as a member of its Honorary Advisory Committee.

I shall discuss some of the techniques which I used to study music in
Africa between 1954 and 1969. These techniques varied according
to the aims and context of the research. Whether or not it is stated or
even recognized, some kind of theoretical outlook directs the course of
field research, so I will discuss the techniques and experiences in relation

to three different objectives, each of which implies a distinct theoretical orientation:

1. The collection of musical samples from different regions, together with documentation related to the recordings. This has been admirably done by Hugh Tracey and Charles Duvelle in particular, and apart from the aesthetic pleasure to be derived from the variety of sounds and styles, it provides a useful basis for subsequent, more intensive research. Even when the documentation is good, I question the reliability or value of any analysis of African music which is based solely on recordings collected in this way. I reject an analysis which is derived from the sound of the music on record, without reference to techniques of performance and the accompanying social situation.

2. The intensive study of a musical tradition, or a number of related musical traditions within a homogeneous area, with special reference to the function of music as an aspect of the behavior of man in society. This is the kind of approach with which I began my fieldwork among the Venda of the Northern Transvaal, and it is in line with work done by Merriam, Hood, Malm, Garfias, McAllester, Kauffman, Nketia, England, Lois Anderson, and many other musicologists trained in the U.S.A. The results of such fieldwork have been very fruitful and have enabled us to place ethnomusicology on a more scientific basis.

However, there are two consequences of this approach which, in my opinion, render it inadequate. First, when we analyze an African musical style "in its own terms" (to quote Mantle Hood), we are in fact analyzing it in the terms of the culture of which it is a part. We cannot regard an African musical system as an "action autonomous" (to quote S.F. Nadel), and I suspect we cannot analyze any musical system this way. Secondly, if we analyze a musical style in terms of its musical rules—without revealing the extramusical processes which generate the music, comparisons with other styles may be automatically irrelevant and invalid. We cannot compare two musical styles which sound the same if the processes which generate the sounds are entirely different. On the other hand, we can compare two musical styles which sound different, if we find that the processes which generate them are similar.

I believe that these inadequacies can be overcome by a more comprehensive approach which treats the analysis of music as part of the analysis of a cultural and social system. This is really the logical consequence of the methodological approach advocated by Merriam in *The Anthropology of Music*,[1] which thus leads us to the third orientation.

---

[1] Evanston: Northwestern University Press, 1964.

3. The intensive study of a musical tradition as a system of musical cognitive and social processes which in turn are part of, or are related to, the social and cultural system of the maker of music. I do not propose to argue the case for this kind of theoretical approach, as I have done so in a number of publications. I shall consider only how it affects the style of fieldwork and the collection of data for analysis.

The task of the fieldworker can be summed up as follows: He must record not only the sounds of the music and the ways in which they are produced, and glossaries of musical terms and details of instrument making, but also the precise contexts of the situations in which music is performed and the responses of performers and listeners, the structures of social and cultural activities, and correspondences between tonal relationships and relationships that are expressed in other fields of social life. In other words, he must live with the people whose music he is studying for at least a year, he must especially be able to communicate in their language, he must participate in non-musical as well as musical activities so that he can appreciate the role of music in the general context of social life, and he must be looking all of the time for patterns of thought or of social interaction that seem to be related to the patterns of music which he hears and performs. The deeper processes which generate the surface structures of music will be revealed only by a degree of total participation and rigorous documentation which involves much more than a collection of documented videotapes, films, and tape recordings.

Obviously a person who has been born and brought up in a country has a certain advantage in studying its music, assuming that he has some training and theoretical orientation. On the other hand, he may have the disadvantage of being so used to his own music that he fails to see the significance of important features which may be more quickly appreciated by a stranger. Thus, although I hope more and more Africans will devote their time to studying and analyzing their own music,[2] I hope that African governments and universities will recognize that European, Asian, and American ethnomusicologists can make useful contributions.

In particular, Black scholars in America would do well to turn their attention to the deep structures of early Black music and of the music in those parts of Africa that were their ancestral homes. My own ex-

---

[2] John Blacking has written tersely and forcefully against *Apartheid* in "The Current State of Anthropological Research in the Transvaal", which was published in *A.S.A.U.K. Proceedings* (September 1969), pp. 77–78. This appeared shortly before he left his post with the University of the Witwatersrand.

perience of music in east, central, and southern Africa convinces me
that there has been a continuous, unbroken tradition of music making
by Black Americans, even in those areas where music was supposed
to have been banned, and that there is much more of African music
systems in, say, the spirituals than their surface sounds at first suggest.
I have heard and read a number of arguments in favor of the African
origins of Black American music which are probably right in theory,
but regrettably wrong in their supporting evidence. That is, some of the
features which are said to be African are derived from superficial
accounts of African music, while truly African features are ignored. For
instance, I have heard "*all* African music" described by a Black-American lecturer as being pentatonic—which it decidedly is not—and *Nobody Knows the Trouble I've Seen* as being in "typically African 2/4
time." Even if White publishers have written out *Nobody Knows* in
2/4 meter, its basic rhythm is the much more typically $3+3+2$.
Again, I have heard Black Americans stress the rhythmic element in
African and Black-American music and go so far as to say "harmony
and melody they knew nothing about," although Richard Waterman
contested this theory as long ago as 1952.[3] For what it is worth, after
fifteen years' exposure to African music, I find the rhythms of the
spirituals the least African characteristic about them, and their harmony
and melody the most African! I am sure that further research will
reveal much closer and much more significant correspondence between
Black-American music and African music than has yet been observed,
but we shall not get far until we start doing intensive fieldwork, in
America and in Africa, and rise above the level of facile and often
inaccurate sloganizing.

Having stated these theoretical premises, I will turn to some of the
practical issues of fieldwork in Africa. I am very conscious of the
inadequacy of my own fieldwork, and I therefore consider my work to
be the very minimum that can be allowed if we are to achieve the
level of description required by the third approach which I outlined.

I neared this intensity of study only during my twenty-two months
in Vendaland between May 1956 and December 1958. Combining the
experience of my training in anthropology and music, I noted the social,
economic, and political relationships between performers with as much
care as I recorded and analyzed the successive patterns of music which
they produced. Thus, in attending the sixty daily rehearsals of a girls'
dance, I observed how kinship affected the development of musical

---

[3] "African Influence on the Music of the Americas" in *Acculturation in the
Americas,* ed. Sol Tax (Chicago: University of Chicago Press, 1952).

ability, and how the changing patterns of music reflected changes in the social situation. Again, I could never have explained the musical and choreographic form of the *domba* initiation dance if I had not spent many hours with masters of initiation discussing the symbolism and the function of the rites: The masters are fine musicians, but like many creative artists, they cannot explain the form of what they do. It is only when musical and extramusical facts are brought together that the logic of the musical system becomes apparent.

Even though this kind of intensive study is ideal (and I consider that every ethnomusicologist ought to undertake it at some time of his life, like a rite of passage), it is possible to produce adequate accounts of musical styles after shorter passages in the field—provided that one works in close cooperation with someone who has detailed cultural knowledge of the area. (I suspect that this kind of fieldwork may only be possible after the experience of a long period in the field elsewhere, but I do not wish to generalize dogmatically from my own experience.)

In August of 1957, I spent a month sampling the music of the Gwembe Tonga before they were moved out of the Kariba Valley. In this exercise I was able to draw on the knowledge of anthropologists who were working in the same area, as well as Hugh Tracey's collection of recordings and his and Elisabeth Colson's information about different kinds of music recognized by the Tonga. I was thus able to ask for specific types of music with the foreknowledge of the social and cultural background, and I was able to concentrate on what were said to be more important aspects of the music.

In August of 1961, I collected about twice the amount of information in half the time when I studied Nsenga music in collaboration with Raymond Apthorpe, who had already done several months' anthropological fieldwork in the Petauke district of Zambia, and with the two Nsenga students who were working with him. Before I set foot in the field, I was able to study an extensive glossary of Nsenga musical terms, together with an almost complete paradigm of Nsenga musical styles, the titles of several songs, information about musical instruments, and so on. Without this preparation and cooperation, it might have taken me as long as six months to collect the information, photographs, and recordings I accumulated in two weeks of very concentrated work. I was also greatly helped, as in my work among the Gwembe Tonga, by my experience of fieldwork with the Venda and by the fact that I was able to understand some Nsenga and they some Venda, though neither could speak the other's language.

In the last quarter of 1965, I had the privilege of teaching a course in African music at Makerere University in Kampala. Although the main purpose of this operation was to train Ugandans to study their own music, I was able to learn much about the different styles of music by the teaching method I adopted. Members of the class who came from, or knew something about, different parts of Uganda were set the task of preparing notes and paradigms on the music of those areas, and then of planning a study tour which would enable us to record a representative sample of the music. In this way we learned much about a wide range of music in a very short period of time and were able to identify a number of general principles of musical structure and relate them to the different cultural systems. We also formed a clearer idea of the directions in which further research might go.

In addition to these four different kinds of research experiences, I was involved for ten years in various aspects of the musical life of Africans who lived in Johannesburg and its environs, and I participated in recording tours of Zululand and Mozambique in 1955. I shall not discuss these experiences because they do not add anything essentially new to what I have already said.

I have deliberately outlined four different kinds of fieldwork which I have undertaken because, although I am convinced that no study of African music can begin to be adequate unless it is accompanied by a detailed knowledge of the language and the social and cognitive processes involved in other features of the culture, I would not insist that studies should be carried out by only one person. I am sure that adequate studies of musical traditions can be achieved by close cooperation between anthropologists, ethnomusicologists, experts in choreography, linguists, and above all, local teachers who have an interest in their own music and regular contacts with students from many different regions. It should be possible for an ethnomusicologist to produce a cultural analysis of a musical tradition, even if he lacks the time or inclination to learn the language and live for an extended period in Africa. It will only be possible as long as he realizes just how little he will learn from the sound of the music alone, and how he must take into consideration extramusical factors which at first may appear to have nothing to do with the organization of the music.

This said, we must now consider one form of cooperation which no ethnomusicologist can avoid, even if he wishes to work away from anthropologists and linguists in the most remote area he can find. Without the cooperation of the people whose music he is studying and without good rapport with those who know most about music, he will achieve nothing that is of any more than superficial interest—no matter how many yards of film or miles of magnetic tape he brings back from the field.

This should not be a difficult task for one who loves music, respects *all* musicians, and is anxious to learn from them, and is not in a hurry to force his plans on others. A successful fieldworker does not have to be the life and soul of the party, a regular guy or gal trained in the techniques of Dale Carnegie or Emily Post. He/she does not have to make an impression on people and advertise the joys of the American or European way of life, nor need a fieldworker apologize for being a foreigner. In fact, in those parts of Africa where I worked, I found that people were rather suspicious of those who were too anxious to please or went out of their way to criticize their own society. This was generally considered to be an unnecessary and abnormal posture. What is required above all is a genuine interest, human compassion and concern, a desire to learn, and a willingness to *listen*.

There are occasions when one's desire to learn may cause some embarrassment, however, or one's willingness to listen may cost some money. For example, after several months' study of Venda girls' initiation schools, I was invited to attend the final rituals of *Tshikanda* in an area where I was not known by the old ladies in charge. They had no objection to my recording the music by putting the microphone through the wall of the initiation hut, and so I sat outside in the cool air of a summer's night, following the sound of the proceedings. Some time after midnight, the old lady in charge came out and expressed surprise that I was still around. "Aren't you going?" she asked. "No," I replied, "I'm enjoying the music. She complained that it was hot inside. "Why not come outside then?" "We cannot while you and your friend are here. Men are not supposed to see what we do." "Oh, I'm sorry about that. However, you did say that we could listen to the music as long as we stayed outside." We did not move, and so the initiation continued inside. The same conversation ensued later on, and eventually they all moved into the courtyard, and I was allowed to take photographs and make recordings through the night and into the next day. On another occasion I returned to the village with copies of the photographs, and the old ladies invited me to make more recordings and volunteered information about the meaning of the songs.

All music of importance has its price, and if a field worker becomes a participating member of a society, he cannot expect to be immune from certain obligations. He must be a giver as well as a receiver; he must become part of the system of reciprocal gift exchange. He must also recognize that people have work to do, whether it be in food production or in social and ritual obligations. To take their time may be depriving them of certain economic benefits, and therefore they should be correspondingly compensated. There are also certain types of information which are, as it were, copyrighted. These must be bought, even from the son or nephew of the man who "owns" them. A fieldworker must not think that his desire to "groove" with the local people absolves him from these obligations.

Assuming that rapport has been well established and the fieldworker has copious information on the "folk view" of the musical tradition (i.e., systematic lists of different categories of music recognized and musical terminology used), he must then concentrate on the main task of recording musical activity in such a way that he can discover the principles which generate it and their relationship to other social activities and cultural forms.

Without doubt, the first and most useful step in this direction is to start singing and playing the music, and to invite criticism of one's performance. I didn't have to wait! The Venda, the Gwembe Tonga, and the Nsenga never hesitated to tell me when I was wrong. They were not always able to tell me exactly why I was wrong, but I persevered until I found out, and in doing so I usually learned something important about fundamental musical principles.

When I first learned to sing a particular Venda children's song,[4] the Venda told me that I was doing well, but that I sang it like a Tsonga, who were their neighbors to the south. I sang all the word-phrases to the melody of the first, and I thought that my fault lay in the pitch of my intervals. When I eventually realized that the melody should vary, they accepted my performance as truly Venda even if I deliberately sang out of tune. I therefore learned that the pattern of intervals is considered more important than their exact pitch because, in certain parts of a melody, they are expected to reflect changes in speech-tone.

On another occasion I was playing one of the drums during a Venda possession dance (*ngoma daz midzimu*). Dancers come into the "arena" in turn, and at first there were no complaints about my efforts. Very soon, however, a senior lady began dancing, and she was expected to go into a trance because the dance was being held by her cult group. After a few minutes she stopped and insisted that another drummer should replace me! She claimed that I was ruining the effect

---

4 No. 38B in *Venda Children's Songs* (Johannesburg: Witwatersrand University Press, 1967).

of the music by "hurrying" the tempo. Thus I learned that a metro-nomic tempo is required for the *ngoma* music.

In 1957, when I was learning the drum rhythms of the Gwembe Tonga *Mankuntu* dance, I was able to bring in the second drum part correctly when we played with sticks on a table but, as soon as we transferred to drums, I was told I was wrong. I discovered that the correct drum tone was as important as the correct rhythm. The iambic meter could be played *tibwi-tibwi-tibwi* or *gwitang-gwitang-gwitang,* and one or the other was selected according to the style of the music.

Again, by cutting and tuning reed pipes, I learned that they were made from smallest to largest, and tuned adjacently down the scale, and that the final tuning was not possible until a group of people played them and adjusted or threw out those pipes which were out of tune, the "mad ones" (*mavhavhi*).

Performance can never be an end in itself if one is making a serious study of the music: It is a means to the end of understanding the music better. Also it is not the only way of sharing a musical experience. Critical listening is of no less importance and is, in many respects, the chief means of perpetuating a musical tradition. Performers are not necessarily the most musical of people. In Venda society, men of the ruling clans tend to stop performing as they take a more active part in public affairs, but they do not lose interest in music or the ability to listen and comment critically. If the purpose of fieldwork is not to study the music of a single instrument or group of instruments, but to discover the principles of a musical system, only a limited amount of time can be spent on performance, enough to get the feel of the music and the problems involved in playing it, to elicit constructive responses from one's teachers and critics, and to have discussions with those who are experts.

Moreover, performance is no substitute for detailed documentation, though it may be an asset in the process of transcription and analysis. After I had made recordings of Nsenga kalimba music and had taken detailed notes on different instruments, I found it helpful to check my transcriptions by playing each tune (badly!) on the instruments I brought home with me. But after I had spent some three and a half hours performing different melodies and dance steps of the Venda pentatonic reed-pipe music and had earned the approval of my fellow performers, I found that I could not note down a single melody or dance step out of the context of the total situation. Now this may simply be an indication of my own musical incompetence (although a Venda musician kindly asked why anyone should be expected to remember music out of context), but at least it warned me always to reinforce my performing experience with different kinds of documentation. I made analytical recordings: in which the microphone was placed close to the different "parts" of the music, such as each drum in turn; in which a xylophone or mbira player, for example, played left- and right-hand/thumb melodies separately as well as together; in which variations in music were accompanied by notes on accompanying variations in the social situation. With a stereo recorder, such notes could be given on the tape with the second microphone. I also made synchronized films which enabled physical movement to be related exactly to sound production, and rough transcriptions in the field, which could be checked back later or on the spot with musicians.

It is important not to interrupt or interfere with a live performance, especially if it is in the context of the correct social situation. If a fieldworker imposes himself on the social event, he may get a "concert performance" rather than the real thing—not because people are irritated or wish to dissemble, but because they are polite and give him what they think he wants. In the context of the situation, without his presence, they might do otherwise. For example, when I asked Venda for the songs which they use to take a girl from her home to the puberty school, they sang the song as requested but, in the context of the school and in the middle of the night, the song was preceded by sounds which are an integral part of the song, but which they had presumed would not interest me.[5]

Analytical recordings and detailed notes, which are essential for analysis, can sometimes be taken during the course of live performances, but more often they must be done afterwards. Playing back recordings and even showing films (if you can get a generator) are important aspects of the cooperative relationship which should exist between a fieldworker and the people whose music he studies. It also gives him a chance to ask questions about the songs and events, to note and check the words of songs, and to inquire about individual and regional variations. This can be corroborated by further recordings or the same song by the same person, by different people in the same area, and by different people in another area. All this kind of information is necessary if we are to discover the principles and rules which apply to musical creation in a society, and what tolerances are allowed. The Venda are quite clear in their own minds about what music is, or what could be, Venda or not. Their judgments are made possible

---

[5] Blacking, John, "Tonal Organization in the Music of Two Venda Initiation Schools" in *Ethnomusicology* [Middleton] 14 (January 1970): 30, song no. 1.

by their experience of Venda society and culture. They have acquired various systems of behavior, of which some are peculiar to music but many are common to several aspects of Venda life. They are able to recognize what is or is not characteristically Venda about musical behavior, but they are not always able to express their reasons for these judgments. It is the task of the musicologist to discover the system by which the Venda, or any other people, are able to make such judgments.

I found it helpful to devise tests in the field by which I might learn more about the Venda system of music. Incidentally, I consider tests of musical ability which have been devised in Europe and America to be irrelevant in the study of African music. I am even doubtful of their relevance in European and American societies! Tests of musical expectancy could be devised for the Venda, provided it is realized that the rules of the system are often extramusical, as in the influence of speech-tone patterns on melody.

For instance, I wanted to find out how Venda children perceived the meter and the "key" of their children's songs, so I set them to the task of clapping to several different songs which are normally sung without clapping, and I asked them to sing songs in sequence or in relation to a given tone so that I could note on which pitch they began the melody.[6] Later, in order to find out about harmonic and tonal preferences, I asked some youths to make several different ocarinas whose size determines different ranges of tones, although their exact pitch can be altered by the position of the mouth. They played special ocarina duets on different pairs of instruments, and their selection of the most suitable pair gave me an idea of their musical preference.

What I should have studied in much greater detail was the development of musical consciousness in Venda society—not simply children's growing responses to music as involvement in the social situations in which it is performed, but also the growth of their awareness of pattern in the sounds that reach their ears. Until a year or so ago, I considered that the growth of musical ability was chiefly a matter of learning certain patterns of behavior in a favorable social and cultural environment. I am no longer sure that music making is essentially a matter of learning techniques. I believe that it may depend on the realization of certain species-specific cognitive, perceptual, and motor processes in the context of a favorable social environment.

The crucial factors to investigate are how much musical behavior a person learns in his society and how much he discovered in himself

---

[6] *Venda Children's Songs,* pp. 157–165, 168, 171.

with the help of his society; and to what extent structured listening is an ability which develops with aural perception as a result of experiences of a structure in society, or a capacity for structuring experience which is a part of man's biological nature. The Venda are one of many African peoples who declare that all normal men are born musical and that it is absurd to talk of some people being unmusical. Perhaps they are right. At any rate, detailed study of musical behavior in these musical societies, and especially of the processes of learning music, may bring us more than a knowledge of many new, exciting styles of music. They may reveal crucial new information about the nature of man.

QUESTION: How strong a relationship do you see between African music and Afro-American music?

BLACKING: I can't pose as an authority on the music of Blacks in this country, but there are a few points which suggest basic relationships. First, African music is always creative, always new, always changing. All oral music is. Music changes with social situations. I'm talking here of surface structures, what we hear with our ears. It is true that, if there has not been an initiation ceremony in five years, the people will get together and work for two or three weeks before they can sing the music to their satisfaction, but this is like language. Every sentence we speak is absolutely new, but the principles on which the sentences are constructed are old. On the surface, there is constant re-creation.

I'm suggesting there are basic principles of music making within a society. These cognitive and social processes were brought from Africa, and in a new environment they gave rise to new sounds, but the underlying processes remain. There is a limited number of musical processes in the world (theme and variation, inversion, retrograde inversion, etc.), and it is the combination of these processes which are unique to different cultures. The basic principles on which these processes are organized are universal to all men. The processes used in British music for the last five hundred years, as an example, are to other human beings, to new social situations and, all the time, creates new sounds out of the same processes. That's a general theory.

I would like to see American musicologists working with Black-American music. From what I have heard during my visits to this country and from what I know of African music, I am personally convinced that the parallels in structure are very profound and are rooted in a common social organization.

I came to America as a stranger, and I found American culture very different and almost incomprehensible. In a sense, I found it a single culture; in other respects I note differences. One of my students in Kalamazoo was from Detroit. I was talking about Venda attitudes to age and old people, and I complained that American and British societies were careless about their old people. This student said to me, "Yes, that's the problem with White people generally: they don't care about their old people." He expanded the point to illustrate the kinds of relationships between older and younger people within Black-American society. This ties in with what I've heard and observed, and reinforces my theory that the processes remain the same while the surface structure changes.

The idea, for example, that African music has not changed in a century is nonsense. Within the two years I was with the Venda, I saw change—but I'm speaking of surface change. There is a common view in Africa among some Whites that the Venda have copied the Western music to which they have been exposed. If you examine the structure of the new Venda music, you will see this is not true. On the surface they have accepted what they wished and rejected what they did not like, but the new music is rooted in the African political system and the society. It might sound a bit like Western music to an undiscerning ear, but it isn't. It has a different principle of chord sequence, of harmonic treatment. It is basically and totally African.

In answering your question, I know I'm posing many more, but I can't give you any answers about Black America. I think you need to investigate how this enormous creativity from African roots fared when it reached American soil and social conditions. Has it really changed, or has it remained basically the same? I have no answers.

QUESTION: How much unity is there in African music?

BLACKING: The idea is that one person on his own has some value, but two people equal more than two people when they come together. This relates to African socialism, which is found all over the continent (but for South Africa). The Venda say that man becomes human when he associates with other men. This can be demonstrated in music. With one man, you have a single beat. The Venda would consider it ridiculous to have two people playing the same beat. That is individuality in community. Each man must maintain his individuality, but something greater than the sum of two parts can be secured through the union of two people.

If you consider the principles found in medieval Western music, in Indian music, and in Japanese music, for example, you find they tend to go with an idea about the role of the individual within a community. Such ideas are very widespread and are pretty fundamental to most philosophies. They are clearly realized in the structure of many African societies. There is the special concept of chiefmanship in Africa, but this is a first among equals, not a leader giving orders to followers.

The unity of the cognative processes means that all men's minds work essentially in the same way. When you have similar minds applying themselves to similar social situations you have a tendency toward similar structures.

● I feel a bit shallow in my appreciation for Mahalia Jackson, William Grant Still, Scott Joplin, and Claudio Monteverdi after hearing John Blacking speak about music. His perspective is broadly based, and he is one of those extraordinary persons who, I suspect, is close to knowing what music is. All I know are some of the tunes.

One particular point should be considered by all persons engaged in Black music research: individuality within community. We have had people digging through early Western music manuscripts in the hope of finding new statistical data which might prove of value to other specialists, and I am not complaining about this. What we have in the area of Black music, however, is a wealth of immediately important information which is desperately needed by educators on all levels, by performers, by scholars, and by society. Duplication of efforts, money, and time is senseless, and procrastination or a rejection of community interests is an unfortunate position.

In order to care for these lacunae, the need of special skills is of great importance. For areas of interpretive sensibility, the researcher should no doubt have empirical knowledge of the Black experience. Under any circumstances, the research must know the techniques of musicological and statistical research and should have far more than the usual concept of bibliographic and classification methods. If it is the responsibility of a graduate school to develop a program which will train such personnel, the curriculum will have to include relatively in-depth studies in Western music, in ethnomusicology, and in folklore, sociology, and linguistics. However ideal such a curriculum might be (particularly with more refinements than presently recommended), it would be quite difficult to find this network of interdisciplinary studies on any campus, and probably very expensive to initiate and staff. In the end we must know that no degree program has fully given its registrants all of the essentials. Formal education can only provide a basic stimulus; the development of individual talents and the compensation for informational and technical shortcomings remains the responsibility of the ambitious and dedicated scholar. We cannot wait for all conditions to be perfect. We cannot always hold off until we have enough time and financial or moral support to move toward some solution, but we must know whatever potentials we might individually have and whatever shortcomings might exist in our experiences so that our projects can benefit from the expenditures to the maximum.

If we lack a massive grant for a staff of ethnologists, we can still take tape recorders to church and document what is happening now. We can interview older people (professional musicians or not) and search for facts and ideas of at least some importance in local history. We can support the publishers of scores, books, and recordings who have given attention to Black music and put these materials to use. For these things you don't need a Ph.D. Once something of value has been captured, it might be published or—if the work has not progressed to that stage—it can be deposited with a local public or university library, or with the Black Music Center, so that others might benefit from these energies and perhaps extend the implications of the tentative results.

What Professor Blacking has done (and the spirit in which the work was accomplished) should prove a model for those of us who may approach a local topic for investigation and understanding, within the perspectives of broad musical and social realities.

17. Conclusion

I titled the final chapter of *Black Music in Our Culture* "Forward" for several reasons. There is perhaps a nostalgic parallel to be reflected now, but it is not my farewell to that commitment which I built into the concept of the Black Music Center. I hope those goals can be retained in high priority during the Center's future, refined by the insights of subsequent administrations and facilitated by the opening of new channels for financial and moral support.

I designed the concept of the Center in 1968 and voluntarily accepted the implicit duties and responsibilities as a superimposition on my contractual responsibilities to direct one of the nation's largest music libraries and to teach those courses assigned me. It was not an imposition, except in the area of schedule. A few non-Blacks began to think of me as a specialist in Black music, but that is a status I could never hope to reach, and it was essential that I never place myself in more than a supportive role. A few non-Black academics gently viewed me as a turncoat musicologist and librarian, "suddenly" afflicted with monomaniacal tendencies for relevancies and vogues. One kind soul (who admitted his profound work with European masterpieces had made him a racist, and I joked that I was one also, for the same reasons) pleaded with me to spend my energies in something "sensible." Some who met me recently find it surprising that I gave the world première of Bellini's oboe concerto under Newell Jenkins, or that I have worked with such other conductors as Serge Koussevitsky, Leopold Stokowski, Heitor Villa-Lobos, Carlos Chávez, or Sir Thomas Beecham, or that I have published more than eighty books and articles on *non*-Black topics. There have been a few Blacks who initially resented my interest in their culture (and I'd like to think that those who explored the nature of my work qualified their surface reservations), but I knew I was obligated to do what I felt *had* to be done as long as I could accomplish something within my various areas of limitations. This is not a conclusion then; it is a foreword through synthesis to stimulate the second quarter century of my professional life. It also is not a resignation from the publications of resource and research materials specifically on Afro-American music, as the future will prove reasonably soon.

One phase of this activity developed very quickly during the final weeks of 1972. Paul Freeman, Conductor-in-Residence of the Detroit Symphony Orchestra, came to see me about our mutual interest in the development of recordings of music by Black composers. In the course of our animated conversation, I showed him some work of Saint-Georges which I had secured while in Paris in 1969. He was deeply impressed with the charm of this music and began plans to include several of the works in his schedule. We went to the Irwin-Sweeney-Miller Foundation, which had supported Dr. Freeman's telecast that year of music by Black orchestral composers and had twice funded my projects with the Black Music Center. We found great interest in the concept, and the Foundation subsequently awarded a grant via the Afro-American Music Opportunities Association for the initiation of a series of such recordings. Dr. Freeman accepted my reconstruction of Saint-Georges' first violin concerto, first string quartet, and an aria from *Ernestine* to be included on the first disc. The scores for these works will be issued by Southern Music Publishing Company in New York. My enthusiasm for the music of Saint-Georges quickly began to occupy much of my free time, and it now appears that his complete works and a thematic catalog may be forthcoming.

For a short time, I considered accepting the offer of a publisher who wished me to prepare a text on Afro-American music for use in the high schools. The most determining factor in my decision not to accept the contract was my acknowledgement that a high school student who had lived in the world of soul music and jazz was potentially in a far better position than I to treat these core areas, but—with respect to concert music—it also entered my mind that students at this level need recordings for musical illustration of any historical facts. Whereas graduate students may be expected to work from scores (and I'm not suggesting that there is an abundance of symphonic or chamber music by Blacks which has been published), the less technically trained must have the sounds presented to them. I was aware that the appendices in *Black Music in Our Culture* were not complete discographical listings and that any earlier work was dated. For acquisitional purposes, I felt we needed a checklist which would survey the entire history of recorded Black music including the forthcoming Turnabout issue of the *Tolson Variations* of T. J. Anderson, and certainly including the Hall Johnson and Harry Burleigh spirituals sung by Eugene Holmes and the Lawrence Brown spirituals recorded by Paul Robeson. That discography is now en route.

Such a project indicates the kind of documentation—really not evaluative—which I felt essential for the Center's work, but it was not just a matter of racial considerations which obligated objectivity. Comprehensive studies designed to care for remedial needs and planned to be flexible enough to satisfy a network of variant interests demand objectivity. Surely all librarians know this premise, even if value judgments, budgets, and local considerations force subsequent considerations. Those factors, however, are antithetic to the concept of the Center's work.

The question of what Black music really is has been raised often. Ardent Blacks will respond that it is that music which is of Black people —the ethnic music of gospel, blues, and soul. When Whites ask the question, the academic types are seeking statistically supported accounts of style, although they might join with others in wondering how it could be possible to consider music by cultural subdivisions (unless speaking of French songs, German symphonies, or Italian operas).

The Black Music Center, even before it formally existed, opted for no *a priori* conclusions. We thus left the door open for the possibility that the composer of a jazz tune and the creator of a string quartet might have something in common, and that music from twentieth-century Africa might share a source with eighteenth-century Brazilian music. We thus said, and still maintain, that Black music is that music which is produced by groups or individuals who are Black. This has remained our *pro tempore* basis.

Furthermore, our work has not been directed only to the composer or arranger. The need for the Center is also sociological, and we suspect not too naively that the problems a composer has in getting his works recognized might relate to the concert pianist who cannot secure a suitable number of bookings, or to the jazzman (well known or not) who seeks a university post or more than occasional gigs. The respect for the performer is further justified by the fact that performance of Black music is not always distinct from the composition of it.

The next question is much harder to answer: What is Black? There is certainly little difficulty in such an identification if the person speaks ghetto and sings blues, if his skin is dark. White America has already established definitions of Blacks and has liberally included those with only one drop of Black blood. In doing this, they have been forced to include their own progeny many times. If it is a matter of skin color, there is no trouble about including most who embrace the culture. And we know they don't all speak ghetto. I have heard Blacks in London with Oxford accents, Blacks in Paris whose French is beautiful, and Blacks in the Caribbean who might say, "Mahn, I love to beat de pahn."

If the definition cannot be restricted by one kind of speech, by skin or hair, what are its limits? The more non-Black in one's veins makes one less Black? Doubtful. If we find someone (and we can) whose ancestry includes Irish, Spanish, and Indian blood, could the music of that person be cited within an Irish Music Center, a Spanish Music Center, and an Indian Music Center? If we find a person without any African ancestry who is darker than a major Black leader, how might this affect our definition?

Perhaps it is a matter of culture, then. If you can really sing the blues, e.g. you are Black. That won't work. It ignores acculturation, such as is manifest in the neo-Delta singer, John Hammond, Jr. It would also sidestep Louise Parker, who can sing German art songs as wonderfully as any German contralto.

The result of this quandry could put us in the state of nondecision, but we are suggesting that the manifestations of the culture are to be acknowledged after the work in documentation has been done, thus throwing us back to the sometimes superficial matter of skin color. But we do not measure Blackness this way; we measure it as we were taught to do by the White racists and find few instances of confusion or indecision. Some of us, the fruit of miscegenation, might have identity problems, but that is also part of the story: to be White or Black, to be forced by social and cultural traditions into electing a side. Tolson refers to this. Perhaps wholesale miscegenation is the answer.

I know I've not answered the question. I'm not qualified to do this. But it is a problem which raises itself only once in a while (as in the case of Gottschalk, depending on which authority you last read). This is just part of the story.

Our survey of this music suggests the presence of certain qualities which might be unique, in context, to Black music. These are certainly generalizations, and they are not offered as standards by any means. Perhaps they might serve as points of discussion.

1. Black music often relates directly to social functions. It is a part of life, not a superimposition on it. It is the agent for social *communication,* not just social commentary. Charles Ellison sees this in Coltrane, and it can be found in protest songs, in freedom songs, in work songs, in satirical music.

2. There is a blurred distinction between the audience and the performer, the composer, and arranger, the music and the dance. This is music for everyone. In speaking to Dave Baker's class recently, T. J. Anderson mentioned the extraordinary variety of melodies used for a the same spiritual text, an experience John Work had in his research. He

noted that the Black arranger takes over the *cantus firmus* and creates his own composition. The almost ubiquitous element of improvisation counts for this, no doubt, but it also suggests that roles in Black music are not as neatly assigned to individuals as they are in White-American music (which has become so structured that performers are wedded to the printed page in every detail—if, indeed, an electronic work has not dismissed the performer altogether). In the Black church, it is often impossible to separate the congregation from the choir, and this encourages all the more the element of improvisation.

3. The "blues" scale is one element of a specific technical musical nature. The persistence of this distinct scale in so much of Black music immediately gives harmonic and melodic flavors not found elsewhere: in jazz, in the blues, in the spiritual.

4. Rhythm is not confined to a supportive role. At its most minimal, it is coequal with melody and harmony. Its vitality and emotional range can be easily seen in African music as well as in the drumming of Elvin Jones and in the performances of Charlie Parker or John Coltrane.

5. Singing is the mother tongue, and Black voices often have special characteristics. In imitation or allegiance, instruments in Black hands do not forget the inflections and sonorities of the voice. As the African has talking drums, Louis Armstrong had a talking trumpet.

6. The Black man is at peace with the earth, and he is bound to it. It is not part of his culture to fly from the earth in extended ballet leaps. In his barefeet, he can feel the soil and caress it. In his life style, he can swing with the realities of life (even if he laments them in his blues) because he has not accepted abstractions and idealizations which religious and social dogma have imposed on the White man. There is then an earthiness which produces a special kind of sophistication, of resiliancy, of bouyancy, of naturalness, and this—with his deeply ingrained respect for the oral tradition—has helped to keep the essentials of his age-old culture alive and vital.

7. He has style. He takes pleasure in his individuality, and it is respected. It is not just a matter of economics that stimulates the Black man to dress in other than flannel suits and tuxedos. Conformity and the absence of individual expression have less merit in Black culture. This, as well as White exploitation, accounts for the ability of the Black musician to move on into new ideas, to retain his individuality. This accounts for the lesser degree of inhibition which the Black man feels and for the joy he has in doing his thing his way, no matter if his football talents are less than Gayle Sayers, his musical imagination less than Sun Ra, his oratorical delivery less eloquent than Ralph Abernathy.

8. There is the matter of "inspired intensity," a factor raised by T. J. Anderson several times in *Black Music in Our Culture*. This relates to the fact that, no matter what obstacles are in the way, the Black musician will manage. If he lacks an instrument, he will build one or use materials readily at hand. If he does not understand the principles of fingering, how to hold an instrument, or the idea of embouchure development (these according to traditional approaches), he'll find a way—and may even start a new school. What he has to express will find expression, even without the blessings of academic discipline. And this very frequently relates to several points cited above: to the social function of the music, to the lack of separation between the performer and audience, to the imitation of Black vocal sonorities, to the Black man's unity with the earth, and to the style and freedom of his individuality.

If these elements might have some degree of validity in the academic exercise of defining Black music, they will certainly not be present in all manifestations of Black talent in the same intensity, and they can also be expected to be present in the music of acculturated societies. It should also be evident that these are not totally musical considerations, and they might be found even in non-musical aspects of Black life.

As the documentation of Black music progresses and intuition and hopes are replaced by factual knowledge, aspects of this music can be cited with greater security. I appreciate the fact that T.J. Anderson alluded to this in his final report to the Center's Honorary Advisory Committee on May 2, 1972: "I am convinced that the potentiality of our Center represents one of the most important musical resources in the history of American music." The realization of that potential rests in the extent to which the Center can complete its basic commitments, and in the extent to which its bibliographies and registers are put to use by persons in all walks and levels of musical life and in areas of music-related activities. It is not enough that such materials and research exist; that work is only the initial step.

There is more than one river yet to cross.

Black Elements in European Music:
A Sample Listing

There are moments with Ravel and Gershwin when these two substantial composers might be confused. The fact that both impressionistic and jazz styles are present is manifest. In these instances, we do not say that Gershwin exploited the French (although it has been stated that he exploited Black music). This is not to say that the evidence of influence is never also possibly one of exploitation. There are economic advantages built into imitation if the quality or marketing is superior (by *quality*, I mean in this instance a spirit or direction which is more digestible by a larger or more wealthy public), but real imitations can rarely hope for the aesthetic quality that validates an original creation. It might be said that exploitation is the conscious acceptance of an influence designed to provide the imitator with greater financial benefit than the model secured, or that exploitation is acculturation on an individual basis when the imitator is deliberately seeking to divert profits from the originator. We can thus point the finger to those who "cover" records, i.e. those who copy an arrangement from a recording and release it as their own work, but we cannot deny the right of a composer to set a text from Shakespeare, orchestrate an organ work of Bach, or incorporate a little jazz in his symphony. If ideas of this sort constitute exploitation, virtually every composer and performer today might be found guilty.

There may be some works cited below which could be regarded as exploitations, but that is certainly not true in all cases. The purpose of this listing is not to call attention to possibilities of exploitation, nor is it offered as if to say, "See, even *good* composers have been influenced by Black music." Rather is the suggestion made that the impact of the Black contribution is so strong that even the analyst concerned only with European music must give more than footnote, token acknowledgement to the Afro-American genius. Appendix 3 will indicate the extent to which authors of textbooks have been willing to see these influences on "their" music, if not to examine Black for its own qualities.

This register of works, initially prepared by Professor John A. Taylor, is clearly restrictive. To cite every twentieth-century composition influenced by Black sources would have been a needlessly exhausting task. Professor Taylor based his information largely on that given in the theses of David Baskerville, Ruth Gillum, Eileen Southern,

Mildred Jenkins, Hazel Kinscella, J. Harold Montague, and Clarence Tocus,[1] supplementing the data provided in *Music since 1900* by Nicholas Slonimsky (New York: W. W. Norton, 1937), *The International Cyclopedia of Music and Musicians* edited by Oscar Thompson and others (New York: Dodd, Mead & Co., 1964), and a mimeographed sheet entitled "Some Examples of Black Influence on non-Black Composers of the West" which Undine Moore offered to our 1971 seminar registrants.

It is interesting to note that virtually all of the non-American composers (but for Hindemith) are largely of some degree of impressionistic persuasion. The alliance of impressionists and non-German nationalists against the power of Wagnerian stylistic imperialism opened the door for new harmonic, melodic, and instrumental resources. It also often permitted the composer to look at music as a sensual delight, not always taking itself so seriously, not always offering itself as a philosophic discourse. This attitude, plus the Franco-American associations which grew strongly after the First World War, encouraged the European composer to acknowledge the distinctive attraction of Black-American music—either in jazz or folk music—and to absorb those stylistic elements with which he could identify, even on a superficial basis. To a large extent it must be remembered that the European support for Black music gave many musicians the employment their own country would not, and it gave an *imprimatur* to the merits of the music in the minds of many Americans (Black and White).

In several instances, publication information has been provided for these works when readily available from the holdings of the Indiana University School of Music Library, the New York Public Library, or the Library of Congress. Parenthetical dates indicate the year of composition in a few instances. Persons desiring more historical information may examine the theses previously cited. Those wishing to examine the scores should consult their local library.

---

[1] David Ross Baskerville, *Jazz Influence on Art Music to Mid–century* (Ann Arbor: University Microfilms [65-15,175], 1965; Dissertation, University of California, Los Angeles, 1965), 535pp.; Ruth Helen Gillum, "The Negro Folk Song and Its influence in America" (M.A. Thesis, University of Kansas, 1940), 144pp.; Mildred Leona Jenkins, "The Impact of African Music upon the Western Hemisphere" (M.A. Thesis, Boston University, 1942), 63pp.; Hazel Gertrude Kinscella, "Songs of the American Negro and Their Influence upon Composed Music" (M.A. Thesis Columbia University, 1934), 43pp.; J. Harold Montague, "A Historical Survey of Negro Music and Muscians and Their Influence on Twentieth Century Music" (M.A. Thesis, Syracuse University, 1929), 52pp.; Eileen (Jackson) Southern, "The Use of Negro Folksong in Symphonic Forms" (M.A. Thesis, University of Chicago, 1941), 42pp.; Clarence Spencer Tocus, "The Negro Idiom in American Musical Composition" (M.A. Thesis, University of Southern California, 1942).

Antheil, George 1900–1959
  Jazz Symphony (1925) for chamber orchestra
  Transatlantic (1929), opera
Arnold, Maurice, 1865–1937
  Amerikanische Tänze; American plantation dances, for
    orchestra. Boston: P. L. Jung, 1894.
  Sonata, for violin and piano
Auric, Georges, 1899–
  Adieu, New York, for piano. Paris: Les Editions de la Sirène,
    1920 (also available for orchestra)
  Fox Trot, for orchestra
Bartók, Béla, 1881–1945
  Suite, Op. 14, for piano. London: Boosey & Hawkes, 1939.
Berg, Alban, 1885–1935
  Lula, opera
  Der Wein, for soprano and orchestra
Bennett, Robert Russell, 1894–
  Abraham Lincoln; A Likeness in Symphony Form. New York:
    Harms, 1931.
Bernstein, Leonard, 1918–
  (As only a sampling, mention should be made of *Age of Anxiety,
    On the Town, West Side Story,* and *Mass,* all of which have
    been published by G. Schirmer)
Blatcher, Boris, 1903–
  Fünf Negro Spirituals, for soprano and instrumental ensemble
Blitzstein, Marc, 1905–1964
  The Cradle Will Rock (1936), opera
Bloch, Ernest, 1880–1959
  America; An Epic Rhapsody (1926), for orchestra
Blomdahl, Karl-Birger, 1916–1968
  I speglarnas sal, for chorus and orchestra. London: Schott, 1955.
Braine, Robert, 1896–1940
  Concerto in Jazz (1930), for violin and orchestra
Busch, Carl, 1862–1943
  Negro Carnival, for orchestra
Cadman, Charles Wakefield, 1881–1946
  Dark Dancers of the Mardi Gras, for piano and orchestra.
    New York: Edition Musicus, 1938.
  Trio, op. 56, for piano, violin and cello. Boston: White-Smith
    Music Publishing Co., 1914.
Carpenter, John Alden, 1876–1951
  Concertino, for piano and orchestra. New York: G. Schirmer, 1920.
  Krazy Kat, ballet. New York: G. Schirmer, 1932.
  A Little Bit of Jazz (1925), for orchestra.
  Skyscrapers, ballet. New York: G. Schirmer, 1927.

Casella, Alfredo, 1883–1947
La giara (1924), ballet
A notte alta (1921), for piano and orchestra
Elegia eroica (1916), for orchestra
Paganiniana (1942), for orchestra
Scarlattiana (1926), for piano and orchestra

Cercós, José, fl. 1960
Concerto on a theme from A midsummer night's dream, for 13 instruments
Perpendicular variations on a theme of Webern
Triple string quartet

Chadwick, George Whitefield, 1854–1931
Symphonic Sketches, for orchestra. New York: G. Schirmer, 1907.
Symphony No. 2 in B Flat Major, for orchestra. Boston: A. P. Schmidt, 1888.

Copland, Aaron, 1900–
(Among the many works by Copland should be mentioned the *Concerto for Clarinet and String Orchestra,* the *Concerto for Piano,* the *Dance Symphony, Four Piano Blues, An Immorality, Music for the Theatre, Nocturne* for violin and piano, *Symphony for Organ and Orchestra, Two Piano Blues, Ukelele Serenade* for violin and piano, *Billy the Kid, Lincoln Portrait,* and *Appalachian Spring*)

Cowell, Henry, 1897–1965
Suite, for clarinet and piano

Debussy, Claude, 1862–1918
Le coin des enfants, for piano. Paris: Durand, 1908.
Préludes, book 1, for piano. Paris: Durand, 1910.

Delamarter, Eric, 1880–1953
Symphony No. 2, after Walt Whitman (1926), for orchestra

Delannoy, Marcel, 1898–1962
Le fou de la dame, opera. Paris: Heugel, 1930.

Delius, Frederick, 1862–1934
Appalachia, for chorus and orchestra. London: Hawkes & Son, 1951.
Overture on Negro Themes, for orchestra. New York: J. Fisher & Bro., 1925.

Dvořák, Antonín, 1941–1904
Quartet for Strings, Op. 96, F. Major
Quintet for Strings, Op. 97, E Flat Major
Symphony No. 9, Op. 95, E Minor ("From the New World")

Foss, Lukas, 1922–
Concerto for Improvising Solo Instruments and Orchestra

Gershwin, George, 1898–1937
  An American in Paris, for orchestra. New York: Harms, 1930.
  Concerto for Piano. New York: Harms, 1942.
  Porgy and Bess, opera. New York: Gershwin Publishing Co.,
    1935.
  Rhapsody in Blue, for piano & orchestra. New York: Harms, 1942.
Gilbert, Henry Franklin Belknap, 1868–1928
  Americanesque, for orchestra (1903).
  Comedy Overture on Negro Themes, for orchestra. London:
    Novello, 1912.
  The Dance in the Place Congo, for orchestra. New York: H. W.
    Gray, 1922.
  Humoresque on Negro Minstrel Tunes, for orchestra.
  Negro Dances, for piano. New York: H. W. Gray, 1914.
  Negro Episode, for piano. Newton Center: Wa-Wan Press, 1902.
  Negro Rhapsody, for orchestra. London: Novello 1915.
  Three American Dances, for piano. Boston: Boston Music Co.,
    1919.
  Two Episodes, for orchestra. Boston: The Composer, 1897?
Goldmark, Rubin, 1872–1936
  A Negro Rhapsody, for orchestra. Wien: Universal Edition, 1923.
Gould, Morton, 1913– .
  American Symphonette, No. 1, for orchestra (1933)
  American Symphonette, No. 2, for orchestra (1935)
  Chorale and Fugue in Jazz, for 2 pianos & orchestra (1926)
  Dance Variations, for 2 pianos & orchestra (1953)
  Derivations, for clarinet & band
  Interplay, for piano & orchestra. New York: Mills, 1944.
  Latin-American Symphonette, for orchestra. New York: Mills,
    1947.
  Minstrel show, for orchestra. New York: G & C Music Corpora-
    tion, 1947.
  Rag-blues Rag, for piano. New York: Lawson-Gould, 1963.
  Sonatina, for piano. New York: Mills, 1939.
  Spirituals, for orchestra (1941)
  Suite, for violin & piano (1943)
Grofé, Ferde, 1892–1972
  Broadway at Night, for orchestra (1933)
  Mississippi Suite, for orchestra. New York: L. Feist, 1926.
Gruenberg, Louis Theodore, 1884–1964
  Concerto, for violin & orchestra (1944)
  The Creation, for baritone & instrumental octet (1923)
  Daniel Jazz, for tenor & instrumental octet. Wien: Universal
    Edition, 1925.

Emperor Jones, opera. New York: Cos Cob, 1932.
Jazz Masks, for piano. Wien: Universal Edition, 1931.
Jazzberries, for piano. New York: Universal, 1925.
Jazzettes, for violin & piano. Wien: Universal Edition, 1926.
Sonata no. 1, for violin & piano. New York: Composers Music
    Corporation, 1922.
Sonata no. 2, for violin & piano. Wien: Universal Edition, 1924.
Guion, David Wendel Fentress, 1895–
Shingandi, ballet (1932)
Hill, Edward Burlingame, 1872–1960
Jazz study, for 2 pianos. New York: G. Schirmer, 1924.
Hindemith, Paul, 1895–1963
Kammermusik no. 1, for chamber orchestra. Mainz: Schott, 1949.
Suite op. 26, for piano. London: Schott, 1922.
Symphonic metamorphosis on themes of Carl Maria von Weber,
    for orchestra. New York: Associated Music Publishers, 1945.
Honegger, Arthur, 1892–1955
Concertino, for piano & orchestra. Paris: Maurice Senart, 1925.
Humiston, William Henry, 1869–1923
A southern fantasy, for orchestra. New York: Breitkopf und Härtel,
    1911.
Ives, Charles Edward, 1874–1954
Orchestral set no. 2, for orchestra (1915). New York: Peer,
    196?.
Set for theatre or chamber orchestra (1911). San Francisco: New
    Music, 1932.
Sonata no. 1, for piano. New York: Peer, 1954.
Sonata no. 3, for violin & piano. Bryn Mawr: Theodore Presser,
    1951.
Jelinek, Hanns, 1901–
Symphony, for brass ensemble.
Kern, Kurt
Jazz symphony
Kramer, Arthur Walter, 1890–
Chant nègre, for violin & piano. New York: G. Schirmer, 191?.
Symphonic Rhapsody on Negro Themes, op. 35, in F minor, for
    violin & orchestra. New York: Carl Fischer, 1922.
Two sketches, op. 37a, for orchestra (1916)
Křenek, Ernst, 1900–
Jonny spielt auf, opera. Wien: Universal Edition, 1926.
Kleine Symphonie, for orchestra. Wien: Universal Edition, 1929.
Das Leben des Orest, opera. Wien: Universal Edition, 1929.
Sprung über den Schatten, opera. Wien: Universal Edition, 1923.
Kroeger, Ernest Richard, 1862–
The American Sketches

Lambert, Constant, 1905–1951
  Elegiac Blues, for chamber orchestra or piano (1927)
  The Rio Grande, for chorus, piano & orchestra. London: Oxford
    University Press, 1929.
  Trois pièces nègres
Liebermann, Rolf, 1910–
  Concerto for Jazz Band & Orchestra
MacDowell, Edward, 1861–1908
  Woodland Sketches, op. 51/7 for piano. Boston: A. P. Schmidt,
    191?.
Mason, Daniel Gregory, 1873–1953
  Prelude and fugue, for piano & orchestra. New York: J. Fischer,
    1933.
  Quartet on Negro themes, op. 19, for strings. New York: G.
    Schirmer, 1930.
  Symphony no. 3 ("Lincoln"), for orchestra.
Milhaud, Darius, 1892–
  Le boeuf sur le toit, ballet. Paris: Eschig, 1950.
  Le boeuf sur le toit, fantasy for jazz band (1920)
  Caramel mou, for piano. Paris: La Sirène Musicale, 1921.
  La création du monde, ballet. Paris: Eschig, 1929.
  Saudades do Brasil, for orchestra (1921)
  Saudades do Brasil, for piano. Paris: Eschig, 1929.
  Le tango de Fratellini, for piano. Paris: La Sirène Musicle, 1920.
  Trois rag caprices, for jazz band. Wien: Universal Edition, 1930.
Morris, Harold, 1890–
  Concerto on two Negro themes, for piano & orchestra. Boston:
    C. C. Birchard, 1932.
  Variations on the Negro spiritual "Dum-a-lum", for chamber
    orchestra (1925)
Poulenc, François, 1899–1963
  Rapsodie nègre, for baritone & instrumental septet. London: J.
    & W. Chester, 1919.
Powell, John, 1882–1963
  Rapsodie nègre, for piano & orchestra. New York: G. Schirmer,
    1921.
  Sonata virginianesque, op. 7, for violin & piano. New York: G.
    Schirmer, 1919.
Ravel, Maurice, 1875–1937
  Concerto in G, for piano. Paris: Durand, 1932.
  Concerto for the left hand, for piano. Paris: Durand, 1931.
  L'enfant et les sortilèges, opera. Paris: Durand, 1925.
  Sonata, for violin & piano. Paris: Durand, 1927.

Riegger, Wallingford, 1885–1961
  Little Black Sambo, op. 40, for chamber orchestra (1946)
Satie, Erik, 1866–1925
  Parade, ballet. Paris: Salabert, 1917.
Schmit, William, 1926–
  Variations on a Negro folk song, for brass quintet. Los Angeles:
    Western International Music, 19??.
Schönberg, Arnold, 1874–1951
  Suite for piano, op. 25.
Schoenfield, Henry, 1857–1936
  In the sunny South (1899)
  Symphony in G minor ("Rural") (1892)
Schuman, William, 1910–
  Judith, ballet. New York: G. Schirmer, 1950.
  Symphony no. 4. New York: G. Schirmer, 1950.
Sessions, Roger, 1896–
  Scherzino and march for children, for piano (1955)
Stravinsky, Igor, 1882–1971
  Ebony concerto, for clarinet & jazz band. New York: Charling
    Music Corporation, 1967.
  L'histoire du soldat, for narrator & instrumental septet.
    London: J. & W. Chester, 1924.
  Piano rag music, for piano. London: J. & W. Chester, 1920.
  Ragtime, for 11 instruments. Wien: Wiener Philharmonischer
    Verlag, 1924.
  Tango, for piano. Mainz: Schott, 1941.
  Tango, for orchestra. New York: Mercury, 1954.
Transman, Alexandre, 1897–
  Sonatine transatlantique, for orchestra. Paris: Leduc, 1930.
Taylor, Deems, 1885–1966
  Through the looking glass, for orchestra. New York: C. Fischer,
    1923.
Thompson, Randall, 1899–
  Symphony no. 2. Rochester: Eastman School of Music, 1932.
Thompson, Virgil, 1896–
  Variations and fugues on gospel hymns, for organ (1930)
Varèse, Edgard, 1885–1965
  Intégrales, for chamber orchestra. London: Curwen, 1926.
Wachs, Paul, 1851–1915
  Negro melody, chanson du petit nègre, for 4-hand piano.
    Philadelphia: Theodore Presser, 1905 (in *Four-hand miscellany*)
Weill, Kurt, 1900–1950
  Aufstieg und Fall der Stadt Mahagony, opera. Wien: Universal
    Edition, 1929.

Die Dreigroschenoper, opera. Wien: Universal Edition, 1928.
Der Lindenburghflug, for chorus & orchestra. Wien: Universal
Edition, 1930.
Weiss, Adolph, 1891–
American life, for orchestra (1930)

Black Artists in Music and the Dance Available for Booking

This listing was prepared in an effort to identify currently available professional Black musical artists and to stimulate their booking by local managers of concert series. The names of these individuals and ensembles were obtained to a large extent from information supplied by their managers, supplemented with research by Sharon B. Thompson and Jean M. Little of the Black Music Center staff. Although intended to be a comprehensive register, this listing is very far from complete (particularly in the "nonconcert" field) but bears no intentional evidence of value judgment. Artists without professional management are listed when they are known to be actively engaged in touring. During the time this list was being prepared, several artists seemingly changed managers. This register is as accurate as possible, but there is no assurance that all booking agents or artists are cited as they might wish. Details on repertoire, fees, and schedules should be requested of the artists' managers, whose full address is provided in the second part of this appendix. Corrections and additions include those brought to my notice as of October 1972.

Manager

Part A: Medium Index
Choruses

Afro-American Folklore Troupe (with dancers, actors, and instrumentalists)	Pruitt
Afro-Boricua Folkloric Company (Caribbean repertoire)	New World
The Albert McNeil Jubilee Singers (Albert McNeil, conductor)	International Concerts
The Beverly Glenn Chorale (Gospel repertoire; Beverly Glenn, conductor)	Charisma
Clara Ward and Her Gospel Singers (Clara Ward, conductor)	Boomer
The Hampton Institute Concert Choir	Barrett
The Jamaican Folk Singers	Tornay
The Howard Roberts Chorale (Spirituals repertoire; Howard Roberts, conductor)	Gould; Alkahest; Kolmar

	Manager
The Staple Singers (Gospel repertoire)	American

Conductors

Baker, David N. (Jazz repertoire)	Indiana
Basie, Count (Jazz repertoire)	Alexander
Byrd, George (Orchestral repertoire)	
de Coteau, Denis (Orchestral repertoire)	
de Paur, Leonard (Choral repertoire)	Westchester
de Priest, James (Orchestral repertoire)	Hurok
Dixon, Dean (Orchestral repertoire)	Pitluck
Frazier, James (Orchestral repertoire)	Pitluck
Freeman, Paul (Orchestral repertoire)	Judson
Hampton, Lionel (Jazz repertoire)	Alexander
Harris, Margaret (Orchestral and choral repertoires)	Schiffmann
Isaac, Roland V. (Orchestral repertoire)	Johnson
Lee, Everett (Orchestral repertoire)	Rile
Perkinson, Coleridge-Taylor (Orchestral repertoire)	
Thompson, Leon (Orchestral repertoire)	Kay

Dance groups

Afro-American Dance Company (Arthur Hall, director)	Shaw
Afro-Boricua Folkloric Company (Caribbean repertoire)	New World
Boot Dancers	Blackfrica
The Chuck Davis Company	Pruitt
Dinizulu Dancers (African repertoire)	Polodi; Hampton
Dukaraus African Dance Troupe (African repertoire)	Expressions
Holder, Geoffrey	Leigh
Ishangi Dancers (African repertoire; Ishangi Razak, director)	Razak
Ivory Coast Dance Company (African repertoire)	Howard
Jean Léon Destiné Afro-Haitian Dance Company	Hampton
The Jamaican Folk Singers	Tornay
The Jamaican National Ballet	New World
Jazz Dance Theater (Mura Dehn, director)	New Arts
La Rocque Bey Dance Company	Fulton
Max Roach Afro-American Dance Theater	American
Morse Donaldson's Dance Company	Tornay
Movements Black	Blackfrica
Otalunji African Company	Hampton

	Manager
Pomare Dance Group	Fulton
Rod Rogers Dance Company	Rodgers
Senegalese National Dance Company	Howard
Sierra Leone National Dance Troupe	Pitluck
Southern Dance Company (Trinidad repertoire)	New World
Uhuru Dancers	Blackfrica
Zulu Dancers	Blackfrica

Flutists

| Jones, Harold | Bernard |

French hornists

| Ruff, Willie | American |

Jazz duos

The International Duo	Emerick
Latimer-Lytle Duo	Frothingham
Mitchell Ruff Duo	American

Jazz trios

Alice Coltrane Trio	Fulton
Billy Taylor Trio	Musical
Don Shirley Trio	Bichurin
Emme Kemp Trio	Emerick
Mitchell-Ruff Trio	Fulton; Musical
Young-Holt Unlimited	Alexander

Jazz quartets

Clark Terry Quartet	American
Modern Jazz Quartet	American
The New Liberation Unit	Franklin

Jazz quintets

Cannonball Adderley Quintet	American
Dizzy Gillespie Quintet	American
Earl Fatha Hines Quintet	Music
Jothan Callins Quintet	Semon
Max Roach Quintet	American
Pharaoh Sanders Quintet	Fulton

Jazz sextets

| David Baker Sextet | Pitluck |
| The New York Jazz Sextet | Tornay |

Jazz bands

Duke Ellington Orchestra	American
Indiana University Jazz Ensemble (David N. Baker, conductor)	Indiana
Preservation Hall Jazz Band	Pryor

	Manager
The President's Band (Phillip Slaughter, conductor)	Douglass
Roland Kirk and the Vibration Society	Music

Music-dramatic ensembles

Al Fann Theatrical Ensemble	Gould

Narrators and lecturers

Anderson, Marian	Hurok
Davis, Ossie and Ruby Dee	American
Latimer, Jim	Frothingham
Middleton, E. Arthur	Seaman
Peters, Brock	American
The Society of Black Composers	Patterson

Organists

Cooper, William S.	Pruitt
Simms, James A.	Pruitt
Spillman, Herndon	Indiana

Percussionists

Latimer, Jim	Frothingham
Otalunji and His Drums (African repertoire)	Fulton
Roach, Max	American

Pianists

Adams, Armenta	Soffer
Barrett, Nerine	Shaw
Bates, Leon	Rile
Brand, Dollar (Jazz repertoire)	New World
Capers, Valerie (Jazz repertoire)	Pruitt
Carter, John	Delman
Dilworth-Leslie, Samuel	Kay
Duke, George (Jazz repertoire)	International Artists
Harris, Margaret	Schiffmann
Hill, Andrew (Jazz repertoire)	Fulton
Hinderas, Natalie	Rile
Jackson, Raymond	Alkahest; Jackson
Jordan, Robert	McClelland; Pruitt
Lytle, Cecil	Frothingham
Middleton, E. Arthur (Jazz repertoire)	Seaman
Miller, Horatio	Franklin
Pritchard, Robert	New World
Robertson, Jon	Alkahest
Robinson, Julius	Bernard

Manager

Santos, Henry	New World
Shirley, Donald	Columbia
Taylor, Billy (Jazz repertoire)	Hampton
Walker, George	Walker
Watts, André	Judson

Saxophonists

Brown, Marion	Fulton
Coleman, Ornette	Fulton

Singers (Sopranos)

Arroyo, Martina	Dispeker
Conrad, Barbara Smith	Pruitt
Davis, Osceola (Coloratura)	Franklin
Davy, Gloria	Dispeker
Dobbs, Mattiwilda	American
Flowers, Martha	Bichurin
Gaither-Graves, Mareda	Grubb
Glenn, Bonita	Franklin
Grist, Reri	Columbia
Hayes, Afrika	Frothingham
Johnson, Alma	Liegener
Jones, Betty	Hoffmann
Lane, Betty (lyric)	Spector
Mathis, Joyce	Young
Nelson, Gail	Johnson
Norman, Jessye	Judson
Price, Leontyne	Columbia
Tyler, Veronica	Columbia
Walker, Annie	American
Walters, Jeannette	Tornay
Weathers, Felicia	Judson; Columbia
Williams, Camilla	Columbia

Singers (Mezzo-sopranos)

Allen, Betty	Columbia
Blackett, Joy	Young
Ballinger, Cathryn	Mays
Bumbry, Grace	Hurok
Johns, Mertine	Franklin
Killebrew, Gwendolyn	Shaw
Mayes, Doris	American
Norwood, Jacqueline	Bernard
Quivar, Florence	Franklin
Verrett, Shirley	Hurok

Manager

Singers (Contraltos)
Parker, Louise — Judson
Patrick, Clementine — Kay
West, Lucretia — Schiffmann

Singers (Tenors)
Brown, William — Tornay
Dudley, Ray Ford — Franklin
Farrar, Reginald (Heldentenor) — Frothingham
Hayes, Roland — Hayes
McCoy, Seth — Barrett
Miles, John — National
Patton, John — Patton
Shirley, George — Shaw
Williams, Reed — American

Singers (Baritones)
Brodwith, Leroy — Pruitt
Carey, Thomas — O'Donnell
Estes, Simon — Columbia
Holmes, Eugene — Pitluck
Pierson, Edward — Liegner
Thomas, Fred — New York
Thompson, Arthur — Young
Warfield, William — Columbia

Singers (Bass-baritones)
Boatwright, McHenry — Shaw
Goodman, George — American
Matthews, Benjamin — Schiffmann

Violinists
Adams, Elwyn — Dispeker
Coleman, Ornette — Fulton

Violists
Thompson, Marcus — Young

Violoncellists
Lipscomb, Ronald — Lipscomb
Moore, Kermit — Pruitt

Vocal trios
Phoenix Singers — Gould

Vocal quartets
Black Arts Quartet — Franklin

Vocalists
Bibb, Leon — Kolmar

Manager

Brady, Victor	Polydor
Brown, James	Brown
Davis, Rev. Gary	Folklore
Davis, Sammy, Jr.	Morris
The Four Tops	International Famous
Franklin, Aretha	Queen
Fuller, Jesse	Folklore
Howlin' Wolf	Alexander
The Impressions	Alexander
The Kars from Uganda (Vocalists, dancers, and instrumentalists)	Pruitt
King, B. B.	Lucas
Kitt, Eartha	Morris
Lord Bill Barnes Trio (Calypso repertoire)	Alkahest; Musical
Mayfield, Curtis	Alexander
Miss Black America Show	Alexander
Muddy Waters	Alexander
Odetta	American
The Originals	International Famous
Pickett, Wilson	Alexander
Simone, Nina	Music
Sunnyland Slim	Folklore
Truesdale, Tad	Podoli
Vaughan, Sarah	Alexander
Wallace, Sippy	Folklore
White, Booker	Folklore
Williams, Marion	Liegner

Part B: Management Index

Willard ALEXANDER, Inc.
333 North Michigan
Avenue
Chicago, Illinois 60601
(312) 236-2460

ALKAHEST Attractions, Inc.
P.O. Box 7130
Station C
Atlanta, Georgia 30309
(404) 892-1843

AMERICAN Program Bureau
59 Temple Place
Boston, Massachusetts
02111
(617) 482-0090

Herbert BARRETT Management
1860 Broadway
New York, N. Y. 10023
(212) 245-3530

BERNARD and Rubin
Management
255 West End Avenue
New York, N. Y. 10023
(212) 877-3735

M. BICHURIN Concerts
Corporation
Carnegie Hall, Suite 109
New York, N. Y. 10019
(212) 586-2349

BLACKFRICA Promotions,
Inc.
P.O. Box 10
New York, N. Y. 10027
(212) 691-4415

Eastman BOOMER Management
119 West 57 Street
New York, N. Y. 10019
(212) 582-9364

James BROWN Productions
1540 Brewster Avenue
Cincinnati, Ohio 45207

CHARISMA Management
Corporation
119 West 57 Street
New York, N. Y. 10019
(212) 582-6988

COLUMBIA Artists Management, Inc.
165 West 57 Street
New York, N. Y. 10019
(212) 247-6900

Judith DELMAN
135 West 79 Street
New York, N. Y. 10024
(212) 799-3707

Thea DISPEKER Artists'
Representative
59 East 54 Street
New York, N. Y. 10022
(212) 421-7676

DOUGLASS Associates
17 Haynes Street
Hartford, Connecticut
06103
(203) 527-4980

Elwood EMERICK Management
596 Crystal Lake Road
Akron, Ohio 44313
(216) 666-2036

EXPRESSIONS in Black
Entertainment Bureau, Inc.
7501 Cottage Grove
Chicago, Illinois 60619
(312) 487-6776

FOLKLORE Productions, Inc.
176 Federal Street
Boston, Massachusetts
02110
(617) 582-1827

FOUNDATION for the Vital
Arts
872 Avenue of the
Americas

New York, N. Y. 10001
(212) 689-4239

FRANKLIN Concerts
2031 Chestnut Street
Philadelphia, Pa. 19103
(215) 563-7874

The FROTHINGHAM
Management
156 Cherry Brook Road
Weston, Massachusetts
02193
(617) 894-7571

Richard FULTON, Inc.
200 West 57 Street
New York, N. Y. 10019
(212) 582-4099

Walter GOULD
609 Fifth Avenue
New York, N. Y. 10017
(212) 752-3920

Thomas GRUBB
1217 Park Avenue
New York, N. Y. 10028
(212) 831-8348

HAMPTON Center of
Contemporary Arts
119 West 57 Street
New York, N. Y. 10019
(212) 586-2747

Roland HAYES
58 Allerton Street
Brookline, Massachusetts
02146
(617) 277-1593

Hans J. HOFMANN Artists'
Management
200 West 58 Street
New York, N. Y. 10019
(212) 246-1577

Mel HOWARD Productions
450 West 24 Street
New York, N. Y. 10011
(212) 243-1488

HUROK Concerts, Inc.
730 Fifth Avenue
New York, N. Y. 10019
(212) 245-0500

INDIANA University Office of
Musical Attractions
Bloomington, Indiana
47401
(812) 337-7047

INTERNATIONAL ART-
ISTS Agency
P. O. Box 978
San Leandro, California
94577
Phone not listed.

INTERNATIONAL CON-
CERTS Exchange Foundation
9015 Wilshire Boulevard
Beverly Hills,
California 90211
Phone not listed.

INTERNATIONAL
FAMOUS Agency
2457 Woodward Avenue
Detroit, Michigan 48201
Phone not listed.

Raymond JACKSON
684 Riverside Drive
Apartment 4E
New York, N. Y. 10031
(212) 368-9191

Theodate JOHNSON
1 West 72 Street
New York, N. Y. 10023
(212) 874-6950

Arthur JUDSON Manage-
ment, Inc.
119 West 57 Street
New York, N. Y. 10019
(212) 586-8135

Albert KAY Associates, Inc.
38 West 53 Street
New York, N. Y. 10019
(212) 765-3195

KOLMAR-Luth Entertainment, Inc.
1776 Broadway
New York, N. Y. 10019
(212) 581-5833

W. Colston LEIGH, Inc.
521 Fifth Avenue
New York, N. Y. 10017
(212) 682-6623

Judith LIEGNER Artists Management
33 Greenwich Avenue
New York, N. Y. 10014
(212) 989-7041

Ronald LIPSCOMB
311 East 105 Street
New York, N. Y. 10029
(212) 369-8645

Victoria LUCAS Associates
1414 Avenue of the Americas
New York, N. Y. 10019
(212) 421-2021

Jim McCLELLAND Associates
756 North 26 Street
Philadelphia, Pennsylvania 19130
(215) 765-5526

Ella Kay MAYS Agency
Suite 201
9350 Wilshire Boulevard
Beverly Hills,
California 90211
(213) 272-8551

William MORRIS Agency
1650 Broadway
New York, N. Y. 10019
(212) 265-3350

MUSIC and Drama Associates
118 West 57 Street
New York, N. Y. 10019
(212) 247-3730

MUSICAL Artists
119 West 57 Street
New York, N. Y. 10019
(212) 586-2747

The NATIONAL Music League, Inc.
130 West 56 Street
New York, N. Y. 10019
(212) 265-2472

NEW ARTS Management, Inc.
33 Wooster Street
New York, N. Y. 10013
(212) 691-5434

NEW WORLD Festival Concerts
The Anchorage Building
Suite 203
1555 Connecticut Avenue, N. W.
Washington, D. C. 20036
(202) 393-1454

NEW YORK Recital Associates
353 West 57 Street
New York, N. Y. 10019
(212) 581-1429

Anne J. O'DONNELL Management
353 West 57 Street
New York, N. Y. 10019
(212) 581-1184

Benjamin PATTERSON, Ltd.
Suite 1203
Carnegie Hall
New York, N. Y. 10019
(212) 246-4362

John PATTON
1569 Ashland
St. Paul, Minnesota 55100
(612) 777-9782

PERFORMING Arts Management, Inc.
Box 44
Ft. George Station
New York, N. Y. 10040
(212) 663-8500

Sherman PITLUCK, Inc.
250 West 57 Street
New York, N. Y. 10019
(212) 247-0660

Michael PODOLI Concert and Lecture Management
171 West 71 Street
Suite 11-D
New York, N. Y. 10023
(212) 877-1001

POLYDOR Incorporated
1700 Broadway
New York, N. Y. 10019
(212) 245-0600

Bess PRUITT Associates
819 East 168 Street
Bronx, N. Y. 10459
(212) 589-0400

PRYOR-Menz Attractions
P. O. Box 455
Council Bluffs, Iowa 51501
(712) 328-2361

QUEEN Booking Corporation
no address determined

Ishangi RAZAK
209-02 Hollis Avenue
Queens Village, N. Y. 11432
(212) 479-1904

John RILE Associates
424 West Upsal Street
Philadelphia, Pennsylvania 19119
(215) 438-0627

David SCHIFFMANN
111 West 57 Street
New York, N. Y. 10019
(212) 245-3010

Norman J. SEAMAN
Box 693
Radio City Station
New York, N. Y. 10019
(212) 245-9250

Eric SEMON Associates, Inc.
111 West 57 Street
New York, N. Y. 10019
(212) 765-1310

SHAW Concerts, Inc.
233 West 49 Street
Suite 800
New York, N. Y. 10019
(212) 581-4654

Sheldon SOFER Management, Inc.
130 West 56 Street
New York, N. Y. 10019
(212) 757-8060

Mary SPECTOR Artists Management, Inc.
250 West 57 Street
Suite 315
New York, N. Y. 10019
(212) 586-3445

TORNAY Management
250 West 57 Street
New York, N. Y. 10019
(212) 246-2270

George WALKER
323 Grove Street
Montclair, New Jersey 07042
(201) 746-2794

WESTCHESTER Symphony Orchestra, Inc.
215 Fox Meadow Road
Scarsdale, N. Y. 10583
(914) 472-450

YOUNG Concert Artists, Inc.
75 East 55 Street
New York, N. Y. 10022
(212) 759-2541

Black Music in College Music History Texts

A graduate piano student at one the nation's foremost universities recently lamented to me her "complete lack of information on the music of her people." While I don't doubt for a moment that she had extensive musical experience in her church and through ordinary social contacts, it was quite evident that her formal education ignored Black music history and literature, and filled her schedule with assignments and concerts which prevented her having the time to get it all together on her own.

After thinking about it, I asked Indiana University's Associate Music Librarian, David E. Fenske, to draw up a list of selected texts which might be adopted in various colleges, both now and in the past. I went through them, looking in the indexes for such entries as jazz, spirituals, William Grant Still, blues, African music, and Duke Ellington. In most instances, jazz (which was rarely discussed *per se,* much less were its major figures cited) was included to account for influences in the styles of Stravinsky, Hindemith, or Copland. It came as no great surprise to find no real coverage of Black music in many of the earlier texts, but it was distressing to see the directions taken by more recent books. In the midst of all this, Edith Borroff's book was a true delight, and it was a pleasure to see that Marion Bauer concerned herself with Black musicians as well as women composers several decades ago.

I've not commented on the quality of information given in these books, and in fact, this is by no means a survey of all major college texts. In offering this information, I suggest it as a worthwhile topic to be more formally pursued and called to the attention of the textbook industry and the nation's music educators.

Bauer, Marion
> *Music Through the Ages; A Narrative for Student and Layman,* by Marion Bauer and Ethel R. Peyser. 2d. ed. New York: G. P. Putnam's Sons, 1946, 1932. 623 p. Substantial attention to American music, with some information on spirituals, call and response, minstrelsy, Handy, Burleigh, Dett, White, J. Rosamond Johnson, and Still, as well as the only special attention in these books to women composers.

Borroff, Edith
Music in Europe and the United States; A History. Englewood Cliffs: Prentice-Hall, 1971. 752 p. Contains much information on African music, ragtime, blues, and jazz, with biographical sketches of Duke Ellington, Jelly Roll Morton, Coleridge-Taylor, Scott Joplin, and Paul McCartney, including a transcript of Charlie Parker's *Improvisation.*

Cannon, Beekman Cox
The Art of Music; A Short History of Musical Styles and Ideas, by Beekman Cox Cannon, Alvin H. Johnson, and William G. Waite. New York: Thomas Y. Crowell Co., 1960. 484p.
A text by three professors from Yale University, with no reference to Black music.

Crocker, Richard L.
A History of Musical Style. New York: McGraw-Hill Book Co., 1966. 573p. (McGraw-Hill series in music) A few references to influences from Black music are cited.

Deri, Otto
Exploring Twentieth-century Music. New York: Holt, Rinehart & Winston, 1968. 546p. No mention of Black music.

Dickinson, Edward
The Study of the History of Music, with an Annotated Guide to Music Literature. New York: Charles Scribner's Sons, 1931. 425p. Only mentions Coleridge-Taylor by name.

Einstein, Alfred
A Short History of Music. 3d. American ed., rev. New York: Alfred A. Knopf, 1947. 438, xii p. The following quotation from page 251 indicates the scholar's attitude: "Fox trot, shimmy, and ragtime are adapted as elements of artistic music, and finally jazz, an orgiastic dance-music in quick-march rhythm—the most abominable treason against all the music of Western civilization —becomes symbolic of the spirit of the times."

Ferguson, Donald Nivison
A History of Musical Thought. 3d. ed. New York: Appleton, Century, Crofts, 1959, 1948. 675p. States on page 503 of 1935 edition that jazz "was borrowed probably from the negroes." Edition of 1959 has brief consideration of jazz, spirituals, ragtime.

Grout, Donald Jay
A History of Western Music. New York: W. W. Norton, 1960. 742p. Contains only brief references to jazz.

Harman, Alec
Man and His Music; The Story of Musical Experience in the West, by Alec Harman, Anthony Milner, and Wilfred Mellers. New York: Oxford University Press, 1962. 1172p. Refers to Black music only with respect to its influences on White music.

Howard, John Tasker
A Short History of Music in America, by John Tasker Howard
and George Kent Bellows. New York: Thomas Y. Crowell Co.,
1967, 1957. 496p. Contains extensive references.
Lang, Paul Henry
Music in Western Civilization. New York: W. W. Norton, 1941.
1107p. Lacks even reference to jazz.
Leichtentritt, Hugo
Music of the Western Nations, edited and amplified by Nicholas
Slonimsky. Cambridge: Harvard University Press, 1956. 324p.
Contains reference to spirituals, Burleigh, Still, Dawson, Kay,
Swanson, Roland Hayes, Marian Anderson, and Dorothy Maynor.
Machlis, Joseph
The Enjoyment of Music; An Introduction to Perceptive Listening.
Rev. ed. New York: W. W. Norton, 1963. 701p. Briefly mentions
spirituals.

Introduction to Contemporary Music. New York: W. W.
Norton, 1961. 714p. Contains some information on Roldán, Kay,
Swanson, Still, and Coleridge-Taylor.
McKinney, Howard Decker
Music in History; The Evolution of an Art, by Howard Decker
McKinney and W.R. Anderson. 2d. ed. New York: American
Book Co., 1957. 749p. Like most books, this gives data on music
of Middle East (not Africa) before consideration of Egypt. Has
brief summary of jazz.
Naumann, Emil
The History of Music, translated by F. Praeger. Vol. 5. London:
Cassell & Co., n. d. 1332p. No information on Coleridge-Taylor,
Saint-Georges, or Bridgetower, although this volume covers that
historical period.
Nef, Karl
An Outline of the History of Music, translated by Carl F.
Pfatteicher. New York: Columbia University Press, 1935. 400p.
(Columbia University series in musicology) Brief, respectful men-
tion of blues and work songs, cites influence of jazz on European
composers.
Portnoy, Julius
Music in the Life of Man. New York: Holt, Rinehart & Winston,
1963. 300p. Include brief history of rock-and-roll, reacts against
generic criticism yet sees "cultural limitations" of jazz.
Prunières, Henry
A New History of Music; The Middle Ages to Mozart, with in-
troduction by Romain Rolland, translated by Edward Lockspeiser.

New York: Macmillan, 1943. 413 p. Lacks entries on Bridge-tower and Saint-Georges.
Sachs, Curt
Our Musical Heritage; A Short History of Music. New York: Prentice-Hall, 1948. 400p. Brief mention of the influence of jazz on European composers by a major ethnomusicologist.
Ulrich, Homer
A History of Music and Musical Style, by Homer Ulrich and Paul A. Pisk. New York: Harcourt, Brace & World, 1963. 696p. Virtually no information, even within the 31 pages on three centuries of American music.
Walter, Don C.
Men and Music in Western Culture. New York: Appleton, Century, Crofts, 1969. 244p. Large areas on Afro-American music, jazz, and pop.
Westrup, Sir Jack Allan
An Introduction to Musical History. London: Hutchinson University Library, 1955. 174p. Brief mention of jazz influences on European composers.
Wiora, Walter
The Four Ages of Music, translated by M. D. Herter Norton. London: J.M. Dent & Sons, 1965. 233p. Some consideration of jazz.

List of Works Publically Performed

The compositions cited below were among those scheduled for our concerts from 1969 to 1972, in Bloomington, Washington, New Orleans, and Boulder. Not included here are those titles spontaneously selected for performance by the Indiana University Jazz Quintet in 1970 and 1972, and in the latter year by Leila Blakey, Wilson Breaker, and the Black Hope Liberation Ensemble. In several instances, only the names of the soloists have been given. Performers for works which were performed more than once during these four years are indicated within the title entry.

It would not be particularly easy to cite those works which, in addition to being outstanding, secured excellent performances, but among those which I shall best remember are David Baker's *Black America* (the 1971 performance, supported with a grant from the Indiana State Arts Council), Bridgetower's *Henry* (and, for that matter, all the rest of those works performed by Bernadine Oliphint and Carol Stone), Robert Morris' *Lyric Suite,* the works of Kalvert Nelson (a very gifted young man), and both premières of works by Saint-Georges. To have been able to have such outstanding guest talents as George Walker, Natalie Hinderas, John Patton, and Louise Parker, was certainly a major attraction. One of the most beautiful performances was that given by Leila Blakey and her solidly gospel-rooted pianist, Daisy Cobb Lawless. And, perhaps, the most moving (within the context of Latin sentimentality at least) was the Crispus Attucks High School performance of *Precious Lord,* with Professor Dorsey in the audience. For me personally, I have deep admiration for those many students—White and Black—who took time from very busy schedules to prepare these works, always on short notice, and particular appreciation to Hans Boepple for the première of T.J. Anderson's *Watermelon,* which the composer had dedicated to me.

Anderson, Marvin
> *God Is Already Here.* College Avenue Baptist Church Choir of Indianapolis.

Anderson, Thomas Jefferson
> *Variations on a Theme of M. B. Tolson.* Bernadine Oliphint, soprano; Jenny Lind, violin; Ronald Crutcher, cello; Barbara Krall, saxophone; John Henes, trumpet; Arlen Eichman, trombone; Linda Walker, piano; T.J. Anderson, conductor

Watermelon (world première). Hans Boepple, piano
Baker, David N.
   April B. IU Jazz Ensemble.

   Black America. Linda Anderson, Beverly McElroy, Bernadine Oliphint, Janice Albright, sopranos; Robert Ingram, tenor; David Arnold, baritone; John Joyner, narrator; IU Chorus; IU Jazz Ensemble; David Baker, conductor.

   Deliver My Soul (world première). Steven Shipps, violin; Paul Parmalee, piano.

   Deliver My Soul. James Compton, violin; Thomas J. Ahrens, piano.

   Early in the Morning. Roberta Dennie, soprano; George Dennie, piano.

   Gebrauchsmusik (Children's pieces for string quartet; Black frontier suite). IU Ensemble.

   The IU Swing Machine. IU Jazz Ensemble.

   One for J.S. IU Jazz Ensemble.

   Roly Poly. IU Jazz Ensemble.

   Settings for Soprano and Piano. Bernadine Oliphint, soprano; Carol Stone, piano. Janice Albright, soprano; Douglas Murdock, piano.

   The Silver Chalice. IU Jazz Ensemble.

   Soft Summer Rain. IU Jazz Ensemble.

   Son Mar. IU Jazz Ensemble.

   Sonata for Cello and Piano (world première). Michael Peebles, cello; Gayle Cameron, piano.
Beethoven Ludwig van
   Sonata for Piano, op. 81a, in E-flat Major ("Les adieux"). George Walker, piano.
Blacher, Boris
   Negro Spirituals. Linda Anderson, soprano.

Bless me, Lord.
College Avenue Baptist Choir of Indianapolis.
Boatner, Edward H.
I Want Jesus to Walk with Me. Crispus Attucks High School Choir of Indianapolis.
Brewster, W.H.
Tell the Angels. College Avenue Baptist Church Choir of Indianapolis.
Bridgetower, George
Henry (American première). Bernadine Oliphint, soprano; Carol Stone, piano.
Brown, Lawrence
Great Gittin' Up Mornin'. Louise Parker, contralo; Susan Peters, piano.
Brown, Oscar
Brown Baby. Crispus Attucks High School Choir of Indianapolis.
Brumley, Albert E.
I'll Fly Away. College Avenue Baptist Church Choir of Indianapolis.
Burleigh, Harry T.
Deep River. Steven Shipps, violin; Robert L. Morris, piano. Steven Shipps, violin; Paul Parmalee, piano.

Lovely Dark and Lonely One. John Patton, tenor; Susan Peters, piano.

Oh, Didn't It Rain? Louise Parker, contralto; Susan Peters, piano.

Oh, Rock Me Julie. John Patton, tenor; Susan Peters, piano.

One Year, 1914–1915. John Patton, tenor; Susan Peters, piano.

Southland Sketches. Steven Shipps, violin; Robert L. Morris, paino. Steven Shipps, violin; Paul Parmalee, piano.
Carter, John
Cantata. Bernadine Oliphint, soprano; Carol Stone, piano. Edythe Jason, soprano; Susan Peters, piano.
Chambers, Stephen A.
Sound-gone. Natalie Hinderas, piano.
Chopin, Frédéric
Ballade in G Minor, Op. 23. Natalie Hinderas, piano.

Nocturne in C-sharp Minor, Op. 27/1. Natalie Hinderas, piano.

Scherzo in C-sharp Minor, Op. 39/3. Natalie Hinderas, piano.

Sonata in B Minor, Op. 58. George Walker, piano.
Clark, Edgar Rogie
Copper Sun. Gordon Greer, tenor; Susan Bishop, piano.

Impression. Bernadine Oliphint, soprano; Carol Stone, piano.
Coles, George
Praise God. College Avenue Baptist Church Choir of Indianapolis.
Cooper, William B.
Meditation on Steal Away. Herndon Spillman, organ.
Cunningham, Arthur
Engrams'. Natalie Hinderas, piano.
Dailey, Anderson T.
In Jesus' Name. College Avenue Baptist Church Choir of Indianapolis.

Steal Away. Crispus Attucks High School Choir of Indianapolis.
Dawson, Willian L.
Ezekiel Saw de Wheel. Crispus Attucks High School Choir of Indianapolis.
Dett, Robert Nathaniel
In the Bottoms. Natalie Hinderas, piano.

Ride on, Jesus. John Patton, tenor; Susan Peters, piano.
Dickerson, Roger
Chorale Prelude on Das neugeborne Kindelein. Herndon Spillman, organ.
Dorsey, Thomas A.
Precious Lord, Take My Hand. Crispus Attucks High School Choir of Indianapolis.
Douroux, Margaret
I'm Glad. College Avenue Baptist Church Choir of Indianapolis.
Duncan, John
Black Bards. Kenneth Ware, flute.
Fax, Mark
May Day Song. Bernadine Oliphint, soprano; Carol Stone, piano.

Pieces for Organ. Herndon Spillman, organ.

Rondel. Bernadine Oliphint, soprano; Carol Stone, piano.
Gaither, William J.
He Touched Me. College Avenue Baptist Church Choir of Indianapolis.
Gershwin, George
Preludes for Piano. Hans Boepple, piano.

Grey, De Sayles
Wildroots! Scott Reeves, trombone.
Hailstork, Adolphus C.
Scherzetto from Organ Suite. Herndon Spillman, organ.
Hairston, Jester
Goin' Down Dat Lonesome Road. Crispus Attucks High School
Choir of Indianapolis.

____

Hold On. Crispus Attucks High School Choir of Indianapolis.
Hall, Frederick D.
Lord, How Come Me Here? Bernadine Oliphint, soprano; Carol
Stone, piano.
Haydn, Franz Joseph
Sonata for Piano, H. XVI 52, in E-flat Major. Natalie
Hinderas, piano.
Hayes, Roland
Lord, I Can't Stay Away. Louise Parker, contralto; Susan Peters,
piano.
Hawkins, Edwin
Oh Happy Day. Crispus Attucks High School Choir of Indianap-
olis.
Hayes, Joseph
Praeludium for Organ. Herndon Spillman, organ.
Hear de Lam's A-cryin'.
Louise Parker, contralto; Susan Peters, piano.
Holiday, Billie
God Bless' the Child. Crispus Attucks High School Choir of
Indianapolis.
James, Willis Laurence
My Good Lord Done Been Here. John Patton, tenor; Susan Peters,
piano.

____

Pity a po' boy. John Patton, tenor; Susan Peters, piano.
Johnson, Hall
The Courtship. John Patton, tenor; Susan Peters, piano.

____

Crucible. John Patton, tenor; Susan Peters, piano.

____

Fi-yer. Bernadine Oliphint, soprano; Carol Stone, piano.

____

His Name so Sweet. Louise Parker, contralto; Susan Peters, piano.

____

Witness. Louise Parker, contralto; Susan Peters, piano.

Johnson, Harrison
I've Decided to Make Jesus My Choice. College Avenue Baptist Church Choir of Indianapolis.
Jones, Isaiah
Fill My Cup. College Avenue Baptist Church Choir of Indianapolis.
Jones, Pearl Williams
Rockin' Jerusalem. Louise Parker, contralto; Susan Peters, piano.
Joplin, Scott
Treemonisha: Slow Drag. Bernadine Oliphint, soprano; Carol Stone, piano.

———

Treemonisha: When villians ramble. Dennis Gillom, bass; Thomas J. Ahrens, piano.
Jordan, George
I'll Make It Home Some Day. College Avenue Baptist Church Choir of Indianapolis.
Kay, Ulysses
Aulos (world première). John Solum, flute; IU Chamber Orchestra; Wolfgang Vacano, conductor.

———

Quartet for Brasses. Larry Wiseman, Walter Blanton, trumpets; Michael Olsavsky, Jay Hildebrant, trombones.
Kerr, Thomas H.
Anguished American Easter. Herndon Spillman, organ.
Lord, I Want to be a Christian.
College Avenue Baptist Church Choir of Indianapolis.
MacLellan, Gene
Put Your Hand in the Hand of the Man. College Avenue Baptist Church Choir of Indianapolis.
McLin, Lena J.
The Torch Has Been Passed. Crispus Attucks High School Choir of Indianapolis.
Merrifield, Norman
Hard Trials. Crispus Attucks High School Choir of Indianapolis.

———

Now Look Away. Crispus Attucks High School Choir of Indianapolis.
Moore, Undine S.
Afro-American Suite. Sally E. Turk, flute; Ronald Crutcher, cello; Linda Walker, piano.

———

The Lamb. Crispus Attucks High School Choir of Indianapolis.

Morris, Robert L.
  Lyric Suite. Cynthia D. Lynch, soprano; Robert L. Morris, piano.
  Ruby Jones, soprano; Robert L. Morris, piano.
Nelson, Kalvert
  Different Worlds. Kalvert Nelson, Robert Minette, trumpets.

  Songs for Soprano and Oboe. Roberta Dennie, soprano; David
  Reichenberg, oboe.

  UUUMMMM. Kalvert Nelson, trumpet; Vesta Maxey, dancer.

  A Whimper, for electronic sounds. Realized at the Center for
  Mathematical and Automated Music, Indiana University.
Newton, John
  Amazing Grace. College Avenue Baptist Church Choir of Indianap-
  olis.
Pickett, Donald
  I Want Jesus to Walk with Me. Edythe Jason, soprano; Donald
  Pickett, piano.

  Songs. Lillian Dunlap, soprano; Joe Matthews, piano.
Price, Florence B.
  Night. Bernadine Oliphint, soprano; Carol Stone, piano.

  Songs to the Dark Virgin. Bernadine Oliphint, soprano; Carol
  Stone, piano.
Price, John E.
  Sonata No. 2 for Piano. John E. Price, piano.
Saint-Georges, Joseph Boulogne, Chevalier de
  Sonata for Violin in B-flat Major (American première). Steven
  Shipps, violin; Paul Parmalee, piano.

  String Quartet in C Major (American première). Jacques
  Israelivitch, Zoltan Szabo, violins; Robert Swan, viola; Suzanne
  McIntosh, cello.
Scarlatti, Domenico
  Sonatas in A Major, D Minor, B-flat Major and G Major. George
  Walker, piano.
Shorter, Rick
  The People Had No Faces. Crispus Attucks High School Choir of
  Indianapolis.
Simpson, Ralph R.
  Two Settings on Negro Spirituals. Herndon Spillman, organ.

Simone, Nina
  To Be Young, Gifted and Black. Crispus Attucks High School Choir of Indianapolis.
Smith, Hale
  Brevities. Sally E. Turk, flute.

———

  Duo. Steven Shipps, violin; Robert L. Morris, piano. Steven Shipps, violin; Paul Parmalee, piano.
Sowande, Fela
  The Negro in Sacred Idiom. Herndon Spillman, organ.
Still, William Grant
  The Breath of a Rose. Helene Oatts, soprano; Robert L. Morris, piano.

———

  Songs of Separation. Bernadine Oliphint, soprano; Carol Stone, piano.
Summers, Myrna
  God Gave Me a Song. College Avenue Baptist Church Choir of Indianapolis.
Walker, George
  Sonata for Piano, No. 1. Natalie Hinderas, piano.

———

  Sonata for Piano, No. 2. George Walker, piano.

———

  Spatials. George Walker, piano.
Wilson, O. Lee
  A City Called Heaven. College Avenue Baptist Church Choir of Indianapolis.

———

  Dry Bones. College Avenue Baptist Church Choir of Indianapolis.

———

  How Long, O God? College Avenue Baptist Church Choir of Indianapolis.

———

  I've Decided to Follow Jesus. College Avenue Baptist Church Choir of Indianapolis.
Withers, Bill
  Ain't No Sunshine. Julie Smith, soprano; Donald Pickett, piano.

———

  Grandma's Hands. Julie Smith, soprano; Donald Pickett, piano.

Afterword

Between the time that a manuscript is submitted for publication and the release of the book, various events can take place—particularly in the dynamic area of Black music. Now at the stage of checking page proofs, I am taking this opportunity to register a few significant developments which have come to my attention.

Very soon after I left my post with the Black Music Center, I accepted the position of Research Consultant to the Afro-American Music Opportunities Association, an offer extended by AAMOA's executive director, C. Edward Thomas. An institutional channel was thus opened for projects and philosophical ideals which I could not desert. The initial phase of the recording project mentioned on page 225 of this book has been realized with Columbia Records, and the first set of the Saint-Georges scores is now available from Southern Music Publishing Co.(1740 Broadway, New York, N. Y., 10019). AAMOA has completed its plans for a symposium on orchestral music by Black composers, involving the Baltimore Symphony Orchestra and Dr. Paul Freeman, and it may be that this will be the start of a series of such events. Persons wishing to keep alert to these important developments are urged to subscribe to *AAMOA Reports* (Box 662, Minneapolis, Minnesota, 55440).

A second periodical publication of unequivocal importance is Eileen Southern's *The Black Perspective in Music,* issued semi-annually by the Foundation for Research in the Afro-American Creative Arts (P. O. Box 11049, Cambria Heights, New York, 11411). The publication of Dett's music, *The Collected Piano Works* (i.e., suites) *of R. Nathaniel Dett,* was issued by Summy-Birchard early in 1973. We have also seen the publication of John Lovell's *Black Song* (Macmillan, 1972), Stephen Henderson's *Understanding the New Black Poetry* (William Morrow & Co., 1973) with its perceptive relationship of poetry and music, and John Storm Robert's *Black Music of Two Worlds* (Praeger Publishers, 1972). Quite soon we may look for Leonard Goines' *The Black Musical Experience,* written in collaboration with the late Ellsworth Janifer and being published by Harper & Row, and Crescendo Publishers' issue of a new study by Hildred Roach, as well as the second edition of my *The Black-American Musical Heritage* and a resource book on Black music research whose availability will be announced in *The Black Perspective in Music.*

These, at least, are a few crossed rivers of the past months.

Index

AACM. *See* Association for the Advancement of Creative Musicians

AAMOA. *See* Afro-American Music Opportunities Association

Abernathy, Ralph: 226

Abrams, Richard: 88; identified, 101; on AACM, 105; on freedom from labels, 108-9; on humanizing nature of Black music, 105, 106; on jazz in education, 119-20; on jazz terminology, 103-4, 107

Acculturation: Black influence on European musical tradition, 228-36; effect of, 30; effect in Nigeria, 124-30; inevitability of, 16, 129-30; role in education, 84

Adderley, Cannonball: 80, 103, 123; identified, 111; on Black identity, 122; on Black *vs.* White in jazz, 115; on blues, 120-1; on education, 115-6, 117, 118, 119, 120; on lack of Black coverage in media, 122; on terminology, 114-5; remembered by J. Lee, 68; taught by J. Lee, 51

Adderley, Nat: remembered by J. Lee, 68; taught by J. Lee, 51

Aesthetics: 141-2; and social responsibility, 87-8; as basis for academic racism, 27; concept of E. Calloway, 131-6; reflects cultural values, 28

Ahrens, Thomas J.: 11, 253, 257

Ailey, Alvin: 132, 136, 137; associated with D. Ellington, 140-1; associated with MODE, 131

African music: experiences and ideas of J. Blacking, 207-21; Nigeria and acculturation, 124-30; question of influence in Europe, 179; summary by D. Baker, 145-52

African traditions in Black-American music: 210, 218

Afro-American Music Opportunities Association: cited by C. Adderley, 118; supports Columbia recording project, 223

Akademie für Musik und Darstellende Kunst, Graz: 22

Akpabot, Samuel: 188; on Nigerian music, 124-29

Alcindor, Lou: 107

American Dance Guild: 139

American Wind Symphony Orchestra: 124, 125, 135

Amram, David: 37

Anderson, Joseph D.: 172

Anderson, Lois: 51

Anderson, Marian: 132, 205, 240

Anderson, Thomas Jefferson: 3, 11, 25, 67, 87, 104, 153, 197, 199, 204n, 225, 252; chairman of Honorary Advisory Committee, 10; identified, 74; his reconstruction of *Treemonisha* published, 206; his *Variations on a Theme by M. B. Tolson* recorded, 223; on Black humanism, 77; on Black pacification projects, 81-2; on Blacks as emotional people, 76; on definition of art, 80; on eclecticism, 78-9; on Joplin, 85; on need for Black unity, 75, 109; on need for Blacks to know wide spectrum, 83-4; on *Variations on a Theme by M. B. Tolson,* 90-5; pays tribute to concept of Black Music Center, 227; serves as example of inspired intensity, 99

Apartheid: 209n

Appa, William: 172

Archives of Traditional Music: 196, 200-1

Armstrong, Louis: 9, 22, 115, 148, 154, 155, 157, 201

Arnold, Ronnie: 138

Art music defined: 162-3

Ashby, Dorothy: 41, 123; on baroque study for jazz musicians, 122; on harp playing, 117; on jazz education and history, 111-4

Association for the Advancement of Creative Musicians: 7, 101, 103, 106; goals, 105